THE POLITICS OF HIGHER EDUCATION
IN MINORITY NATIONS

The Politics of Higher Education in Minority Nations

Insights from Quebec

HANNAH MOSCOVITZ

UNIVERSITY OF TORONTO PRESS
Toronto Buffalo London

© University of Toronto Press 2025
Toronto Buffalo London
utppublishing.com
Printed in the USA

ISBN 978-1-4875-5854-3 (cloth)   ISBN 978-1-4875-5856-7 (EPUB)
                                   ISBN 978-1-4875-5855-0 (PDF)

Library and Archives Canada Cataloguing in Publication

Title: The politics of higher education in minority nations : insights from
    Quebec / Hannah Moscovitz.
Names: Moscovitz, Hannah, author.
Description: Includes bibliographical references and index.
Identifiers: Canadiana (print) 20240461622 | Canadiana (ebook)
    20240461665 | ISBN 9781487558543 (cloth) | ISBN 9781487558550 (PDF) |
    ISBN 9781487558567 (EPUB)
Subjects: LCSH: Higher education and state—Québec (Province) |
    LCSH: Nationalism—Québec (Province)
Classification: LCC LC176.2.Q8 M67 2025 | DDC 378.714—dc23

Cover design: Mark Byk
Cover image: iStock.com/cerber82

We wish to acknowledge the land on which the University of Toronto
Press operates. This land is the traditional territory of the Wendat, the
Anishnaabeg, the Haudenosaunee, the Métis, and the Mississaugas of the
Credit First Nation.

This book has been published with the help of a grant from the Federation
for the Humanities and Social Sciences, through the Awards to Scholarly
Publications Program, using funds provided by the Social Sciences and
Humanities Research Council of Canada.

University of Toronto Press acknowledges the financial support of the
Government of Canada, the Canada Council for the Arts, and the Ontario
Arts Council, an agency of the Government of Ontario, for its publishing
activities.

   Canada Council   Conseil des Arts
                       for the Arts   du Canada

Contents

Acknowledgements vii

Introduction 3

1 When (Minority) Nationalism Meets Higher Education: Concepts and Issues 17

2 *Maîtres Chez Nous*: The Quiet Revolution, Higher Education, and the Consolidation of Quebec Nationalism 33

3 The University as Public Good: Towards the 2012 Maple Spring Protests 51

4 McGill University and Quebec's Nationalist Politics 72

5 Higher Education as a Catalyst to Quebec's "Identity Paradiplomacy": The French Connection 89

6 Branding Minority Nations: Marketing and Promoting Quebec as an International Study Destination 107

7 Promoting the Quebec Nation through Education Diplomacy 126

Conclusion: What Implications for the Study of Minority Nationalism? 145

Appendix: List of Primary Sources 161

Notes 171

References 173

Index 187

Acknowledgements

I am deeply grateful to the University of Toronto Press for their dedication and hard work in bringing this book to life, with special thanks to Daniel Quinlan for his exceptional support and guidance throughout the process. I would also like to thank the two anonymous reviewers for their insightful and constructive comments on the manuscript.

Since embarking on this project, I have had the privilege of working within remarkably supportive academic environments. I would like to thank the Simone Veil Research Centre for Contemporary European Studies and the Department of Politics and Government at Ben-Gurion University, the Knowledge Power Politics research cluster at the Faculty of Education, University of Cambridge, and the Policy Futures Program at the Danish School of Education, Aarhus University. I am especially grateful to Prof. Sharon Pardo, Dr. Hila Zahavi, Prof. Susan Robertson and Prof. Katja Brøgger for their mentorship and encouragement.

I would also like to thank the McGill University Library (rare books and special collections) and the MacMaster University Library (archives and research collections) for access to their resources. Finally, I am grateful to the Social Science and Humanities Research Council of Canada for supporting the publication of this book through the Awards to Scholarly Publications Program grant.

THE POLITICS OF HIGHER EDUCATION
IN MINORITY NATIONS

Introduction

In the spring of 2012, Quebec made headlines around the world as a student-led protest fought against growing government austerity measures. Catalysing the movement was the Liberal Party of Quebec (PLQ) government's announcement of an impending tuition fee hike. Described in the international press as "the most powerful challenge to neoliberalism on the continent" (Lukacs 2012), the period became known as the "Maple Spring"/printemps érable, a play on words on the Arab Spring movement sweeping the Middle East and North Africa a few months prior. The red square became the symbol of the Maple Spring, a nod to the French expression "being in the red" (être dans le rouge) to describe the increasing debt incurred by students. While sparked by student grievances, the movement quickly galvanized Quebec society, challenging broader neoliberal policies enacted by the Liberal government in preceding years. The protests were underpinned by a strong nationalist sentiment, with concerns framed in nationalist terms, a trend visually evidenced by the juxtaposition of the fleur-de-lys to the red square in the crowds of protestors taking part in marches across Quebec. Discursively, arguments against the tuition fee hike were aligned with Quebec's ambitions to carve distinct policy choices for itself, in line with the values characterizing its nationhood. It was emblematic of Quebec's right to distinctiveness as a minority nation within Canada.

The Maple Spring protests represent a pivotal moment for Quebec society. The event will undoubtedly go down in history books as one of its most impactful social movements. It is also indicative of the strong intersection between nationalism and higher education in Quebec, the underlying theme of this book. Illustrating the nationalism/higher education policy nexus, the Maple Spring follows a long trajectory of mutually reinforcing links between Quebec's higher education system and its nationalist ambitions as a minority nation within Canada. *The Politics of Higher Education in Minority Nations* delves into the long-standing intersection between higher education policy and nationalism in Quebec, tracing the evolution of this relationship from the 1960s until 2022. Taking Quebec's Quiet Revolution (révolution tranquille) as a point of departure and highlighting specific policy arenas and events in which nationalism and higher education have intersected over time, the book traces how this specific policy sphere has come to serve as a symbol of Quebec's distinctiveness and a tool for the cultivation of a distinct national identity.

Quebec's Quiet Revolution is a natural starting point for any discussion of its higher education policy. This period of large-scale societal, economic, and political reforms saw Quebec shift from a traditional, Catholic value–based society to a "modern" society with strong political institutions taking charge of issues previously undertaken by the church. Education became a focal point of the Quiet Revolution reforms with sweeping changes occurring in this sphere. These changes coincided with the cultivation of Quebec's territorially based nationalism and the rise of sovereigntist ideals. Evolving in parallel, Quebec's modern education system and its contemporary nationalism are closely intertwined. Investigating the permeation of nationalist interests in higher education policy discussions over time, *The Politics of Higher Education in Minority Nations* provides a longitudinal analysis of the sustained relationship between Quebec's higher education system and Quebec nationalism.

Unpacking the Relationship between (Minority) Nationalism and Higher Education

This book delves into the mutually reinforcing relationship between nationalism and education by focusing exclusively on the higher education domain. While the links between school-level education and nationalism have been the focus of more extensive research, less attention has been paid to the relationship between nationalism and higher education specifically (exceptions to this include Davies and Aurini 2021; Harvey 2010; Kerr 1991; Koch 2014; Tannock 2007). The relatively limited scholarship on higher education and nationalism is surprising given the superseding role the university has played for national governments, since the advent of the Westphalian state system to its function as a linchpin for the "knowledge economies" of today (Ruegg 2006). Higher education systems are currently at the forefront of crucial policy decisions, intersecting with a host of additional policy fields at the crux of political decision-making processes, including economy and trade, foreign affairs, and immigration.

The relative dearth of scholarship linking nationalism to higher education has been attributed to an overemphasis on globalization and internationalization as frames of reference for exploring this policy domain (Koch 2014). Examining higher education projects in Saudi Arabia and Qatar, Koch (2014) demonstrates how the internationalization agendas are intertwined with nationalist ambitions, making the case for considering nationalism as a significant force in higher education projects. Additional studies have delved into the connection between nationalism and globalization/internationalization and how the two come together in the higher education policy sphere (see, e.g., Hsieh 2020; Lo and Chan 2020).

Recent research has explored how the re-emergence of nationalism in the global landscape and the strengthening of populist, isolationist, and "nation-first" ideologies in recent years are impacting higher education policy and practice. Scholars have investigated the influence of "new" nationalist movements on higher education in different parts of the world, including in Denmark (Brøgger 2022; Tange and Jaeger 2021), India (Gupta 2019), South Africa (Lee 2017), Brazil (Balbachevsky and Guilhon Albuquerque 2021), the Netherlands (Van der Wende 2021), the United Kingdom (Weimer and Barlete 2019; O'Malley 2021), and the United States (Douglass 2021). Evidently, the rise in neo-nationalism seen in different parts of the world is leading to a renewed interest in the intersection between nationalism and higher education, which has, until now, been overshadowed by the discussion of higher education internationalization.

If the scholarship on nationalism and higher education remains limited, there is an even larger gap in research connecting higher education and *minority* nationalism (on Scotland, see Arnott and Ozga 2010, on Quebec, see Moscovitz 2020, 2022). *The Politics of Higher Education in Minority Nations* addresses this gap by exploring how Quebec's higher education system has been influenced by nationalism and vice versa. More broadly, the findings and discussions presented here advance the scholarship on the link between public policy and minority nationalism. Higher education is considered a pivotal arena through which to investigate nation-building and national identity–building practices as it touches on both explicit features of nationalist projects (language, culture, history) and more "banal" (Billig 1995) forms of nationalism (policy distinctiveness, social welfare ideals).

Higher education also sits on the seams between domestic and foreign policy and, in this way, offers a useful vantage point to explore the different manifestations of nationalism by minority nations in both their domestic and foreign policy ambitions. By highlighting this specific policy sphere, the book provides new empirical support to the symbiotic relationship between public policy and minority nations. Investigating the nationalism/higher education connection in Quebec also addresses the call for higher education scholarship to consider the political and power dimensions of this policy sphere and its actors (Cantwell et al. 2018; Pusser 2018; Weimer and Nokkala 2020). It does so by focusing on a particular form of political actor – the minority nation.

Minority Nationalism as a Conceptual Lens

The study approaches Quebec as a minority nation and investigates the higher education/nationalism relationship against its unique position within Canada's multinational federation. As defined by Gagnon, "multinational federalism stands for the advancement of nations – albeit these nations are often times contested political communities – within the confines of an existing state" (Gagnon 2021, 102). In states where multiple nations coexist, multinational federalism allows for "the expression of national diversity within complex democratic settings" (Gagnon 2021, 101). Such a system recognizes the existence of multiple (at least two) "nations" or *demoi*, within one territorial state, and provides institutional empowerment for these to promote their distinct policy and governance interests within a larger state.

As cultural communities "sharing a common past, attached to a clearly demarcated territory and wishing to decide upon their political future which lack a state of their own" (Guibernau 1999, 1), minority nations, or as Guibernau calls them "nations without states," jostle for authority over policy decisions deemed in the best interest of their nations. As the case of Quebec substantiates, competing nation-building agendas between Canada's "majority" nationalism and Quebec's "minority" nationalism constitute an underlying tension within Canada's federal system. Accordingly, the balance between self-rule for minority nations and shared rule with the majority nations with which they share territory is constantly negotiated.

Through the prism of Quebec as a minority nation within Canada, the book showcases the unique position of minority nations as policy-makers, as well as the different ways in which higher education policy becomes entangled in the relations between majority and minority nations in the country.

Minority nations also find themselves navigating their interests and ambitions beyond the confines of their broader state structures, engaging in the international arena, through their foreign policy endeavours and their economic and trade relations. The engagement of minority nations in the global economic landscape raises an additional set of opportunities and challenges, as they strive to strengthen their attractiveness and competitiveness all the while maintaining their national distinctiveness.

The Premise

Exploring the Quebec case, *The Politics of Higher Education in Minority Nations* points to a deep and sustained alignment of higher education policy with nationalist agendas. A core argument put forth is that nationalism continues to influence higher education policy decisions and processes and should therefore be considered as an explanatory factor for how higher education policies are articulated, negotiated, and ultimately implemented. Adjacent to this, the book also makes the case for considering the specificities of the nationalism–higher education nexus in minority nations.

Revealing a strong permeation of nationalist discourse and ideals in higher education policymaking supports and extends the argument that the "state" (in this case a non-sovereign state) continues to play a fundamental role in higher education policymaking. This challenges the growing conception of the public role of higher education as waning, due in part to globalization processes and marketization trends. Moreover, the scholarship on higher education policy tends to view it as linked to the nation-state scale, prompting accusations of methodological nationalism (Shahjahan and Kezar 2013). By shedding light on the impact of nationalism on higher education in Quebec, it is my hope that the book provides new insights into this connection through the exploration of *minority* nationalism and policy processes below the nation state. More broadly, however, the book aims to contribute to the understanding of minority nations and their unique modes of territorial mobilization in the contemporary globalized system.

While the permeation of nationalist interests in higher education policy decisions is found to be constant over time, the book also reveals a tension between Quebec's nationalist ambitions, on one hand, and its desire to become a competitive player in the global economic landscape, on the other. More specifically, the tensions that arise between efforts to compete in the global economy and the preservation of national distinctiveness are underscored. Through this lens, the book offers an important account of the unique challenges faced by minority nations in the articulation of their global engagements.

The intensification of globalization in the last two decades has "markedly contributed to the uncertain future of minority nations" (Gagnon 2014, 34). For Gagnon, minority nations find themselves in an "age of uncertainty" both because of the pressures of globalization, as well as the limited scope of institutional arrangements to manage diversity in multinational states. Just as globalization can constrain the capacity of minority nations to flourish, it can also open avenues for them to pursue political goals (Gagnon 2014). The move towards transnational integration and subsequent re-territorialization of politics and policymaking creates new sets of opportunities for minority nations (Keating 2001). Through an investigation of the relationship between nationalism and higher education policy in Quebec, the book sheds light on how Quebec navigates its nationalist ambitions within the confines of the global economic system and the constraints and opportunities that come with it.

The focus on a minority nation offers an important contribution to the existing literature on economic nationalism by drawing out its specific manifestations at the substate scale. Higher education policy is increasingly difficult to decouple from broader economic policy interests. This is evidenced throughout the chapters of this book, which show the deep economic rationales behind Quebec's higher education policy decisions. The sphere of higher education is thus uniquely positioned to advance the understanding of how minority nations promote their interests in an increasingly globalized economy and how the protection of their national distinctiveness might come at the expense of economic gains. The findings presented here point to an at times mutually beneficial relationship between nationalism and economic competitiveness, and, at times, a contradictory one, lending weight to the notion that "[t]he political economy for the expression of minority nationalism is therefore favorable only up to a point" (Graefe 2005, 541).

The Politics of Higher Education in Minority Nations contributes to the discussion of Quebec's economic policy as a reflection of its nationalism as advanced by Rioux (2020), with particular attention paid to the balance of scales between economic interests and nationalism. It also answers the call for more nuanced approaches to the study of economic nationalism, beyond its understanding as synonymous with protectionist economic policy to considerations of its broader ideological implications on how economy and nationalism interact (Fetzer 2022; Helleiner 2021; Nakano 2004; Pickel 2003; Rioux 2020). Economic nationalism, the argument goes, should not be viewed solely in terms of the instrumental relation of economy to nation; rather, it should be understood as an example of the "interiority" of economy to nation (Crane 1998; Fetzer 2022). In other words, these scholars are interested in exploring the interconnection between "economy" and "nation" and the way nationalism shapes economic processes.

Exploring the Quebec context from a longitudinal perspective, the findings reveal the persistent embeddedness of higher education in territorial politics and nation-building agendas, despite seemingly countering trends. Indeed, while historically linked to nation-building projects, universities are increasingly engaged in cross-border activities intensified by the growing internationalization of higher education.[1] Adding to this the enhanced private/market interests in the field, the "national" function of higher education is reconfigured (Beerkens 2003). Recent decades have witnessed a growing, politically supported internationalization and globalization of academia, characterized by increased student/faculty mobility, the formation of regional alliances in higher education, the establishment of international satellite campuses, and growing global competition, among other features. Accordingly, universities and their stakeholders are operating transnationally, contributing to a certain change in sovereignty over higher education policy away from the nation state towards the supranational/international realm. To enhance competitiveness within the internationalized higher education arena, states are also harmonizing their policies to be congruent with international standards. In this way, universities become "disembedded" from their national context (Beerkens 2003). This is not to say that the nation state's role in higher education governance is obsolete, it remains engaged, although it is increasingly accompanied by a plethora of additional actors below (local) and above (supranational, global) it (Marginson 2022).

At the same time, the higher education policy field is also affected by marketization trends and the growing role of private and commercial actors in decision-making and policy design. Around the world, the public character of higher education is receding to market incentives and commercialization. The "economic ethos" (Washburn 2008) in higher education is characterized by a reshuffling of priorities by which corporations and private actors take on financing functions to fill the void of public financing in academia. This is in line with an overall global trend towards the downgrading of welfare-state models and the consequent decline in state authority over social programs. These trends are commonly discussed as antithetical to the nation-building function of higher education by downplaying their public characters. The decline in public/state engagement in the higher education policy sphere has important implications for the perceived role of higher education in society and its anchoring within the nation state. By showcasing the sustained connection between higher education policy and nationalism, the findings presented in this book challenge the idea that the state is losing relevance in this policy sphere. Furthermore, it argues that additional territorial governance scales, in this case the subnational governments of minority nations, are themselves promoting nationalism through their higher education policy. In this way, the book calls for a more nuanced reading of where higher education policy is heading, one that recognizes the increasing pull towards the global and the permeation of market forces, all the while considering the continued territorial interests involved.

Analytical and Methodological Framing

Recognizant of the multitude of actors participating in higher education policy discussions, this book focuses on the role of political actors engaged in the formulation, design, and implementation of policy decisions. More specifically, the study uncovers the interests and rationales of government and parliament representatives, elected officials, and party leadership. It also considers, albeit to a lower degree, the interests of lobbyists, student movements and other societal organizations engaged in the policy discussions at stake. In this way, the analysis follows Van Dijk's (1997) conceptualization of "political actor" as one "engaged in politics," although with a focus on political actors working at an official capacity in state spaces.

The study draws on critical discourse analysis (CDA) to examine the political discourse surrounding higher education policy discussions in Quebec. The data under investigation include policy documents (white papers, policy strategies, annual reports, policy evaluations) and political discussions surrounding them (parliamentary debates, political speeches, media interviews/editorials, party positions, electoral platforms). Primary data includes publicly available policy documents found through various Quebec ministry websites as well as through the Bibliothèque et Archives nationales du Quebec (BANQ) archives. Given that higher education policy discussions are undertaken across policy domains, including immigration, labour, foreign affairs, and trade, the documents under analysis correspond to different government bodies and agencies, including a range of ministries engaged in higher education policy decisions.[2] A smaller number of documents were retrieved through archival sources.[3] Most documents under analysis are published in French and excerpts translated to English by the author.

The approach draws from the understanding of discourse as constituting a form of social practice and a reflection of power dynamics (Fairclough 2001, 2013). The CDA examines how notions of nationalism and national identity are articulated in higher education policy discussions in Quebec from 1960 to 2022. To this end, a systematic reading of the materials was conducted (drawing on Reisigl and Wodak 2009), with a focus on the interdiscursive themes linking higher education and nationalism, the immediate language (how is nationalism/national identity discussed?), the consideration of the socio-political and historical context in which the discourse is found, and the relation of the discourse to "meta-range" theories on minority nationalism. "Working in dialogue" (Fairclough 2013, 365) with theories of minority nationalism and multinational federalism, the analysis underscores how these are discursively constructed.

Moving beyond the Domestic/Foreign Policy Binary

The study's broader analytical framework incorporates a dual lens on higher education policy, one that considers both its domestic and foreign policy dimensions. With the growing internationalization of higher education and research, policy decisions in this sphere are increasingly related to foreign policy alongside the domestic governing bodies responsible for education internally. This is evidenced in the policy initiatives geared towards recruiting international students or the enacting of bilateral education cooperation agreements, which are typically conducted by ministries of foreign affairs and international trade. Hence, alongside ministries of higher education and research authorities working within a specific territory, ministries of foreign affairs, global affairs, and international trade are increasingly engaged in the decision-making around higher education. Sitting on the seams between domestic and foreign policy domains, higher education policy offers a particularly valuable subject of inquiry.

The importance of highlighting both the domestic and foreign policy spheres is motivated by the understanding that the "domestic/foreign polarity" in the conceptualization of world politics is largely unproductive (Agnew 1994). A government's domestic policy cannot be fully detached from its international policy goals and vice versa. Inspired by Agnew's (1994) "territorial trap" discussion, this study proposes to investigate the domestic and foreign in conjunction as opposed to separate analytical categories. In his seminal piece, Agnew argues that the common view of a "domestic/foreign polarity" in international relations has contributed to a "territorial trap" in the literature. For Agnew (1994), "showing how the domestic and foreign come together under different historical circumstances rather than separating them into permanent opposition becomes the overriding task ... the main point is that the domestic/foreign opposition constitutes a shifting interaction rather than a fixed polarity" (67).

The scholarship associating (sub-)nationalism with different policy domains tends to dissociate between domestic and foreign policy spheres. On one side of this gamut are studies interested in how minority national governments promote solidarity and a sense of distinctiveness through the policies they advance within their borders. On the other are those examining the nationalist interests behind the *paradiplomacy* of minority nations, that is, their engagement in international relations. This book bridges these two schools by exploring both the domestic and foreign policy implications of higher education for Quebec's nationalist ambitions.[4] As evidenced throughout the different chapters, the domestic and foreign policy interests are difficult to disentangle. Such an approach also allows for a discussion about how nationalism is promoted both internally and externally and how these efforts might differ or converge.

Contribution and Significance

The Politics of Higher Education in Minority Nations contributes to the scholarship on Quebec nationalism by highlighting a unique lens through which to investigate its manifestation and the challenges it faces. By focusing on the permeation of nationalist interests in higher education policy, the book offers the first comprehensive account of this relationship in Quebec. The limited attention paid to the interface between higher education and nationalism in Quebec is surprising considering the inherent and long-standing connection between them.[5] Decisions over higher education were integral to the evolving of Québécois nationalism during the Quiet Revolution and have intertwined with its nationalist ambitions ever since. From the Quiet Revolution to the 2012 Maple Spring protests and beyond, higher education policies in Quebec have been aligned with nationalist interests. As the book aims to substantiate, scrutinizing major policy decisions and events in this sphere offers a particularly unique vantage point to advance our understanding of Quebec nationalism, specifically, and of minority nationalism, more broadly.

The book's novelty also derives from its consideration of the higher education/nationalism connection through both the domestic and foreign policy spheres. Examining both domestic and foreign policy arenas in conjunction, as opposed to viewing them as separate analytical frames, allows for a coupling of two important sets of literature on minority nationalism; the public policy/sub-nationalism connection (Béland and Lecours 2008; McEwen 2006) and the discussion surrounding paradiplomacy and its nation-building potential (Lecours 2001; Paquin 2004, 2018; McEwen and Moreno 2008). The literature on sub-state nationalism has yet to effectively consider its promotion from both domestic and foreign policy perspectives, and as such, the book provides a unique approach that is potentially applicable to other territorial contexts or other policy domains.

Finally, by highlighting how higher education policy and nationalism intersect in Quebec, the study provides a look at how nationalism is perpetuated through different public policy arenas, including those which shy away from the "usual suspects," notably culture and language (Béland and Lecours 2008). In their important discussion on the connection between nationalism and social policy, Béland and Lecours (2008) make the case for exploring how sub-nationalism is perpetuated through arenas not necessarily associated with "cultural markers" (23). Social policy, they contend, is included in the "mix of identity markers" used by minority nations to promote nationalism. The focus on higher education allows for an understanding of both the cultural aspects (most notably language) as well as those more structural, institutional nationalism levers and how they coincide. By relating to critical moments and policy events where higher education and nationalism intersect from the Quiet Revolution era until today; the book offers a unique historical and socio-political perspective not only of nationalism in Quebec but also of higher education policy and the perceived role of the university in society.

Outline of the Book

The book opens with a theoretical exercise in chapter 1, outlining key conceptual issues at the root of the nationalism/higher education connection. It starts by situating the study on Quebec within the wider literature on multinational federalism and minority nationalism. The discussion then narrows to a consideration of the connection between nationalism and policymaking, as it pertains to minority nations. Although the book is focused on the policy field of higher education, an extended understanding of how policymaking and nationalism are connected in the literature on minority nations provides an important backdrop to some of the key themes advanced in the book. The chapter also fulfils a contextual exercise, outlining the socio-political and historical background of Quebec's higher education governance and its connection to its status as a minority nation.

The remainder of the book provides an empirical account of the way Québécois nationalism has permeated higher education policy over the past six decades. Chapter 2 explores the roots of the higher education/nationalism connection in Quebec. More specifically, it centres on the Quiet Revolution era (1960–1966) to outline how Quebec's modern higher education system became entangled with its nationalist politics and national awakening. The chapter considers how the *modèle Québécois* for higher education, developed during this time and largely still intact today, is connected to its nationalist ambitions and ideals.

Chapter 3 focuses exclusively on the policy issue of tuition fees, problematizing how it became so closely associated with Quebec nationalist politics. The permeation of nationalist ideals in policy decisions around tuition fees came to the fore during the 2012 Maple Spring protests. Yet debates over Quebec's tuition rates and their implications for its collective mobilization and identity have been a point of contention for decades. The chapter investigates the discursive alignment between nationalism and the tuition fee issue from the Quiet Revolution to the Maple Spring protests. A central theme emerging from the analysis is the significance of maintaining the public character of higher education imbued with values of accessibility and democratization. The question of tuition fees is coupled with the importance of maintaining the public character of the university, a value anchored during the Quiet Revolution era. The findings reveal a strong discursive connection between low tuition rates and issues of collective identity and nationalism. It also points to this policy issue as an example of Quebec's distinctiveness within Canada.

Chapter 4 takes a focused approach to the nationalism/higher education connection in Quebec by considering its manifestation in policy debates and discussions surrounding McGill University. As an anglophone institution situated in Quebec's cultural metropole of Montreal, McGill University represents a microcosm of the linguistic and nationalist tensions in Quebec and has long been at the centre of nationalist concerns over the status of the French language in the province. From the 1969 *McGill Français* movement calling for the university to become a French-language institution to a 2020 debate over the funding of McGill's expansion project, the discussion situates the University in Quebec's nationalism debate with a focus on the linguistic battles

Introduction 15

inherent to it. The findings outlined here point to an important tension arising between the desire to maintain Quebec's francophone identity and the need to ensure its economic competitiveness globally.

Chapter 5 launches the portion of the book dedicated to uncovering the nationalism/higher education policy connection in the foreign policy sphere. The chapter takes readers back to the Quiet Revolution era and highlights the catalysing role of higher education for the development of Quebec's international relations and the consolidation of its status as a paradiplomatic actor. Through an investigation of Quebec's international education activities and a focus on bilateral schemes with France, the discussion advances an understanding of how higher education, international relations, and nationalism interact in Quebec. The findings presented in this chapter point to the use of international education for "identity paradiplomacy" over time. Yet a tension is also observed between Quebec's nationalist interests and its economic rationales in this sphere, coinciding with the findings outlined in previous chapters.

Chapter 6 considers the nation branding function of international education in Quebec by exploring how Quebec promotes its international image through international student recruitment and marketing campaigns. It takes Quebec's unique position as a minority nation within a multinational federation as a backdrop to investigate how nation branding practices are realized in contexts in which nationalisms coincide and even compete. The chapter addresses how Quebec's education marketing rationales reflect the majority–minority tensions vis-à-vis the federal level. It also considers how Quebec juggles its desire to project a distinct, national (francophone) image with its need to remain competitive and appeal to a wide "market" of potential international students. In this way, the chapter provides further indication of the precarious position held by minority nations in the global economic landscape.

Chapter 7 explores the public diplomacy function of Quebec's higher education policy and how it intersects with its nation-building agenda. The discussion centres on education-oriented government initiatives aimed at promoting Quebec internationally. The chapter opens with an investigation of the Quebec studies programs developed internationally and traces these from the very first Quebec studies centres in Europe (1971) to more recent budget challenges faced by these initiatives (2018). The chapter then moves on to outline the education diplomacy efforts specific to Quebec's regional ambitions in the Americas. It considers the role of the Centre de la francophonie des Amériques inaugurated in 2008 by the Liberal Party of Quebec (PLQ) government to promote the

16 The Politics of Higher Education in Minority Nations

French language in the Americas and foster ties between their francophone communities. Education-oriented activities feature prominently among the centre's initiatives, providing a valuable lens to delve deeper into Quebec's education diplomacy and consider the implications of its role in the *francophonie*, as well as its sense of attachment to the wider American space, or its *américanité*.

1 When (Minority) Nationalism Meets Higher Education: Concepts and Issues

This introductory chapter sets the stage for the discussion of the higher education/nationalism nexus in Quebec, outlining key conceptual issues at the root of this relationship. It starts by situating the study on Quebec within the wider literature on multinational federalism and minority nationalism. The discussion then narrows to a consideration of the connection between nationalism and policymaking, as it pertains to minority nations. Although the book is focused on the policy field of higher education, an extended understanding of how policymaking and nationalism are connected in the literature on minority nations provides an important backdrop to some of the key themes advanced in the book. The chapter draws parallels to previous works on the minority nationalism/public policy connection and highlights how minority nations cultivate and promote their nationalist agendas through their higher education policymaking. The chapter ends with a contextual exercise, outlining the socio-political and historical background of Quebec's higher education governance.

Multinational Federalism and the Re-Territorialization of World Politics

The rise of sub-state movements is cited as an indication of the changing nature of territory and sovereignty, or of what Ruggie (1993) termed the "unbundling of territoriality." Territorial politics in the current era is "re-configured" and emerging in "new and potent forms" (Keating 1998, 3). The "re-territorialization" literature emerging in the 1990s challenged the notion of a "de-territorialization" (Badie 1995; Ohmae 1995) of world politics that saw the eroding of territory and the status of the nation state as the primary holder of territoriality questioned. As a counterweight to this pessimistic view of the future of territoriality, the re-territorialization school emphasizes how territory is reordered and how sovereignty is increasingly migrating both below and above the nation-state apparatus (Brenner 1999; Keating 1998). While global forces have had an undeniable impact on the contemporary world order, it has become clear that territory remains significant. As noted by Michael Keating (2013), "euphoria did not last long" (6) for the "end of territory" argument.

Central to the idea of a "re-territorialization" of world politics is an understanding that governance and policymaking are increasingly dispersed among territorial scales, migrating from the nation state towards additional territorial entities both below and above it. The world might be entering a "post-sovereign order" (Keating 2002), according to which sovereignty is "increasingly shared and divided and cannot be said to inhere purely in the state" (362). As the argument goes, the nation state has not receded as the principal organization of territory and identity; rather, it is rescaled as responsibilities traditionally confined to it are dispersed between different territorial scales and actors (Biswas 2002; Brenner 1999; Keating 2013).

The growing salience of minority nations in the global order is but one manifestation of this rescaling. Of note, the existence of sub-state territorial units is not a new phenomenon. Tendencies to devolve state authority to subunits can be traced back to the emergence of the Westphalian state itself (Van Langenhove 2011). The decentralization of state power to sub-territorial units occurs at different degrees and for different reasons. In some cases, they are established by a "top down" decision aimed at creating more effective bureaucratic and administrative systems (Keating 1997). Referred to as forms of "territorial federalism," these are attributed to cases like Germany, Australia, and the United States (Gagnon 2010).

Diversity within states and the associated tensions are another central push factor for decentralization. At the heart of this discussion is the notion that in a world of "so many nations, so few states" (Keating 2001), state and nation are not always congruent. Most states today include a certain degree of diversity, whether along cultural, linguistic, ethnic, or religious lines. Certainly, diversity within states does not automatically lead to decentralization of authority. Yet, in cases in which divisions run deep and two or more nations coexist, measures for managing this diversity are often put in place. Federalism assumes this role, and in the context of multinational states, it allows for a recognition of the existence of distinct national groups within one territory. The appeal of federal systems as described by Burgess (2012) is their ability to "accommodate and reconcile different forms of unity with different forms of diversity" (25). In his seminal work on the Canadian case, Taylor proposes "deep diversity" to address the country's divisions (Taylor 1991). For Taylor, within federal systems like Canada's, diversity should be embraced, and multiple forms of belonging encouraged. In this way, a balance between diversity and commonality is promoted.

The establishment of a multinational federal system is viewed as essential to protect national minorities and to promote ideals of justice and stability in diverse liberal democracies (Gagnon 2010). As defined by Kymlicka (2000), multinational federations

> embody a model of the state in which national minorities are federated to the state through some form of territorial autonomy and in which internal boundaries have been drawn, and powers distributed, in such a way as to ensure that each national group is able to maintain itself as a distinct and self-governing societal culture (212).

The intricacies related to these systems are attributed in part to the existence of two or more nation-building projects within one territory, where "rival" nations are "competing for the hearts, minds and identities of the same citizens" (Norman 2006, 29). Although the arrangement of multinational federalism can appease separatist ambitions and conflict, there is a constant tension and contestation of power structures between central and subnational levels of government. Alluding to this paradox, Burgess (2012) notes, "[i]t is surely a curious set of circumstances that leads to the formation of a federation deliberately founded upon strong cultural-ideological differences, such as distinct nations, which will also constitute one of the major fault lines in its subsequent evolution" (24).

The Plight and Prospects of Minority Nations in Multinational Federations

In this book, I follow Gagnon (2013) in viewing the terms *stateless nation* (Kymlicka 2000), and *nation without state* (Guiberbau 1999) less applicable to the Quebec context as it "has developed major state apparatuses active in paradiplomacy, education, culture, economy, and intergovernmental matters that would make many existing countries very envious of its accomplishments" (40). In this way, Quebec can be considered a non-sovereign state. I consider the term *minority nation* more appropriate to describe and explain Quebec's position within Canada, all the while recognizant that Québécois consider themselves less a minority nation and more akin to a founding nation (Gagnon 2013). The use of the term *minority* to describe Quebec is intended to highlight the unequal power relations and dynamics at play within Canada and the tensions between Quebec's minority nationalism and the "majority" or "dominant" nation-building project pursed at the federal level. For Rioux (2020), minority nationalism involves the "collective commitments *to* and demands *for* significant policy self-determination caused by national communities forming demographic minorities within sovereign nation-states" (15).

Terminology aside, a common thread found in these portrayals of minority nations is the notion that they aspire for greater political control in the confines of the territory in which their national community lives. Minority nations jostle for influence and political legitimacy within the larger state in which they operate. They find themselves in a constant search for the most effective ways to pursue their interests as a distinct national group within a larger whole. This leads many to seek full sovereignty through self-determination and independence movements, more often pursued these days through political referendums. While aspirations for independence are often percolating in the background, they are not always at the forefront of political issues facing minority nations. Between full independence and full integration into the federal system are degrees of tensions between majority and minority nations, which evolve over time. At the core of their functioning, minority nations aspire to gain legitimacy both within the multinational federation, and outside it, as the rightful provider of their citizens' needs and the "protector" of the national culture they represent. One of the most powerful tools at their disposal to achieve this is through their policymaking.

Promoting Minority Nationalism through Domestic Policy

Federal systems are predicated on power-sharing models whereby authority over different policy domains is distributed between the central state apparatus and territorial subunits. This decentralization of authority is of heightened significance in cases in which authority is relegated to minority nations, where a parallel can be drawn between institutional boundaries and a distinct political community and territorial identity (McEwen 2005). The governance and policymaking decisions made by a minority nation government are geared towards the national community in its territory, a minority nation in the broader federal system yet forming a majority within said territorial unit. The desire to increase political authority and legitimacy leads minority nations to articulate their policy decisions around the specific needs of their citizens, understood as distinct from the rest of the state.

The connection between public policy and minority nationalism has been explored through the prism of different policy spheres, notably regarding social policy and welfare (Béland and Lecours 2006, 2008; Dupuy and Ingelgom 2014; McEwen 2005, 2006; McEwen and Moreno 2008). These studies highlight the territorial politics of social and welfare policy through an investigation of how minority nations cultivate and promote their nation-building agendas through these policy domains. Of note, is that it is not necessarily the content of the policies themselves that take on a nation-building role but, rather, the symbolic attributes around policy control.

As pointed out by McEwen (2006) in her study on Quebec and Scotland, "the nation-building role of the welfare state is, in part embodied in the symbolic significance of its institutions" (62). McEwen (2005) also refers to the significance of "policy ownership" for minority nations. The very fact that a subnational government takes control of a specific policy field works to enhance its legitimacy vis-à-vis its citizens and ultimately heightens a sense of solidarity between them. Examining education and media policy in Flanders, Erk (2003) makes similar contentions noting the Flemish slogan "what we do ourselves we do better" was used to promote a deeper decentralization of authority along linguistic lines in Belgium. Policy "ownership" is the first step towards mobilizing nationalist ideals through specific policies. Once "owned" policy structures can be moulded to be congruent with the interests and desires of the national community. For McEwen (2006), "the emotion and sentiment that underlies national identity, and the mutual sense of belonging together it engenders among the people, underpins much of the discourse used to justify public policy making and governmental action" (42).

The policy/nationalism link advanced in the scholarship on minority nations echoes Habermas's (1975, 1991) discussion of political legitimacy. Habermas's (1975) thesis on legitimacy in the modern capitalist era contends that the state's economic function runs a risk of encountering a "crisis of legitimacy" if it fails to meet the demands of its citizenry. Habermas (1991) defines legitimacy as "a political order's worthiness to be recognized" (178) and notes its instability as it is heavily dependent on recognition. Gaining control over policy domains through federalization, minority nations enhance their legitimacy as "state-like" entities. This legitimacy can be strengthened through the political discourse used to promote specific policies. In their study on Flanders, Dupuy and Ingelgom (2014) found that the public discourse around social policy served important legitimatizing purposes by emphasizing solidarity between Flemish citizens, one based on a political culture distinct from the Belgian state. Similarly, in their comparative research on social policy and nationalism in Canada, the United Kingdom, and Belgium, Béland and Lecours reveal, how in each context, the sub-state nations have articulated and mobilized a distinct national identity through social policy programs. Because social policy is so closely connected to the concept of community, it is a prime gateway to pursue nationalist goals (Béland and Lecours 2008).

The appeal for policy ownership is often attributed to the desire of a national minority government to promote and preserve the distinct character of its cultural community. In their analysis of the link between social policy and nationalism, Béland and Lecours (2006) note that "[i]n seeking control over social policy, nationalist movements can project powerful images about how their community is different from another because it espouses different values"(80). Distinctiveness is often pronounced as a rationale for demanding more policy control from the central state apparatus. It is also used to explain the very structure and outcomes of policy decisions. It follows that the desire to showcase distinctiveness can lead to the design of policies which diverge from the central state serving to emphasize the different needs and desires of the minority nation. Yet, as McEwen (2006) notes, the concept of distinctiveness is not necessarily tied to divergence in policy decisions but, rather, to the way they are presented and discussed. The previously cited literature linking nationalism to the policymaking of minority nations tends to focus on policy issues within the realm of domestic politics. Indeed, the permeation of nationalist interests in policy processes is most explicit in areas of direct concern to citizens. Yet, as discussed next, nationalism is also cultivated and promoted through foreign policy decisions and considerations.

Promoting Minority Nationalism through Foreign Policy

The connection between a state's foreign policy and its national identity promotion has been the subject of important scholarly attention, with several seminal works on the subject published in the early 1990s (Bloom 1990; Campbell 1992; Wallace 1991). These studies depict a mutually reinforcing relationship between foreign policy and nationalism. In his work on the United States, Campbell (1992) describes foreign policy as "one of the practices that contingently constructs through stylized and regulated performances the identity of the state in whose name it operates" (85). An analysis of American post-war foreign policy documents reveals that beyond offering strategic insights into policy threats, they also "concerned themselves with the scripting of a particular American identity" (Campbell 1992, 32). In a discussion of Britain's foreign policy, Wallace attributes the country's foreign policy downfall to its difficulty in projecting a clear national identity internationally. For Wallace (1991), "foreign policy is about national identity itself: about the sources of national pride, the characteristics which distinguish a country from its neighbours, the core elements of sovereignty it seeks to defend, the values it stands for and seeks to promote abroad" (65).

Britain's "crisis of national identity" significantly circumvented its foreign policy capabilities as foreign policy is, in part, "a reflection of that search for identity" (Wallace 1991, 68). Accordingly, a strong national consciousness domestically is construed as a critical tool to increase a country's power and credibility as a foreign policy actor. Bloom uses the term "national identity dynamic" to describe how states galvanize their national public through their foreign policy decisions and discourses. Examining American Cold War foreign policy, Bloom (1990) demonstrates the "domestic manipulation" of national identity in its framing of the Soviet threat at the time.

These studies have been followed by additional research investigating the nationalism/foreign policy connection in more recent years, highlighting different case studies including Turkey (Hintz 2018), Korea (John 2015), Russia (Tsygankov 2019), and India (Wojczewski 2020). Describing the Turkish case, Hintz (2018) shows how foreign policy is used as an alternative arena to promote national identity, where domestic struggles over identity politics exist. John's (2015) study on South Korea reveals how the cultivation and dissemination of a strong international image as an "advanced nation" is also a site for the consolidation of national identity domestically. The intersection between nationalism and foreign policy lends further support to the notion that domestic and foreign politics should be studied in conjunction. As noted by Bloom (1990), "[a] government's foreign policy is thus dictated by internal domestic political realities in as much as by the actual nature of international relations" (81). For Campbell (1992), "the construction of the 'foreign' is made possible by practices that also constitute the 'domestic'" (69).

The Nationalism/Foreign Policy Dynamic in Minority Nations

While much of the literature on the nationalism/foreign policy relationship centres on the nation state as a unit of analysis, the international role of minority nations supports the need to inquire into this relationship at the subnational scale. Indeed, the re-territorialization of world politics is characterized by the multiplication of actors engaged in foreign policy and international relations, including minority nations. The international relations of subnational entities are referred to in the literature as *paradiplomacy*. Denoting the pursuance of foreign policy conducted in *parallel* to a central state, paradiplomacy is commonly associated with the subnational scale. The study of paradiplomacy as it relates to minority nations specifically has gained significant scholarly attention (Bélanger 2002; Criekemans 2010; Keating 1999; Lecours 2002, 2008; Lecours and Moreno 2003; Rioux Ouimet 2015; Paquin 2004, 2005; Paquin and Lachapelle 2005).

The literature on paradiplomacy cites three primary motivations behind the pursuit of international affairs for minority nations: economic, cultural, and political (Keating 1999; Lecours 2008). In the "economic layer," subnational entities seek to establish an international presence to attract foreign investment and enhance economic competitiveness. From a cultural standpoint, they will often develop international ties with their cultural counterparts, aiming to foster common linguistic, educational, and other endeavours. Finally, the political driving forces behind paradiplomacy involve the expression of a distinct identity within the international arena, an affirmation of cultural distinctiveness, and the desire to highlight the national character of the entity in question (Lecours 2008).

This "political layer" (Lecours 2008) is closely tied to nationalism. According to Lecours and Moreno (2003) "nationalism logically leads regional governments to seek international agency" (2). There is an inherent connection between paradiplomacy and nationalism in that through their pursuit of international engagements, minority nations as able to "both behave like nations and present themselves as such" (Lecours and Moreno 2003, 4). International agency provides minority nations and their leaders with legitimacy and strengthens their sense of nationhood. In this way, the paradiplomacy literature echoes the discussion on policy ownership found in the literature on minority nations' domestic policymaking. Parallels can also be drawn with the notion of policy distinctiveness outlined above. Paradiplomacy allows minority nations to promote their distinct interests on the world stage. In line with the studies linking foreign policy to nationalism at the nation-state scale, minority nations are also found to utilize their foreign policy activities towards territorial mobilization goals, gaining a certain degree of prestige domestically through their strong international presence (Lecours and Moreno 2003). In a study of Quebec, for example, Rioux Ouimet (2015) shows that underlying its commercial paradiplomacy is the desire to strengthen the image of an international entity as distinct from the federal level and, through this, mobilize its nation-building internally.

Paquin (2004) coined the term "identity paradiplomacy" to describe the nation-building role and potential of paradiplomacy. For Paquin, sub-state governmental actors act as "identity entrepreneurs" (30) striving to gain recognition on the international stage. The presence of paradiplomacy in multinational societies is not without contention. It is, as Lecours (2002), writes "tied up in power struggles between levels of government" (95). The paradiplomacy of minority nations is rooted in contestations over who has the right to act as a representative of a particular nation.

Public Diplomacy and Soft Power

Within the broader foreign policy domain, minority nations conduct what can be described as public diplomacy initiatives, that is, "attempts to conduct its foreign policy by engaging with foreign publics" (Cull 2008, xv). The focus on higher education as a subject of foreign policy pursued in this book leads to an inevitable discussion of public diplomacy. Educational and cultural exchanges are pivotal to public diplomacy, through which governments cultivate strong relationships with foreign publics and by extension foreign governments (Nye 2008). The sphere of higher education, including international student and staff exchanges and the promotion of university research centres aimed at promoting the understanding of a particular territory, are valuable assets for making connections and communicating with foreign publics. Ultimately, public diplomacy is geared towards promoting a positive image of the country, region, or territory in question. It is an exercise of "soft power," described by Nye (2004), as "the ability to get what you want through attraction rather than coercion or payments. It arises from the attractiveness of a country's culture, political ideals and policies" (4).

"Middle powers" are especially susceptible to relying on soft power as their capacity to exert influence on world politics by other means is limited (Potter 2003). In his discussion of Canada's public diplomacy, Evan Potter (2003) states that "middle powers such as Canada, with limited ability to influence the global public discussion, must give its image serious attention because Canada's global influence today depends increasingly on factors that transcend raw economic or military power and that appeal to public perceptions abroad" (45). The reliance on soft power is also relevant for minority nations, as like "middle powers" described by Potter, their ability to exert change on the global scale is in many ways circumvented by their non-sovereign status. By investigating Quebec's education diplomacy initiatives, this book contributes to an understanding of how soft power is manifested in minority nations. In this way, it makes an explicit link between the study of paradiplomacy and soft power.

Quebec in Canada's Multinational Federation

Education and Canada's Federal System

Understanding the implications of federal dynamics on Quebec's higher education policy requires a discussion of Canada's federal structure and Quebec's unique position as a minority nation therein. Quebec's multinational federal model is often described as asymmetrical. As discussed by Gagnon (2001), such systems serve

> as an instrument of equity rather than strict equality, and a tool of communitarianism rather than procedural liberalism. In this way, the equality of individuals and nations in a federation should be considered in light of their particular needs and historical developments, not in terms of their identical relation with other individuals or member states in a federation (330).

This accurately describes the Canadian context. Home to a national minority with a distinct historical context and distinct needs, Quebec is set apart from other provinces making up the Canadian entity. Quebec's cultural distinctiveness vis-à-vis the rest of Canada is based on the French language, its Catholic heritage, and the use of the Napoleonic civil code (instead of the Common Law). For Gagnon (2001), "Quebec being the primary provider of culture for Quebecers, it deserves more power than a political unit which is simply a subdivision of a larger cultural unity" (321).

The distribution of powers between the federal government and provinces/territories was first outlined in the 1867 agreement on confederation, the British North American Act (BNAA) passed by the British Parliament. At the time, four "colonies" took part in the negotiations on the structure of this confederation; the eastern territories of Nova Scotia and New Brunswick and the two "Canadas" (today's Ontario and Quebec). Additional territories were gradually incorporated into the federal state, the most recent being the territory of Nunavut, officially becoming part of Canada in 1999. The debates and negotiations on confederation took place in 1864, in Charlottetown and Quebec City. The main point of contention revolved around the degree of centralization/decentralization the confederation would take. Two competing visions were proposed. The first, advocated by the man who would eventually become the country's first prime minister, John A Macdonald, foresaw a centralized system, with the authority concentrated with a central government that would be responsible for the different territories. For the province of Quebec, as well as the Maritime provinces, the greater degree of autonomy provided to each territorial unit, the better. A compromise was reached, according to which the power-sharing model of Canadian federalism was sculpted (Gagnon and Iacovino 2006). While this arrangement devolved powers between federated units, it is viewed as a weak form of decentralization, with the territories remaining largely subordinate to the central government (Gagnon 2009).

Although the final federal model may not have been as decentralized as the Quebec delegates desired, it provided them with a sense of security as a "founding" nation. For Quebec, confederation was viewed through the prism of dualism, as a "pact" between two founding nations (Gagnon 2009). Interpretations of the confederation agreement have varied over the years, including scepticism vis-à-vis the actual intention of "English/French" dualism at the time. Yet, for Quebec intellectuals, there is steady agreement that Confederation legitimized the founding role of the province as well as its existence as a distinct nation within Canada (Gagnon 2009; Laforest 2005). This conception of Quebec's role in the Canadian establishment and history will guide the province's ethos in the post-Confederation era.

The BNAA stated that powers granted to the federal government were those deemed to pertain to "peace, order and good government" of all Canadians, including defense and security, trade and commerce, foreign affairs, and federal taxing. The provinces were granted authority over various aspects of their internal functioning, including direct taxation in the province, education, welfare, and hospitals. Several areas are of joint competency, namely, immigration, pensions, marriage, and agriculture. The constitutional arrangements also mandate that a certain proportion of judges on the Supreme Court and senators be from Quebec.

While the distribution of powers determined in 1867 has largely been maintained, tensions over control of certain areas have surfaced over time, often instigated by various governments in Quebec. An important component of the federal–provincial arrangement involves the "federal spending power." While provinces and territories have extensive authority over numerous policy areas, their ability to raise funds to implement said policies is much lower than the federal government's. Various arrangements have been implemented to allow the federal government to transfer payments to the provinces for different programs or to centralize certain areas in a common framework. The concept of federal spending power emerged in the years following the Second World War. Having assumed control over taxation at the income level, the federal government was able to use its financial status to implement programs in areas otherwise under provincial authority. While these initiatives were welcomed by smaller, poorer provinces, others, especially Quebec, criticized their intervening character (Webber 2015). It has since featured as one of the most contentious aspects of Quebec–Ottawa relations. The university sphere is at the centre of this tension as discussed in the following chapters.

Quebec's Quiet Revolution and Consolidation of its Modern Nationalism

The consolidation of Quebec's modern nationalism can be traced back to the Quiet Revolution (révolution tranquille) era, which saw vast socio-economic reforms and modernization agendas implemented in Quebec throughout the 1960s.[1] This period saw important changes in the way Quebec defined itself and its population. Three major shifts are discernible; from a Catholic to secular ethos, from traditional and conservative values to more progressive ones, and from a linguistically based to a territorially based identity. Until the 1960s, the Catholic Church and the values underpinning it were a central feature of French Canadian identity and nationalism. Following the British conquest of Lower Canada, the status of the Catholic religion in the territory was secured through the 1774 Quebec Act, acknowledging Quebec's distinct religious affiliation (Balthazar 1986). Prior to the Quiet Revolution, nation and Catholicism were intractably linked. As discussed by Balthazar (1986), "[i]t was unthinkable to proclaim oneself nationalist in French-Canada without at the very least accepting the essential role played by the Church" (94). Church elites had an overarching function in the social, economic, and political spheres affecting the French Canadian population – including education and social security (Balthazar 1986, 54). Prior to the Quiet Revolution, French Canadian nationalism was, in large part, concerned with defending these values and traditions against the anglophone Protestantism characterizing the rest of North America (Zubrzycki 2013).

Closely related to the drift away from Catholic traditions, is the shift from a more conservative political stance to a progressive vision of society and politics. Indeed, the church's authority was largely dependent on the maintenance of a conservative ethos in the province, which was supported by elected officials in power until the Liberal Party was first elected in 1960. As the church's grasp weakened with the modernization processes of the 1960s, the traditional values it espoused were also on the decline. With the electoral victory of the Liberal Party and the ouster of Maurice Duplessis' close to forty-year Conservative rule, Quebec was in a state of transformation during the 1960s. Since then, Quebec's politics have been largely characterized as left-leaning (Erk 2010). The "left-leaning political identity of Quebec nationalism" (Erk 2010) is evidenced in part by the significance of social democratic values for Quebec identity. Indeed, egalitarian and social democratic values are often cited as important identity markers for Quebec nationalists (Béland and Lecours 2005). This has implications for policymaking, as noted by Gagnon (2018): "Over the years, the notion of distinct society has been transformed to mean a deeper commitment to public policies founded on a more pronounced solidarity in the areas of education, daycare, third-sector economy as well as regional development and fiscal policy" (67). It should be noted that the political landscape in Quebec has shifted in recent years, especially following the election of the Coalition Avenir Quebec (CAQ) party in 2022, the first non-PLQ or PQ government in power in over fifty years (Graefe and Rioux 2020). While policy decisions around immigration and secularism have been compared to ideological tenants of the radical right in Europe, it has also been argued that "Quebec independentism does not fit the mould of right-wing populist movements" (Blanchet and Medeiros 2019, 817).

Undoubtedly, the most striking change to French Canadian nationalism was the shift to a territorially based conception of identity. Prior to the Quiet Revolution, identity in Quebec did not have the strong territorial focus it has today. As noted by Balthazar (1986), while not void of reference to ancestral lands and to the St. Lawrence River specifically, the territorial space was never given concrete or legal specificity. The French language and culture were the primary identifying traits, and the main concern was their preservation within Canada (Breton 1988). This period was characterized by an identification with "French Canada," thus advancing the perception of a minority defending its threatened culture (Breton 1988). The Quiet Revolution led to a perceptual shift in which the territorial and political dimensions of Quebec nationalism were highlighted. The term *French Canadian* was replaced by *Québécois*, and nationalism was pursued first and foremost within the confines of the Quebec territory. According to Breton, this shift was accompanied by a reversal from a perception of minority status to one of majority status within the province.

While language remained a central feature of identification, a shift towards a territorial and civic conception was evident (Caron 2014). A pan-francophone Canadian vision of identity based on ethnicity was replaced by a territorially defined collective membership with civic connotations (Breton 1988). Quebec nationalism was thus given a territorial focal point engendering with it a separatist ideal. In his 1965 assessment of Quebec's modern nationalism, Taylor highlights the notion of separatism as its central marker. Acknowledging that the notion of separation is not new to this era (the Quiet Revolution), Taylor (1965, cited in Laforest 1993) explains that the symbolic weight given to the idea of independence is a crucial component of the post-1960s' Quebec nationalism. Consequently, the desire to gain increased control over the economic, social, and political affairs affecting its population was heightened. The slogan "maîtres chez nous" (masters in our own home) became synonymous with the demands for greater autonomy.

While fundamentally different, what brought the two versions of identity together was their connection to the French language. As described by Taylor (1965, as cited in Laforest 1995), "In its pure form, practically the only value it had in common with the old was the French language itself" (6). The French language and Quebec's francophonie is its star identity marker, around which policies are designed, including in the sphere of higher education as this book demonstrates. While language is most commonly cited as an identity marker of *ethnic* identity, in the case of Quebec, it is used as a symbol of the civic nation, one in which "an otherwise ethnically diverse population expresses its 'collective will to live together'" (Oakes and Warren 2007, 83).

While much of the discussion on Québécois identity is concerned with the province's sub-national identity, studies have also highlighted Quebec's continental identity, its sense of affiliation to the wider American hemisphere (Bouchard 2000; Lachapelle and Gagné 2000; Lachapelle 2011; Lamonde 1999; Thériault 2005). In his 2000 book, *The Making of Nations and Cultures of the New World*, Quebec historian Gérard Bouchard outlines his argument for the emergence of "new collectivities" in the new world, a process by which collective identification to the "American" space is developed through customs and discourse (Bouchard 2000). According to Bouchard (2000), a historical account of Quebec necessitates a look beyond a "narrow and slightly distorted perspective of a cultural minority and its French heritage"

(12, translated from French), to include an account of its *américanité* – its attachment to the American space. For Lachapelle, Quebec's américanité is a testament to the role it intends to play in the American space (Lachapelle 2011). Describing this process, Lachapelle (2011) observes that "[t]he Québécois are no longer the French of the Americas nor French Canadians. They have, at the beginning of this 21st century fully assumed their américanité, on economic, political and cultural levels" (9, translated from French).

Américanité underscores a certain distance from Quebec's European (and particularly French) heritage and culture (Lamonde 1999). The concept of Quebec's américanité is not without its critics. For Thériault (2005), américanité represents an "anti French-Canadian ideology" (27), which essentially erodes what is left of the ethnic understanding of the Quebec nation. Thériault (2005) also firmly criticizes the use of *américanité* as a political tool "born within the technocratic project of the 1960s, *américanité* is the affirmation of an identity which refuses to see itself as such, thus revealing the identity impasse of contemporary Quebec" (27 translated from french).

In the post–Quiet Revolution era, Quebec politicians are leaning on its américanité as a core tenant of its "geopolitical endeavours" (Lamonde 1999) as they work to increase their global engagement and relevance. The strong political reference to Quebec's role in the Americas is grounded in its desire to assert its place in the global economy as well as ensure its prosperity in the event of secession (Gagné 2004). The promotion of Quebec's américanité as a feature of its national identity is also aligned with the notion that Quebec constitutes the sole francophone majority within the American hemisphere. In this way, it sees itself as bearing a certain responsibility to ensure the vitality of the French language in the larger American region. Hence, Quebec's américanité is also closely tied to its francophone identity. Quebec's américanité has also been noted as a marker of its distinct identity within Canada, as a "a way to differentiate Quebec from the rest of Canada and to reaffirm its national status within and outside the Canadian federation" (Dupont 1995, 11). For Oakes and Warren (2007), attaching itself to a greater hemispheric cause in the Americas has served Quebec's "local" needs by "bringing new legitimacy to Quebec's efforts to protect and promote its language and culture" (79).

The investigation of the nationalist discourse associated with higher education policy decisions in Quebec pursued throughout this book reveals a reliance on américanité as a feature of Quebec nationalism. In developing this further, the book aims to contribute to the until-now opaque discussion on Quebec's américanité and offer timely insight into how this specific feature of national identity makes its way into the Québécois discourse on higher education.

As delineated in the next chapter, the Quiet Revolution marked a critical point of departure for the establishment of Quebec's modern higher education system. It was also the period in which nationalism and (higher) education became entangled, a connection that remains to this day. The profound transformation in Quebec's collective awareness and consolidation of a strong and, importantly, *separate* nationalism is intricately linked to concurring transformations occurring in the sphere of education policy. The changes incurred in Quebec's education and higher education systems are a quintessential symbol of its wider modernization and the "national awakening" attached to it.

2 Maîtres Chez Nous: The Quiet Revolution, Higher Education, and the Consolidation of Quebec Nationalism

A discussion of Quebec's contemporary education system inevitably brings us to the 1960s' Quiet Revolution as a point of departure. The period of large-scale socio-economic reforms brought significant changes to Quebec, including the secularization of government, the establishment of a welfare state, and the consolidation of a territorially based "national" identity. Underpinning this all was a broad modernization agenda aimed at stimulating Quebec's socio-economic status and allowing it to "catch up" to the rest of the country, which had modernized at a faster pace in the post-war period. Education became a focal point of the government's agenda during this time, and it is fair to say that Quebec's education system today is a direct product of the political discussions and policies emanating from the Quiet Revolution era. The development of Quebec's modern education system went hand in hand with the consolidation of a Québécois nationalism, grounded in a territorially based conception of identity and belonging. It follows that education and nationalism are strongly intertwined and mutually reinforcing in Quebec. This chapter explores this connection, focusing on the higher education sphere and shedding light on the roots of the higher education/nationalism connection in Quebec. Presenting the backstory to the important connection between Quebec's higher education policy and its nationalist ambitions, this discussion sets the scene for the chapters to follow.

Towards the Quiet Revolution: *la grande noirceur* and its impact on Quebec

The socio-economic reforms rolled out by Quebec's prime minister Jean Lesage during the Quiet Revolution were a direct response to the traditionalist and conservative ideology of Maurice Duplessis, in power in Quebec from 1936 to 1939 and again between 1945 and 1959. Quebec under Duplessis was "fixed in the past" while the rest of Canada modernized (Laniel and Thériault 2018, 69). With its agriculture-based economy and the strong Catholic values permeating its political structure, the Duplessis government was seen as impeding the potential for cultural, political, and economic progress. Duplessis's ultra-conservative stance impacted Quebec's economy, which trailed behind other provinces. This inevitably affected the university sphere, which was itself underdeveloped. Noteworthy here is the fact that it was the francophone universities and students in Quebec who were most affected. In lieu of a centralized authority for coordinating education in Quebec, the Church was the primary provider of education in the province. A dual system of education ensued according to which anglophones were educated under the Protestant Church and francophones under the Catholic Church. This division deepened the disparities between the two language groups, with the latter having the highest elementary school drop-out rate in Canada and the former the lowest (Donald 1997). Higher education rates among Quebec's francophone communities were subsequently low.

Overcoming the burdens of this period, coined as the *grande noirceur* (the great darkness), became the overarching goal of the Quiet Revolution reforms. The Quiet Revolution was the point of no return for the actors of this movement, led by Prime Minister Jean Lesage. The Quiet Revolution would ultimately represent a shift from tradition to modernity for Quebec and its people (Laniel and Thériault 2018). Importantly, through its broad socio-economic reforms, the changes aimed at providing Quebec with the means to enhance its economic competitiveness and political image on an international stage. At the heart of the modernization agenda promoted by Lesage was the importance of gaining control over crucial policy arenas for Quebec to manage its "own destiny."

Lesage's slogan *maîtres chez nous* (masters in our own home) came to epitomize this period, reflecting the PLQ government's overarching appeals for increased autonomy vis-à-vis the federal government. Education policy was brought to the fore in the struggle for heightened policy control. It was perceived as a crucial linchpin to modernization, and an overhaul of this sphere was deemed essential for the "catching up" objective underpinning the reforms. Quebec's contemporary education system is a product of the Quiet Revolution reforms and is often described as the quintessential symbol of this critical juncture in Quebec's history. As this chapter reveals, the discussions around the education reforms taking place at this time were closely aligned with nationalist ideals building up concurrently. Importantly though, the ideals of policy control over education did not begin with Lesage. The idea that Quebec should retain full control over its education system and avoid any federal interference was well established under Duplessis. While the *maîtres chez nous* appeal was consolidated under Lesage, clashes with the federal government over policy control were apparent decades earlier.

The 1950s' Row over Federal University Grants and the Tremblay Commission

As outlined in chapter 1, while the decentralization of education governance to provinces dates to the 1867 BNAA, the federal government has maintained a certain level of involvement in this sphere, through areas deemed of "national interest." While in the inter-war period, the federal role in higher education was limited to military colleges and vocational training, this would shift after 1945 with the massification of higher education. In the aftermath of the war, the Department of Veteran Affairs launched a new funding program for veterans enrolling in university programs across the country. Transferred directly to universities, the funds led to a significant increase in the number of university students in the country (Fisher et al. 2006). The success of the veterans' program prompted university leaders (mainly in English Canada) to acquiesce to the idea of federal involvement in the higher education sphere and lobby for a more permanent arrangement (Cameron 1997). Their appeal was later answered with the recommendations outlined in the Royal Commission on National Development in the Arts, Letters and Sciences (named the Massey Commission), mandated by Canadian prime minister Louis Saint-Laurent in 1949. Among the Massey Commission report's recommendations was the need to increase federal funding to the provinces' universities. The significance of instilling a federal dynamic in the country's higher education was justified as follows:

> The universities are provincial institutions: but they are much more than that.... They also serve the national cause in so many ways, direct and indirect, that theirs must be regarded as the finest contributions to national strength and unity (Royal Commission on National Development in the Arts, Letters and Sciences 1951, 132).

While answering an appeal by anglophone universities for federal support, the Massey Commission's recommendations pertaining to higher education were met with rebuke in Quebec. While initially accepting the federal arrangement, the Duplessis government eventually decided to reject the aid, directing its universities to refuse the funding. In a letter to the federal minister of justice Stuart Garson, Duplessis reproached the federal funding to universities accusing the federal government of "encroaching in the domain of education, an exclusive competency of the provinces" (Letter from Maurice Duplessis to federal justice minister Stuart Garson, 15 September 1954). In an earlier letter addressed to Canadian prime minister Louis Saint-Laurent in 1951, Duplessis underscores the importance of maintaining provincial competency over education:

> We do not doubt the good intentions of the federal government and in particular your desire to express your respect of provincial autonomy on educational matters, but we are strongly convinced that this project is a dangerous overreach of power by the federal government in a fundamental area, exclusively reserved to the provinces (Letter from Duplessis to Saint Laurent, 17 November 1951).

The controversy over federal university subsidies was among the propelling factors leading the Duplessis government to mandate the Royal Commission of Inquiry into Constitutional Problems (1954; also referred to as the Tremblay Commission) to assess constitutional issues and study tax sharing between the provincial and federal levels of government (Foisy-Geoffroy 2007). The commission resulted in several recommendations, emphasizing the importance of decentralization of authority, specifically the devolving of social security back to the provinces, and the active support of the French Canadian culture by the Quebec government (Foisy-Geoffroy 2007). While English Canada was becoming less skeptical about centralizing authority, the Quebec government maintained a fervent desire for more autonomy, outlined in the various recommendations of the Tremblay Report (Gagnon and Iacovino 2006). Ultimately, the report reiterated the notion of dualism promoted in Quebec since Confederation and highlighted Quebec's status as a distinct national group in Canada, deserving of a distinct status within the federal structure (Gagnon and Iacovino 2006).

The education sphere, and universities specifically, take centre stage in the four-volume report. Education is described as intimately connected to culture and the need to acknowledge and preserve the distinct French Canadian culture in Quebec is highlighted:

If there is one area where the cultural distinctiveness of the province of Quebec should be affirmed with full awareness of itself, it is surely education at all levels.... It is thus first and foremost through the school that the province of Quebec will fulfil its mission of guardian of French-Canadian culture and will justify its desire for autonomy ... (Royal Committee of Inquiry on Constitutional Problems, 1956. Vol 3 Part I, 213).

The importance of maintaining authority over the university sphere (and education more broadly) is discursively linked in the report to Quebec's distinctiveness as a separate "national group" within Canada:

In the current state of affairs, it is dangerous for the province of Quebec and for the future of the French-Canadian collective to fully concede that the fields of education and culture be open to initiatives and activities of the federal government ... The Canadian state is not only a federation of provinces, it is a federation of two national groups, and it is especially because of this characteristic that education was given to and should remain with the provinces (Royal Commission of Inquiry on Constitutional Problems, 1956. Vol 2, 243).

[T]he constitutional debates engendered in Quebec by the federal grants to Canadian universities highlighted the role of universities in the economic, social and cultural life of the nation and the country. For French-Canadians in particular, this awareness of the role of universities is all the more important in that they must make an effort to better consolidate their economy and participate more broadly to the development of their territory – and that only the universities can provide them with the personnel apt to accomplish such an important task (Royal Commission of Inquiry on Constitutional Problems, 1956. Vol 3 Part I, 193).

Similar arguments advocating for Quebec's "fiscal liberty" were outlined by a member of the Tremblay Commission, Esdras Minville, in an editorial for *l'action nationale* in 1956. Minville associates the university subsidy issue with a wider debate in Canada's constitutional politics, viewed as another example of the federal government hiding behind a "façade of federalism and promoting a unitary state." For Minville, "Quebec's loss of its fiscal liberty is equivalent to the loss for French Canada of its most powerful means to preserve itself and take its place as a distinct cultural community within the Canadian state" (*l'action nationale*, 4 December 1946).

Minville further argued that a people cannot preserve their culture if "it cannot benefit from the ability to build its own institutions" (ibid.).

The battle between the Duplessis government and the federal government over university subsidies lasted close to a decade with a final agreement reached following Duplessis' death in 1959. The agreement between Ottawa and Quebec City saw the financial grants intended for universities transferred directly to the Quebec government instead. The solution was touted as a major victory for the Quebec government and as a crucial example of it taking control of its "own destiny." It would also be the first time a province "opted out" of a federal program (Cameron 1997), leading to wider constitutional implications. Coming on the heels of the Quiet Revolution, the decision on university funding would spearhead Quebec's quest for further policy control. The row over university subsidies would provide an important impetus for the *maîtres chez nous* aspirations of Lesage's government.

Maîtres chez nous: Policy Ownership, National Identity, and Higher Education[1]

As the various chapters of this book elucidate, Quebec nationalism is cultivated and perpetuated via different thematic areas around the governance of higher education, including issues related to tuition fees, university language policy, the recruitment of international students, and education diplomacy schemes. Yet, beyond these concrete policy issues, the very existence of a higher education structure at the subnational scale is discursively connected to nationalism and national identity in Quebec. The *maîtres chez nous* aspiration at the heart of the policy development occurring during the Quiet Revolution is a prime illustration of McEwen's (2005) "policy ownership" premise summarized in chapter 1. As discussed in this current chapter, Quebec's policy "ownership" appeals surrounding the university sphere, are discursively linked to the consolidation of its national identity in the postwar period.

Considered an indispensable linchpin to modernization, education became a pillar of the Quiet Revolution reforms and a key policy priority for Lesage following his election in 1960. One of his very first acts as prime minister of Quebec was to mandate the Royal Commission on Education to initiate reforms in this sector and align it with his broader modernization agenda. Presiding over the commission was the vice-rector of the University of Laval and priest Monseigneur Alphonse-Marie Parent. The decision to appoint a clergy member as head of the commission alludes to the critical role of the church in educational affairs in the years preceding the Quiet Revolution and the difficulty in abruptly dissociating the two. The presence of a respected representative of the clergy appeased the fears of the church, private institutions, (including universities) and the more conservative-leaning segments of Quebec society (Corbo 2002). The following years would nevertheless see a heightened government involvement in the education sector at the expense of the church. The Royal Commission on Education laid the groundwork for this shift.

The Parent Commission, as it came to be known, involved a large-scale examination of the state of education in Quebec, accumulating insights and testimonies from a wide range of education stakeholders across the province. The commission's wider aim was to develop an education policy for Quebec embedded in a global perspective and take into consideration the massification of education at the time (Beaulieu and Bertrand 1999). Discussions on the modernization of Quebec's economy were coupled with the desire to widen access to higher education and develop a modern education system which would support and invigorate the economic reforms. The commission's conclusions were outlined in the five volumes making up the Parent Report, which, together, incorporated six hundred recommendations for modernizing Quebec's education system. A core ideal recurring in the report is the importance of democratizing the education system, with a particular emphasis on supporting its public character. If prior to the Quiet Revolution, education, and specifically higher education were accessible to only a minority of francophones in Quebec, the Parent Report called for a shift towards a democratization of the education system, wherein all Québécois would have equal chances to attend. Such a goal necessitated a strong state involvement in the development of Quebec's higher education system and its valuation as a public institution. The strong connection between higher education policy and nationalism in Quebec is heavily rooted in these early discussions and, specifically, in the Parent Commission's reports. An understanding of how notions of nationalism saturate these discussions thus provides an important backdrop to the nationalism/higher education nexus uncovered throughout this book.

Within the Parent Report, education is described as playing a pivotal societal role that necessitates the instilling of an education system that is implanted in its "national" surroundings:

In short, the benefits of education extend beyond the individual and locality; the progress of education primarily serves the general interests of society in such a way that we can indeed consider education to be a **national enterprise** (Royal Commission of Inquiry on Education in the Province of Quebec, 1966. Volume IV, 33, my emphasis).

On the surface, *maîtres chez nous* denotes a desire to take control of policy arenas that have direct implications for the Québécois people. It is about presenting the image of a state in control of its own affairs and as the legitimate entity responsible for ensuring the well-being of its citizenry. Perhaps inevitably, however, once a policy sphere is "owned," it can be moulded to align with the specificities of the communities it serves. One of the underlying rationales behind the education modernization agenda outlined in the Parent Report is one of distinctiveness. Establishing a modern and, importantly, independent system of education is touted as a prerequisite for respecting Quebec's distinctiveness within Canada:

> The **Province of Quebec is distinct** from the other provinces in almost all aspects. As the core of the oldest settlement, its history covers three and a half centuries. Populated by a francophone and catholic people from the beginning of the 17th century, it became bi-ethnic and multi-faith following the ceding to England ... These traits suffice to give the province a distinct character compared to the rest of the country. It is in this **context of originality** that the history of its education system lies (Royal Commission of Inquiry on Education in the Province of Quebec, 1963. Vol. I, 20, my emphasis).

Of the six hundred recommendations outlined in the Parent Report, one-tenth relate specifically to university policy (Corbo 2002). An underlying premise put forth is that the state should take a more prominent role in both university financing and the development of the higher education system through a coherent policy. The university is described in the report as a vital institution for supporting Quebec's newfound industrialization and urbanization. It should also reflect the growing aspirations towards cultivating a democratic, prosperous, modern, and socially just society (Corbo 2002). The report also highlights the critical role of the state apparatus in financing universities, referencing the importance of ensuring their public character:

> Even if the government did not subsidize universities, they could not detach themselves from their social function. This is why they find themselves to a certain extent as **associates of the State** in its specific function of **guardian of the public good**. When the universities and the state are called to work together it is nevertheless the state which retains the responsibility over the public good (Royal Commission of Inquiry on Education in the Province of Quebec, 1966. Vol III 187, my emphasis).

The Parent Report set an important precedent with regards to the role of the university in Quebec society. With education so closely tied to Quebec's socio-economic transformation, government involvement was deemed essential. In the higher education sphere, the need for substantial government involvement was also tied to the democratization agenda pursued at the time. The question of the university's public character and accessibility stemming from the Parent Commission is addressed in the next chapter. Of note in this current discussion is the commission's role in establishing the institutions which would allow the Quebec government to take on its role as "guardian of the public good."

The Establishment of Quebec's Ministry of Education: 'The Most Important Bill of the Century'

Prior to the Parent Commission, Quebec lacked a governmental body responsible for education. Education was coordinated by different government offices with much of the responsibility held by church organizations and officials. The Parent Report solidified the trend towards further governmental authority over education with its recommendation to establish the Quebec Ministry of Education. As per the report, if the Ministry of Agriculture was given a heightened role a decade prior, a Ministry of Education should be prioritized in 1960s' Quebec (Royal Commission of Inquiry on Education in the Province of Quebec, Vol. I, 1961, 105). Taking inspiration from the mandate of the British Ministry of Education at the time, the Parent Report suggests the following role for the ministry: "to promote education, ensure the progressive development of educational institutions in order to offer varied and complete education services to all, in all regions" (105).

In late 1963, Quebec's Legislative Assembly introduced Bill 60 for the creation of the Ministry of Education. The bill also included plans to establish the Superior Council of Education (conseil supérieur de l'éducation), a consultative organ to provide recommendations and opine on matters referred to it. During the second reading of the bill, Jean Lesage described the initiative as being of "great importance for the future of Quebec" (Legislative Assembly of Quebec, 23 January 1964). union nationale member Albert Gervais called it "the most important bill of the century for our province." It was described as aligned with the desire to "provide our people, in accordance with its aspirations and characteristics an efficient instrument for its intellectual growth."

Discussions around the creation of the Ministry of Education echo earlier arguments made when opposing the federal subsidies to universities a decade earlier. Inaugurating a government ministry responsible for education policy in Quebec was the pinnacle of the education policy ownership ideal promoted in their own ways by both Duplessis and Lesage. During the bill's final reading, Paul Gérin-Lajoie, Liberal Party member and Quebec's first minister of education, defended the importance of instituting a separate ministry in Quebec:

> The best ally, the most useful and powerful ally for Quebec citizens is the government of Quebec. This is why important actions of the present government have been geared towards providing the State with the necessary means, the tools and levers to fulfil its function as server and protector of Quebec (Legislative Assembly of Quebec, 5 February 1964).

Gérin-Lajoie's statement enhances the conception of Quebec as the legitimate entity responsible for the well-being of its citizens. A separate ministry of education is deemed essential for the government to take this function on and to develop its policies independent of the federal government. Gérin-Lajoie's vision of the government of Quebec as constituting the "best ally" for its citizens supports the literature associating legitimacy and identity. For Habermas (1984), "the claim to legitimacy is related to the social-integrative preservation of a normatively determined social identity. *Legitimations* serve to make good this claim, that is to show how and why existing (or recommended) institutions are fit to employ political power in such a way that the values constitutive for the identity of the society will be realized" (182). A ministry of education for Quebec would not only ensure that policy ownership is secured but would ultimately provide structural manifestation to the fact that it was "Quebec rather than Canada that provided for the citizens of Quebec" (McEwen 2005, 540).

The need for a ministry of education was also discursively aligned with Quebec's status as a "minority people." Quebec's distinctiveness within North America is described by proponents of the bill as being in peril, with education offering a potential solution to securing it. For Gervais,

> [w]hen it comes to a minority people like ours, a people who lives one against forty on the North American continent, its education system must hold, exert a more direct and more decisive fighting strength. An ethnic minority which seeks to survive and flourish according to its own characteristics does not have the luxury to stagnate in education. ... An ethnic minority which does not excel in the field of education is destined to very quickly see the elements which characterize it crumble, see it disintegrate

and lose value until it eventually dies. And this risk is all the more important for us, French Canadians, as the other 195 million in North America surround us, besiege us so to speak through modern communication, a formidable linguistic and psychological armor which present a serious challenge to Quebec (Legislative Assembly of Quebec, 5 February 1964).

The establishment of the ministry helped solidify the idea that state institutions should be congruent with Quebec's distinct status and character. While, as an institution, the ministry was a symbolic attribute of Quebec's distinctiveness, the policies it advanced concretized this distinctiveness. Underlying these policies were ideals of democratization and accessibility, values that became staples of Quebec's distinct model of higher education. The Parent Commission's report included several recommendations for fulfilling the accessibility and democratization agendas at the core of its investigation. The following section discusses two policy initiatives deriving from the Parent Commission's recommendations which have had a profound impact on Quebec's higher education system as we know it: the creation of the Cégep (College for Professional and General Education) and the establishment of the University of Quebec network. The discourse around these two policy initiatives is demonstrative of the connection between Quebec nationalism and its higher education structure.

Concretizing Quebec's Distinctiveness through Policy Initiatives

THE CÉGEP: A ONE-OF-A-KIND QUEBEC MODEL

Among the Parent Commission's recommendations for ensuring greater accessibility to higher education was the establishment of a new level of education to serve as a bridge between high school and university. Motivated by aspirations of accessibility underpinning the commission discussions, the idea was conceived as critical for reaching the democratization and accessibility goals of Quebec's "revamped" education system. The high school–to–university trajectory common to Canada and the United States was considered inadequate to prepare students for higher education (Rocher 2006). An intermediary between the two was needed to ensure students are better prepared for university. The Parent Commission recommended the creation of a new cycle of preuniversity and professional studies – distinct from high school and university (Gingras 1992). The new education level – the "Institute," as the Parent Commission suggested it be called – would reflect Quebec's newfound ambition to create a "larger, richer, simpler, more generous and more democratic education system" (Royal Commission of Inquiry on Education in the Province of Quebec, 1964, Vol. II, 191).

The newly established Ministry of Education embraced the Parent Report's guidance on the establishment of institutes. Soon after the second and third volumes of the report were published, Gérin-Lajoie announced the creation of a planning committee for the "Pre-University and Professional Studies" (COPEPP) to assess the challenges of preuniversity learning in light of the Parent Report's recommendations (Dassylva 2006). It was during the COPEPP's deliberations that the report's suggested name "Institute" was replaced with Collège d'enseignement general et professionnel (Cégep). In 1965, the newly elected l'union nationale continued the groundwork for the establishment of the Cégep system, putting in place a directorate general for preuniversity and professional studies and a special mission composed of bureaucrats and education representatives interested in taking part in the reform (Dassylva 2006). Deliberations ultimately led to the loi des collèges d'enseignement general et professionel – Bill 21 – introduced to the Legislative Assembly on 27 January 1967.

As outlined in the bill, with the establishment of the Cégep system, following their high school graduation, students in Quebec would enrol in Cégep for either two years of general studies before entering university or for a three-year professional program before entering the workforce (Donald 1997). Intensifying the links between high school, higher education, and the workforce, the new structure was aimed at increasing participation rates among francophone Québécois (Donald 1997). It was by far the most ambitious project outlined in the Parent Report, and the commission members were conscious of the challenges it would entail (Rocher 2006).

Amid its rampant education reforms, the government of Quebec was now committing itself to creating a whole new level of education – establishing buildings, hiring teachers, developing curriculum, and quality assurance mechanisms. Not only was this novel to Quebec, but it was also novel to the world. After three readings, Bill 21 was unanimously passed by Quebec's Legislative Assembly on 29 June 1967. That fall, the first twelve Cégeps were opened. Today, forty-eight Cégeps are dispersed throughout the province, including forty-three francophone and five anglophone institutions. Cégeps constitute an exemplary dimension of Quebec's unique education system. The establishment of the Cégep system is undoubtedly one of the most palpable outcomes of the education modernization agenda outlined in the Parent Report. From a structural perspective, the reforms around collegial education culminated in a new model, one unique to Quebec. In this way, it became an institution associated with the Quebec state and Québécois society more broadly.

The Cégep system is described in early political discussions as an indispensable tool for Quebec's collective development. With no tuition fees, Cégeps played a crucial role in widening accessibility and promoting education in Quebec's peripheral regions. The significance of the Cégep model for Quebec was described by Guy Rocher, one of the members of the Parent Commission, fifty years later as tied to the fact that

> Cégeps, especially in regions, are closely tied to their social environment. The classical colleges which preceded them were turned inwards. On the other hand, Cégeps are deeply anchored in their environments, they have become the pillars of economic, social and cultural development (Rocher 2017).

The notion that post-secondary institutions should be "deeply anchored in their environments" echoes the Parent Report's discourse on the significance of an education system congruent with the needs of the national community it serves. Established in large cities as well as more peripheral regions in Quebec, Cégeps extended the idea of territorial embeddedness to more local/regional levels. Yet their declared significance for regional development around Quebec was also connected to a collective mobilization of Québécois more broadly. Implanting Cégeps in more remote regions of Quebec was crucial to promoting the accessibility of higher education among Québécois. It also served an important mobilizing role, making the Parent Reforms more visible to the public and facilitating the collective attachment to these uniquely Québécois institutions.

The development of the Cégep system reflected Quebec taking control of its destiny and designing policy which corresponded to its needs and aspirations as a collective project. The creation of the "intermediary" level of education was described as a decisive yet difficult choice which was made to "better serve the interests of Quebec" (Quebec Ministry of Education 1978). By instituting a completely new scale of education, the Quebec government was deviating from the common policy of "most Western countries" of enhancing accessibility through the university system itself (Quebec Ministry of Education 1978, 10). While the challenges of this approach were acknowledged, the groundbreaking appeal of such a policy decision was highlighted and linked to the nation-building agenda pursued at the time. The fervour surrounding the creation of the Cégep system went hand in hand with

Quebec's broader collective development and anchoring of a collective consciousness around common values and aspirations. As outlined in a Ministry of Education policy document reviewing the state of Cégeps ten years after their establishment: "[t]he creation of the Cégep ... quickly took on the character of an immense 'national project,' with all the enthusiasm and fervour of such a collective enterprise as well as resistance and clashes" (Quebec Ministry of Education 1978, 10). In the same report, Jacques-Yvan Morin, minister of education at the time, noted the significance of Cégeps for Quebec's "collective project":

> Education cannot be defined in isolation. It only takes on its full meaning in relation to the overall collective project of a society. In Quebec, as in all countries, no sustainable national project can be built without quality education. The Cégep "québécois," through its position in our education system is one of the keys to our collective future (Quebec Ministry of Education 1978, x).

The development of the Cégep system is one of the success stories of the Quiet Revolution and the Parent Commission reforms. Reflecting on the legacy of the Cégep system fifty years after its establishment, former member of the Parent Commission, Guy Rocher, noted the anchoring of the Cégep in Quebec's very identity:

> It is remarkable that in the entire Quebecois education system, it is undoubtedly the Cégep that best protects and realizes the objectives of the reforms of 1960 and the intentions of their designers. This might explain how it has survived various attacks and threats over its very existence. It is today anchored in Québécois society, inserted in its fabric to the point of being part of its identity (Rocher 2017).

Alongside these structural arguments linking the Cégep system to Quebec's collective national project were discussions of how the curriculum in these institutions could enhance young Québécois' understanding of Quebec history, culture, and political institutions. Cégeps are connected by a shared core curriculum, including obligatory courses on Quebec literature and history. Among a series of new compulsory courses introduced in 1979 was a two-credit course on "Quebec Civilization," to address the recent "neglect of teaching national history" (Quebec Ministry of Education 1978, 110). Explaining the rationale behind the new course, the ministry report states:

> The government considers it essential to offer all students at the collegial level the possibility of deepening the reflection gained in high school on

the origins, culture, and institutions of the Quebec nation ... The aim is twofold: at the individual level, to allow students to develop a personal understanding of the principal historical factors which created the community in which they live and have nourished the culture which coincides significantly with what they aspire to become. At a collective level, to cultivate a feeling of attachment in the student, to enlighten and enrich their participation in national life, thanks to the strength of the institutions which frame and guide society (Quebec Ministry of Education 1978, 110).

Beyond its important domestic impacts, the Cégep system was viewed as an example of Quebec's ingenuity and the source of a certain international notoriety. By creating a new model of education, Quebec garnered the attention of the international community and concretized its distinctiveness within Canada and globally. In a report marking the fifty-year anniversary of the first Cégeps, the Superior Council on Education (2019) describes the initiative as "a singular model" and an "added value to Quebec's education system" (1). It also highlights the distinct feature of the Cégep system: "As much as this level of education in Quebec is distinct from other education systems in North America and around the world, the Council believes that the Québécois model is the envy of certain jurisdictions" (1). In a 1978 report, the Ministry of Education referenced the endorsement from the Organisation for Economic Co-operation and Development (OECD) of Quebec's Cégep system as an indication of the international notoriety it engenders. The fact that the OECD is putting a spotlight on Quebec's Cégep system and referring to it as "an educational and socio-political model of utmost importance on an international scale " reflects the strong external impression the reform brings with it (Quebec Ministry of Education 1978, vii).

THE UNIVERSITY OF QUEBEC NETWORK

The Parent Commission voiced concern over the impact the massification of higher education would have on francophone universities, which would be unable to cope with the increased numbers in student enrolment. Among its recommendations to widen accessibility among francophone Québécois was the immediate establishment of a second French-language university in Montreal along with the gradual establishment of additional universities and university centres to address the eventual shortage of university spaces (Royal Commission of Inquiry on Education in the Province of Quebec, Vol. 2 1964). These institutions were meant to be of limited charter, meaning that they would only offer first-degree courses to respond to the surplus of students enrolling in their first cycle of studies. While this vision for the expansion of

Quebec's university system was by no means trivial, the government's eventual policy decisions in this area took it even further. In 1968, plans for the establishment of a network of affiliated universities across Quebec, which would be of full-chartered scope, were introduced in the Legislative Assembly.

The 1968 law on the University of Quebec, Bill 88, was described by Prime Minister Jean-Jacques Bertrand as a "capital act for the development of Quebec's education system and for the progress of Quebec society as a whole" (Legislative Assembly of Quebec, 9 December 1968). The network's establishment addressed three central issues brought forth by the Parent Commission: to widen university participation rates, promote the development of scientific research in Quebec, and enhance accessibility to higher education in Quebec's peripheral regions. To this end, the bill called for the establishment of a new francophone university, Quebec's first public university, which would be made up of affiliated campuses dispersed across its regions, each with its own judicial autonomy (Ferretti 1994). The territorial dimension would have a profound impact on Quebec society by providing access to higher learning in remote regions otherwise lacking academic institutions. In its initial plan, the network would be made up of institutions in Montreal, Trois Rivières, Rimouski, and Chicoutimi. There are currently ten affiliated campuses dispersed throughout Quebec.

Akin to the Cégep example, the intersection between the establishment of the University of Quebec Network and Quebec nationalism is two-fold. First, through its development and success in widening accessibility in Quebec's more peripheral regions, the network is perceived as a key instrument in collective societal development and broader collective mobilization efforts. This is of particular importance in the post–Quiet Revolution era, the crux of Quebec's modernization and societal development agenda. The creation of another French-language academic institution, one which would extend across Quebec and provide learning opportunities to a vast proportion of its population, was discursively connected to the societal transformation occurring in Quebec at the time. During a reading of the bill for the establishment of the network, PLQ member Pierre Laporte stated:

> We have had many occasions in recent months and years to make our case for the promotion of French culture, the progress of various projects which we would like to see through within the French community which we are forming in North America. All we can say about the importance of the French language, its defense, the means to ensure its quality, all we can imagine for the future of Quebec in 1978, is summed

up more than ever in already used statement "battle of the brains" ... Who will we be, us Québécois, in this world? Where will we fit in this knowledge society? I believe this is a question that all Québécois should be asking. We will have only two answers: education and research ... The ability to survive, since this is what is at stake, has a direct link to the level of scientific research of a society (Legislative Assembly of Quebec, 9 December 1968).

Like the Cégep, the University of Quebec network became a symbol of Quebec identity. During the parliamentary reading of Bill 88, the future network was described by the prime minister at the time Jean-Jacques Bertrand as a potential source of collective development:

The University of Quebec is an organization which will impact the future of Quebec society ... in the intermediate we can envision that the University of Quebec will achieve much more than this. It can become one of our most important instruments of collective development, like Hydro-Quebec, the general society for financing, caisse de dépôt (Legislative Assembly of Quebec, 9 December 1968).

The University of Quebec's main purpose was "the promotion of equality, linguistic, social and economic equity in order to allow more francophone, more women and more individuals from disadvantaged backgrounds, citizens from peripheral regions, to have access to university" (Ferretti 1994, viii). For over fifty years, the University of Quebec network has maintained a consistent core mission described today as "contributing to the scientific advancement of Quebec society; to its economy prosperity and its social and cultural fulfilment; to the development of its communities and regions and to its international influence"(University of Quebec network webpage).[2] The network continues to be described by politicians as an indispensable instrument to Quebec's development and collective future. The significance of the network for Quebec's political arena is reflected in the 2018 parliamentary motion to mark the fiftieth anniversary of its establishment. Introduced by Minister of Education Hélène David, the motion

outlines the contribution of these universities to Quebec society and particularly its regions as well as notes the importance of continued investment in the University of Quebec network for it to be able to continue to promote the advancement of knowledge and the development and prosperity of Quebec (National Assembly of Quebec, 13 June 2018).

The "*modèle Québécois*" of Higher Education: The Nationalism Connection

The Parent Commission constitutes a defining event within a broader critical juncture for Quebec. If the Quiet Revolution marks a turning point for Quebec society, on a micro level, the Parent Commission marks a turning point for its education system. The Parent Commission allowed Quebec to promote its distinct values around accessibility and social welfare and, in this way, held tremendous symbolic power. It led the way for the Lesage government to reimagine the features and contours of Quebec's education system to align with the ideals underpinning the Quiet Revolution. It also held a significant material function by paving the way for the realization of unique policy paths for Quebec, notably the development of the Cégep system and the University of Quebec network. These concrete policy initiatives served to solidify the diverging policy decisions taken by Quebec and highlight its distinctiveness vis-à-vis the rest of Canada as well as globally. The Quebec model of higher education, based on values of accessibility and democratization, and materialized through network systems like the Cégep and the University of Quebec, is a hallmark of Quebec's distinctiveness as a nation within a nation. For Quebec, gaining control over higher education policy decisions is deemed necessary for the elaboration of policies which are in line with its specific identity markers and interests. Notably, the political discussions around tuition fees in Quebec have also been permeated by nationalist discourses from the Quiet Revolution until today. In chapter 3, the relationship between tuition fees and Quebec's minority nationalism is investigated.

3 The University as Public Good: Towards the 2012 Maple Spring Protests

The alignment between nationalism and higher education policy in Quebec came to the fore during the 2012 Maple Spring protests, marking the largest student strike in its history and engendering a social movement of unprecedented scope (Ancelovici and Dupuis-Déri 2014). The unparalleled domestic crisis also garnered significant international attention, putting Quebec on the map in relation to broader global discussions around austerity occurring at the time. The Maple Spring protests and the government's response to them connected Quebec to global themes around inequality sprouting in different parts of the world (Garland 2012), including the Arab Spring, and Occupy Wall Street movements. As noted by Giroux (2013), "[e]volving into a major, broad-based opposition movement against neoliberal austerity measures, the Quebec student strike initiated one of the most powerful, collectively organized challenges to neoliberal ideology, policy and governance that has occurred globally" (521).

Prompted by Prime Minister Jean Charest's announcement of an impending tuition fee hike, and against the backdrop of mounting neoliberal reforms, the protests quickly extended past student grievances to galvanize Quebec society. The tuition fee hike was viewed as an affront to the *modèle Québécois* solidified during the Quiet Revolution. Opponents of the proposed reforms perceived affordable tuition as integral to the Québécois ethos. Threats to this ideal were ultimately viewed as threats to the Québécois societal model in place since the 1960s. And, as outlined in this chapter, the discussions around tuition fees were permeated with a strong discourse of nationalism.

The chapter takes the Maple Spring protests as a backdrop to problematize how the issue of tuition fees came to be so closely associated with Quebec nationalist politics. An investigation into the discursive alignment between the tuition fee issue and nationalism/national identity is laid out. A central theme emerging from the analysis is the significance of maintaining the public character of higher education imbued with values of accessibility and democratization. Indeed, the tuition fee question is coupled with the need to maintain the public character of the university, a value anchored in the five volumes of the Parent Report. Through an analysis of policy texts and discussions from 1960 to 2012, this chapter traces how the importance of maintaining the public character of academic institutions is discursively linked to collective identity and questions of nationalism in Quebec. It also demonstrates how it is used as an example of Quebec's distinctiveness within Canada and as a staple of Quebec's distinct society.

Higher Education as a Public Good: The Case of Minority Nations

The characterization of higher education as a public good is not clearcut (Marginson 2018). A good is categorized as "public" when it is "non-excludable" and "non-rival." Put another way, its consumption by one does not deny its consumption by others, and no one can be denied access to it (Samuelson 1954). While knowledge is a quintessential example of a non-rivalrous and non-excludable good, access to knowledge produced in universities is not guaranteed across the board (Enders and Jongbloed 2007). Access to higher education is also contingent on financial status, making it difficult to define it as a "pure public good" (Enders and Jongbloed 2007). As noted by Marginson (2014), alongside their public features, higher education institutions also "produce private goods for students and industry; that is, rivalrous and excludable benefits distributed on a zero-sum basis, such as the social status of graduates, earnings attributable to higher education and income generated by intellectual property originating from university research" (52).

While the public character of higher education may be ambiguous, and the very notion of "public good" as it pertains to this policy sphere problematic (Pusser 2006), it is traditionally perceived as constituting the public responsibility of the state, and as a contributor to the public good. The very term *public* is often equated with that of *government* (Calhoun 2006). Historically, the establishment of universities was part and parcel of state-formation processes and relied on for the cultivation of national consciousness (Ruegg 2006). Accordingly, funding and governance of higher education systems are traditionally under the responsibility of the state (Enders 2004). Universities have and continue to serve *national* needs and, as such, are considered important agents in the pursuit of state interests.

The perceptions of the university as both a "state" and a "public" institution are closely connected. As described by Enders and Jongbloed (2007), the "publicness" of higher education, or the notion that it fulfils a public service is often used to legitimize the state funding and state ownership of this sphere. The discourse of "public" in state services generally implies a state-driven process according to which national governments are responsible for safeguarding these public institutions, whether through public financing or government regulation and decision-making (Marginson 2018). Accordingly, the public good connotation of higher education assumes a collective process of some kind, one that serves the benefits of a particular community. For Kwiek (2005), the "public" roles of the traditional university, which in the globalized era are being re-negotiated, include to "train citizens subjects of the nation-state, watch over the spiritual life of the people, produce and inculcate national self-knowledge and provide the social glue necessary to keep the citizens of the nation-state together" (41). This is in line with broader notions of welfare-state politics, which are predicated on a strong sense of solidarity within national communities. Indeed, the challenge to the public character of higher education falls within the ambit of broader threats facing welfare-state models around the world.

The rise in neoliberal values and permeation of market logics challenge the traditional view of the university as a public good. Critics of the neoliberal turn in higher education describe an antagonistic relationship between the economic imperatives and the civic function of education, which universities fulfil. In their book, *Academic Capitalism and the New Economy: Markets, States and Higher Education*, Slaughter and Rhoades (2004), argue that there has been a conceptual shift from a "public good knowledge/learning regime" to an "academic capitalist knowledge/learning regime (6)," whereby networks of higher education stakeholders create new paths of learning which connect academic institutions to the new neoliberal and capitalist-leaning economy.

The marketization trends affecting higher education institutions in recent decades have deepened the divide between public and private interests while at the same time contributing to their blurring. For Slaughter and Rhoades (2004), "the boundaries between private and public are fluid: higher education institutions, corporations and the state (of which public universities are part) are in constant negotiation. Contradictions and ironies are rife" (27). Ultimately, however, the universal trend towards "academic capitalism" has weakened the conception of "public" in higher education. This reflects broader transformations in the understanding of the public sector and the "renegotiations" of the post-war welfare-state model moulded in industrialized countries (Kwiek 2005). Relating this back to the Quebec case, the government's appeals for policy control and the *maîtres chez nous* ideal are threatened by the turn to private stakeholders in the financing of higher education institutions and activities.

The Nationalism Connection

What are the implications of the precarity of welfare-state models on nationalism, and what can we infer on the relationship between (minority) nationalism and higher education policy? Scholars of liberal nationalism, relate to a bidirectional relationship between the welfare-state and national identities. In an account of the "ethics of nationality," Miller (1995) describes national identity as a fundamental feature of the welfare state as it requires a sense of community, trust, and solidarity between citizens. According to this logic, states that "aim to be welfare states and at the same time to win democratic legitimation must be rooted in communities whose members recognize such obligations of justice to one another" (93). Similarly, Tamir (1995) views the liberal welfare state as "predicated on certain 'national beliefs'" (147).

McEwen's (2005) study of nationalism and the welfare state in Quebec and Scotland, redirects the causal relationship between them by emphasizing the role of the welfare state for sustaining and strengthening national identities. Contrasting her work to Miller's and Tamir's, McEwen (2006) writes that "[i]f the development of a welfare-state is dependent upon a sense of national identity and mutual belonging, can it also be credited with generating and sustaining it?" (66). McEwen's book points to the way in which "public policy designed to recognize the rights and status granted by virtue of one's membership of a national community may in turn reinforce the national identity and sense of national solidarity upon which they are founded" (66). On the Quebec case, Béland and Lecours (2006) similarly highlight the identity building role of welfare politics in Quebec arguing that "to undermine the welfare state is to undermine the *national* state" (85).

Relating specifically to higher education policy, Arnott and Ozga (2016) make similar claims in their study on Scotland. Examining the Scottish National Party's (SNP) discourse around the public mission of universities, the authors reveal how it is geared towards engaging these institutions in Scotland's nationalist project. The article points to the fact that "SNP policy for higher education uses inward referencing to embedded and shared ideas of the public nature of universities in Scotland

and their democratic and intellectual traditions to help in 'steering' of the universities towards their identification with a national 'project'" (Arnott and Ozga 2016, 262). The Scottish case is particularly valuable as a comparative perspective to Quebec. Analogous to the Quebec case, tuition fees are markedly lower in Scotland than in the rest of the United Kingdom, contributing to a "distinctive narrative of education" (Arnott and Ozga 2016, 256) that is based on Scotland's unique culture and social values. In the French context the significance of higher education as constituting a public good has been attributed to a "re-nationalization," whereby the notion of public emphasizes domestic students over international students (Carpentier and Courtois 2022).

The discursive connection observed in this chapter between the public character of the university and nationalism in Quebec corroborates these discussions. The public character of the university and its value for Quebec's collective future and national identity are used to justify the need for greater government involvement in this field. For Quebec to maintain a university system which aligns with its welfare-state ideal, safeguarding control over this policy domain is paramount. The early *maîtres chez nous* aspirations and struggles for policy ownership are connected to the desire to see Quebec's higher education system congruent with the values of accessibility distinguishing the Quebec nation. Hence, in this case, policy ownership is also a springboard towards policy distinctiveness, as appeals for maintaining affordable tuition rates are coupled with discussions of Quebec's distinct values within Canada and the world.

While the weakening of the public character of higher education is a universal trend, this chapter advances the idea that the challenges related to the public character of higher education are distinct in Quebec, given its status as a minority nation. The political discourse advancing the significance of the university as a public good is coupled with an explicit discourse of nationalism. The idea of the university as constituting a public good is related to its critical function in the public sphere and for achieving the collective goals of a particular community (Giroux 2010). It follows that there is an important connection between the ideals of maintaining the public character of higher education and nationalist interests.

Higher Education as a Public Good: Core Principles of the Parent Commission

As laid out in detail in chapter 2, the Parent Commission had an incalculable impact on Quebec, laying the foundations for its modern education system. At the heart of its recommendations pertaining to higher education were ideals around accessibility and democratization based on the understanding that universities were critical agents in Quebec's social, economic, and cultural modernization. Adjacent to these values was the notion that universities are public institutions, and as such, the state should play a significant role in their development, and importantly, their financing. The Parent Report concretized the *maîtres chez nous* argument underpinning the Quiet Revolution reforms by calling for the Quebec government to take over the reins in the higher education sphere. As described in the report, universities are "associates of the state in its specific function of guardian of the public good" (Royal Commission of Inquiry on Education in the Province of Quebec, 1966, Vol. III 187). Against the backdrop of the Quiet Revolution and the reappraisal and modernization of Quebec's state system, the state was the most apt player to support Québécois in becoming "masters in their own home." To ensure that universities become effective partners in the nation-building project, a substantial government investment in the university sphere was warranted. Discussing the various modalities of university financing, the Parent Report further notes:

> Universities are the brain of a nation, the motor of its development; by shaping minds, the university propagates the power of reflection, creation and invention which are unrealized in a nation. This is why investing in universities is investing in human resources the return of which is almost unlimited (Royal Commission of Inquiry on Education in the Province of Quebec, 1966. Volume III, 159).

Attributing a human quality to the "nation" by referring to universities as its "brain," the report's authors rely on a personification metaphor emphasizing a sense of identification to the nation (Wodak 2009). Personification is common in nationalist discourse, as it "evoke[s] our attitudes, feelings and beliefs about people and applies them to our attitudes, feelings and beliefs about political entities" (Charteris-Black 2011, 61).

The university's role for producing the next generation of Quebec professionals is also tied to notions of collective solidarity (albeit gendered) and public good: "the university must prepare men to respond to the needs of a society undergoing rapid transformation; it should show a closer solidarity with the community and the public good" (Royal Commission of Inquiry on Education in the Province of Quebec 1966, Vol. III, 161). A theme of community and collective mobilization is apparent throughout the report, with the university described as critical to this mobilization:

> The normal development of large public or public-oriented organizations requires an inter-dependent collaboration towards common objectives; only an organic collaboration of this kind can enable institutions which were previously self-dependent and self-financed, to pursue their development in line with the needs of society, while also safeguarding their autonomy which is essential to any university (173).

Connecting the university to notions of "collective," "societal," and "community" benefits, the Parent Report also underscores the indispensable role of government in defining its role, and specifically its responsibility to ensure affordable tuition rates. Equating education to other "essential social services," like health, the Parent Report emphasizes the importance of ensuring free access to primary, secondary, and Cégep levels of education. The issue of free schooling at the university level is deemed more complex in the report, with a section dedicated to outlining the arguments for and against offering free tuition to students in Quebec. The need to "democratize university education" by "eliminating psychological and financial barriers" and the importance of "forming the scientific and professional cohorts which the community so urgently needs" are cited among the arguments in favour of free schooling at this level (Royal Commission of Inquiry on Education in the Province of Quebec 1966, Vol. III, 205). Arguments against include, among others, the notion that a tuition rate provides a motivating impetus to postsecondary studies, as well as the idea that universities need this financing to ensure their functioning. In its recommendations, the commission in its report cites that "[w]e recommend that at the university level, while free schooling is preferable in the long-term, tuition rates be maintained" (238). Ultimately, the Parent Commission took a non-committal approach to the tuition fee issue, whereby rather than pledging the Quebec government to a system of free tuition, it called for a freeze on fees (Ratel 2006).

Questions around university financing have gained political salience in the decades following the Quiet Revolution. While the general tendency has been to maintain the tuition freeze, attempts and decisions to raise the cap on tuition have emerged over the years. A comprehensive account of university financing in Quebec being beyond the scope of this discussion, the next section puts the spotlight on two policy events prior to the 2012 Maple Spring protests, where the tuition fee issue emerged in Quebec. The nationalist discourse permeating these discussions and the role of party politics in the debates will be highlighted. Indeed, apparent in the analysis of the policy discussions around tuition fees is the significant tipping of scales occurring alongside electoral shifts. In this way, the study lends weight to the idea that party politics have an important bearing on higher education policymaking (Jungblut 2015).

1980s: A First De-Freeze

Notwithstanding the enormous strides made in Quebec towards economic modernization throughout the Quiet Revolution, subsequent decades brought severe financial strains and a depletion of public financing. In the early 1980s, on par with global trends, Quebec's economy was in a deep state of recession characterized by soaring inflation, rising interest rates and unemployment rates reaching close to 16 per cent (Berubé 2008). The university sphere suffered important losses and was in a state of chronic underfunding by the time the PLQ under Robert Bourassa took office in 1985. Adamant to balance the budget and revitalize Quebec's economy, Bourassa set forth a neoliberal agenda with wide-ranging implications. Higher education was centre stage in the PLQ's discussions on the need to reduce the deficit and balance the budget. The party's electoral program for the 1985 election referenced its pledge to provide financing solutions to the sector (PLQ 1985). Solving the "crisis" over university financing was among the pillars of Bourassa's neoliberal economic policy once elected.

To address the crisis, Bourassa's minister of education, Claude Ryan, established a parliamentary committee on "Orientations and Financing of Universities" to discuss and "find realistic solutions for a strong university recovery" (Conseil des universités 1986). The Committee brought together representatives of student organizations, university leadership, the conseil des universités (Council of Universities),[1] union leaders and members of professional associations to present opinions and evidence on the state of university financing in Quebec (Ratel 2006).

The report produced by the superior council on education for the parliamentary committee outlined the financial difficulties incurred by universities and put forth several recommendations. Within the report, the notion of accessibility and low tuition rates are discursively connected to the idea of an existential threat posed on Quebec, as a francophone minority within Canada, whose "survival" is at risk:

> This issue [of university financing] takes on a particular significance for francophone Quebec, which cannot count as much as its neighbours on exchanges and alternatives to ensure the education of its population. If it

is to ensure the survival of its culture and the development of its population, Quebec must first count on its own strengths and among them, its universities (Conseil des universités 1986, 4).

The report further relates to university accessibility as essential to "a society's survival as a distinct entity (3)". The report signals the council's support for widening accessibility in higher education, noting that "[e]fforts must be made to raise the enrolment and graduation rate of the Québécois population, and in particular its francophone population. Acting any other way would be irresponsible and suicidal" (8).

While promoting the idea of accessibility, the council also referenced the need to raise tuition fees to address the budgetary crisis. Among its recommendations was a call to raise the tuition fees in Quebec to match the rates in the rest of Canada. Recognizant of the implications for accessibility, the council highlighted the importance of ensuring that disadvantaged students would not be impacted by the decision calling for maintaining fees for the student aid bursary schemes.

During the parliamentary discussions of the committee on university financing, Quebec's distinct model of higher education financing, and in particular, its low tuition fees is highlighted. As remarked by the rector of the University of Quebec:

> Barring unforeseen changes, Quebec could soon be celebrating the twentieth anniversary of the tuition fee freeze for its university students. It should be noted that this makes Quebec, in terms of higher education financing, an exceptional case in Canada; Quebec is the only province where the costs incurred on students is reduced from year to year (National Assembly of Quebec, 16 September 1986).

During an earlier debate on university financing, a representative of Quebec's student organizations equated the low tuition to a "societal choice" and references Quebec's distinct status as a rationale for maintaining these low fees:

> I think that as Quebec society, we made a choice in 1960 to democratize as much as possible our secondary and postsecondary education. Accordingly, we believe it remains crucial for Quebec, if it sees itself as a distinct society, to reaffirm these distinct societal choices, that is the choice to not necessarily follow those of others, which is the case, as you have alluded to in Ontario (National Assembly of Quebec, 11 October 1984).

The tuition system is also described as a "collective treasure" (*richesse collective*) which is being "attacked" by the government. The idea of raising tuition fees is perceived as an affront to the values around accessibility emanating from the Quiet Revolution. These values and their role in shaping Quebec's higher education system are part of what makes Quebec distinct both in Canada and internationally. Yet, with the rise in neoliberal ideals in the 1980s, the values associated with the university's public character were tested, challenging the university financing strategy set out in the Parent Report (Maroy et al. 2014). In 1989, four years after the parliamentary committee on university financing, the PLQ government announced its decision to break the tuition freeze in place for the preceding twenty years. While much of the evidence presented during the 1986 committee promoted the need for a hike in tuition fees, the ministry did not explicitly reference a decision in this direction at the time (Ratel 2006). The 1989 decision marked an important departure from the status quo grounded in the Parent Report's legacy for Quebec's higher education system. It also saw the PLQ government backtrack on its initial pledge not to raise tuition fees.

Justifying the decision, Claude Ryan introduced a government declaration stating that the tuition hike is necessary to ensure the quality of Quebec university education and noting that the government "does not have the right to condemn Quebec to mediocrity in terms of higher education" (Quebec Ministry of Higher Education and Science 1989, 9). The declaration foresees a stagnation in the university sphere as "potentially disastrous for Quebec's future" (Quebec Ministry of Higher Education and Science 1989, 7). This corresponds to advice outlined by the Council of Universities in a 1989 advisory statement on university financing which noted that the government freeze "indeed favoured accessibility, but without ensuring that the resources would suffice to maintain the quality of teaching" (Conseil des universités 1988, 34). The rise in tuition was accompanied by a reduction in state subsidies to public education as well as a diminished budget for government ministries responsible for education and higher education and research (Ratel 2006).

In this debate, accessibility and quality are at odds, squaring with broader debates on the quality of higher education occurring around the world at the time. Yet the tension between them takes on a different meaning in Quebec, given the permeation of nationalist discourse within the debate. Arguments against the tuition fee hike were based on the significance of Quebec's low tuition for its national character, societal choices, and overall distinctiveness. To a certain degree, proponents of the hike also rely on a discourse of national well-being to state their claims. Quebec's future survival and the ultimate success of its collectivity will largely depend on the quality of its academic institutions. Nationalist discourse thus permeates both sides of the debate.

1998: PQ/PLQ Debate over Tuition

A decade following the first de-freeze, the university "crisis" saw no signs of waning. The PLQ continued to favour neoliberal solutions and austerity measures to address it. This approach was heavily criticized by the PQ opposition, which promoted a renewed outlook on higher education policy in its electoral platform in the run-up to the 1998 elections. In it, the PQ set out its agenda for a strategy for universities, which would represent the first of its kind in Quebec. In its platform, the PQ also lamented the PLQ's reductions in public financing referring specifically to its repercussions on the university system. The PLQ's approach to the university financing issue is described as superficial and lacking proper investigation. If elected, the PQ pledged to take a more stringent approach citing: "[t]he issue of education financing is evidently one of the major preoccupations of Quebec society. ... A PQ government will make reinvesting in education one of its major priorities" (PQ 1998, 48).

The PQ's objections to the sitting government's higher education policymaking were accompanied by calls against the Canadian federal government's "intrusion" in Quebec's higher education affairs. Specifically, the federal government's Millennium Scholarship program was the target of critique:

> The federal government, motivated by political visibility and constitutional interventionism, decided to immerse itself in Quebec's student financial aid program. The PQ government will continue to do everything in its power to make sure the federal government comes to its senses and transfers Quebec's portion of the Millennium scholarships towards the financing of its higher education (PQ 1998, 48).

The Millennium Scholarship fund was established in 1997 following Canadian prime minister Jean Chrétien's announcement of a CAN $250 million annual endowment for needs-based financial aid across the country (Wellen et al. 2012). The fund was mandated to run for ten years, with a total budget tallied at CAN$2.5 billion. The initiative was predicated on the desire to widen accessibility to higher education and address the mounting student debt faced by Canadian youth. The establishment of the Millennium Scholarship fund struck a nerve with the Quebec government, which viewed the initiative as another example of federal intrusion in a competency which is strictly under provincial jurisdiction.[2] Indeed, not since the Massey Commission decades earlier had the federal government taken on a "pan-Canadian" policy concerning higher education at this scope. For Quebec, the legislation of the scholarship fund represented a blatant denial of its policy ownership in the education sphere (Secrétariat du Québec aux relations Canadiennes 27 May 1998).

The PQ opposition under Lucien Bouchard accused both the ruling PLQ government and the federal government of contributing to the deterioration of higher education in Quebec. On one hand, the challenge to the federal government reflected long-held ideals around constitutional authority and policy ownership. Inside Quebec, the party politics are significant. The PQ saw itself as the necessary leadership to renew the Québécois ethos of the Quiet Revolution era, which has been denigrated by the PLQ leadership. For the PQ, the PLQ's decisions and actions are not in line with Quebec nationalism. This corroborates Béland and Lecours's (2006) assertion that "[r]eferences to welfare retrenchment and neo-liberal restructuring tend to be seen as attacks on Quebec's nationhood, especially when they come from the PLQ whose nationalist credentials are often considered suspect" (85).

Bouchard emerged victorious on the night of the 30 November 1998 Quebec elections. In his victory speech, he laid out his plan for the creation of an "original society, a Québécois model, neither better nor worse than that of our neighbours, but a model that is true to our personality and which requires that we be our very best" (Bouchard 30 November 1998). In his speech, Bouchard also accused the federal government of intrusion in provincial spheres of competencies and reiterated his government's pledge to prevent further federal impositions in Quebec's social affairs. For Bouchard, Quebec should have the option to opt out of the Millennium Scholarship project and "to regain our freedom to conceive and implement our social solidary project in line with our values and priorities" (Bouchard, 30 November 1998). Here, the theme of institutional congruence is once again apparent, with Bouchard associating Quebec's distinct values and priorities with the need to promote its own policies. At the opening of the thirty-sixth legislature in the National Assembly, Bouchard related specifically to his government's plans for Quebec's education system, with the tuition fee issue featuring prominently in his discussion:

> Preparing for the new economy in North America there is one place where young people from all backgrounds have access to higher education at an affordable price, that is Quebec. We made this societal choice together. We

plan to preserve this accessibility, reduce the student debt, improve the student aid program and open it to part-time students. We intend to create through legislation a consultative committee on financial accessibility and to maintain the current rate of tuition fees during our entire mandate. And I state loud and clear that in order to maintain accessibility to higher education for Quebec youth, we will resist pressures from the North American market, we will resist the political pressures of English Canada, and we will resist the pressures of lobbies and of the official opposition. For this issue, like in others, we will defend Quebec's societal choices, we will defend our right to be different (Throne Speech 3 March 1999).

The PQ government's plans for revamping the university financing system led to the production of an official policy strategy, a first of its kind for Quebec. The strategy's title, "To Ensure Our Collective Future" is indicative of the perceived role of universities in Quebec's nation-building agenda. The strategy is described as embedded in a broader societal project for Quebec. Underpinning it is the conviction that "an investment in our universities is an investment in our collective future" (Quebec Ministry of Education 2000, 7). A discourse of collective mobilization is recurring in the policy document and linked to the importance of the university as a public institution. In its opening pages, the document describes the university's function in Quebec as critical for its collective development, and the shaping of Quebec's "identity":

> The university is one of the most important institutions of contemporary Quebec. It plays a pivotal role in the development of many of the capabilities that are shaping Quebec's identity. It offers all of society social, cultural and economic benefits. Indeed, the major government funding it receives shows that it is considered a public service.
>
> [V]iewed from a collective perspective, the university has a strategic role to play in positioning Quebec within a changing world; universities stimulate our economic, social and cultural development. It follows that an investment in our universities is an investment in the future of our society. That is the conviction on which this policy statement is based (Quebec Ministry of Education 2000, 7).

The importance of maintaining accessibility in higher education is one of three action lines in the strategy, alongside university performance and the societal and global role of higher education. The document outlines the government's plan to change the structure of university financing to promote accessibility. As per the policy, the PQ government would increase its allocated funding to universities by CAN

$750 million in three years, attaching to it a requirement for universities to provide a "performance contract" based on a set of predetermined targets to reach (Doray 2016). The reform also significantly enhanced the weight attributed to university financing according to its student enrolment numbers. This new formulation for financing created a more competitive inter-institutional environment whereby universities vie for a larger number of students (Doray 2016). This formula applies to all universities in Quebec.

2003: PLQ in Power

Policy priorities would shift once again following the election of the PLQ under Jean Charest in 2003. In its electoral platform, the PLQ pledged to maintain the freeze on tuition fees and announced plans to establish a parliamentary comittee on university financing if elected (PLQ 2003). True to its pledge, once elected, the PLQ government established the committee and embarked on a consultative process bringing in various actors within the higher education sector to support the discussion on issues of university financing and accessibility. Several policy decisions were made following the committee's discussions. Having pledged not to de-freeze the tuition fees domestically, the PLQ's actions included a de-freeze on the fees of international students, as well as a reform in the grant and loan system for Quebec students.

In 2005, the Charest government announced that it would be converting CAN $103 million earmarked for student grants and loans. The decision led to Quebec's largest student strike to date (to be followed by the Maple Spring protests), lasting between February and April 2005. Twenty-five thousand Cégep and university students were absent from classes, protesting the government's decision and calling out its repercussions for the growing student debt. In the National Assembly, the opposition denounced the reform and called on the Charest government to "correct this stupidity, this blunder" (P. Marois, National Assembly of Quebec, 9 March 2005). Consistent with the rhetoric around the 1989 tuition de-freeze, the PLQ decision on student loans is described by PQ representatives as a breach to the values of accessibility and solidarity solidified during the Quiet Revolution era.

The PQ's position on accessibility is discursively aligned with notions of Quebec nationalism. This link is most explicit in the statement of PQ leader Bernard Landry, who called out the government for going against "the majority of Quebec society" and the "fundamental cultural-political lines of the Quebec nation" (National Assembly of Quebec, 9 March 2005). For Landry, accessibility to higher education is symbiotic with

Quebec's very identity as a nation. The PQ discourse also highlights how the values of accessibility are part and parcel of Quebec's distinctiveness within Canada and within the North American continent.

> Quebec's political culture is not Ontario's nor New England's or Texas. It is a national culture of solidarity which characterizes us, and it is time for those sitting in front of us [PLQ] to understand it ... And we fought in solidarity to create equal, or almost equal conditions for success for every person, no matter their place or conditions of their birth ... How? ... through education, through education accessible to all, in a generous and universal way. And it is true that we are exemplary on our continent, and we are proud of this. But it seems like, when Quebec is exemplary in an area, the Liberal Party is obsessed with bringing it back to its continental fantasies. It doesn't like that Quebec is Quebec, it would rather it be Ontario or New England (National Assembly of Quebec, 9 March 2005).

Describing Quebec's national culture as one of "solidarity," Landry's statement echoes the link between nationalism and welfare politics made in the literature. Striking students demanded the government walk back its decision to turn CAN$103 million of aid in loans. An agreement was eventually reached between the student organizations and the government according to which CAN$103 million would be re-invested to the student grant program within the next four years. Noteworthy here, is the role played by the Millennium Scholarship fund in the final agreement. According to the agreement, CAN$40 million would be provided by the funds allocated for the federal initiative. While an agreement was reached between student organizations and government authorities, many student groups opposed the agreement and maintained their stance against the government's plans. The deep divisions within the student movement were indicative of the delicate nature of the issue raised. While the strike ultimately died down, this would not mark the end of the Charest government's encounter with the tuition fee conflict. In many ways, the 2005 student strike and debate over loans sowed the seeds for the PLQ to raise tuition fees during Charest's second term, leading to the Maple Spring protests.

The 2012 Maple Spring Protests: The Tipping Point

The PLQ under Prime Minister Jean Charest's near-decade rule in Quebec (2003–2012), brought a shift towards starker neoliberal economic policies. In line with global trends, neoliberal ideals were permeating different policy arenas, with higher education taking centre stage. As part of its broader 2010 budget plan, the Charest government announced its intention to implement an incremental hike of CAN$325 per year in tuition fees from 2012 to 2017. The plan was described as necessary to ensure the quality of university teaching and to provide universities with the means to compete both within Canada and internationally (Finances Québec 2011):

> Thanks to this plan, universities will be provided with the necessary means to improve the quality of the teaching offered to their students. This plan will therefore contribute directly to improving university training, considered a key to success in a modern society and economy. It will provide new means to universities, key pillars of our knowledge economy(3).

This declared rationale behind the PLQ decision echoes the wider neoliberal agenda pursued by the party during this time, advanced through its platform to "rebuild Quebec" (Hurteau and Fortier 2015). The welfare-state model emanating from the Quiet Revolution era was perceived by the PLQ as "passé" and not up to the challenge globalization poses on national economies. The 2008 financial crisis served as an impetus for the Charest government to enact neoliberal reforms and pull back the welfare-state model that had characterized Quebec society for decades.

The tuition hike announcement was met with stark opposition by student organizations as well as political opponents, arguing that a rise in tuition would lead to a significant decline in student enrolment, hindering the values of accessibility and democratization which had so strongly characterized Quebec's education system since the 1960s. The opposition to the decision extended beyond its repercussions for the university sphere. It was perceived as bearing heavily on Quebec society, as the argument against the hike was embedded in the social-democratic values deriving from the Quiet Revolution (Bégin-Caouette and Jones 2014). As noted by Giroux (2013), "it soon became apparent that the students viewed the tuition increase as only one symptom of an ailing and unjust social order about which they could no longer be silent" (520). The PLQ's plan was described by its opponents as an affront to the "Quebec model" for higher education, imbued with values of equality, welfare, and accessibility. They were ultimately an affront to the values of the Quebec nation instilled since the Quiet Revolution.

The student-led grievances against the PLQ led to lengthy demonstrations across the province and to a massive student strike, lasting close to ten months. As an ode to the Arab Spring protests of 2011, the demonstrations became known as the Maple Spring (printemps érable). They were part of a broader globalized mobilization of students and youths across different contexts including the Arab Spring and the Occupy Wall Street movements. The strike saw a large proportion of classes cancelled as demonstrators poured into the streets demanding a reversal of the tuition hike decision. The Maple Spring protests constituted one of Quebec's largest and most impactful social movements. What began as a tuition issue quickly extended past student grievances and galvanized Quebec society more broadly. The red square became the symbol of the movement against the tuition hike and wider austerity measures pursued by the PLQ. Concerns against the government's neoliberal policies were framed in nationalist terms, a trend visually evidenced by the juxtaposition of the fleur de lys alongside the red square.

The nationalization of the tuition issue was reinforced by the declared support of the student strikes by members of the PQ. The PQ was quick to confront the PLQ's budget decision. PQ members showed their support for the movement by joining protest camps as well as calling for an end to the hike in parliament. The tuition hike became a featured topic in the National Assembly's Committee on Education and Culture during the 2011–2012 year. A close reading of these debates reveals the reliance on national identity markers by the PQ opposition in its challenge to the hike as well as its emphasis on Quebec's low tuition fees as constituting a key feature of its distinctiveness. In their political discourse on the subject, PQ representatives related to the province's "distinct" policy regarding higher education fees, associating it with the uniqueness of Quebec. As stated by Mathieu Traversy in a 2011 debate,

> I would also like to know why the Minister must also constantly try to compare apples with oranges by comparing Quebec to other Canadian provinces? The other Canadian provinces have **another culture of education**, another history, **another way of doing things**. ... And Mr. President, I would conclude by saying that Quebec has always had its **own way** of doing things, has always had its **own image and difference**. It is not because we are not necessarily like the others that we absolutely need to conform and to compare ourselves to other provinces. Thank You (National Assembly of Quebec, 11 November 2011, my emphasis).

Similarly, Marie Malavoy noted:

> When we are a people, when we are a society, when we have our own history, culture and language, can we not afford to give ourselves the freedom to make different choices? (National Assembly of Quebec, 11 November 2011)

And according to Pauline Marois,

> One of the favourite arguments of the Liberals and the Caquistes, consists of comparing Quebec to other Canadian provinces ... **Quebec is not and will never be a province like the others**. Quebec is a nation and nations worthy of this title **make their own choices** ... If the Harper government continues to deny us our values, our interests, our choices, this will make Québécois think. Why should the Quebec nation accept to have choices imposed by another nation? What will enrich Quebec society more, 500 million in prisons or investment in education? ... This is the fundamental change which we want and propose for the Québécois, make our own laws, deciding ourselves how to use our taxes and speaking on the world stage in our own voice. In fact, we are proposing to Québécois to act in full freedom M. President (National Assembly of Quebec, 28 February 2012, my emphasis).

The underlying assumption in each of these statements is that Quebec is distinct and that this distinctiveness is partly attributed to its unique higher education system and notably its low tuition fees. A hike in tuition fees would thus present a serious affront to the Quebec model for higher education which ultimately represents its social-democratic character and associated image. Quebec's separate interests are also cited as justification for its distinct tuition system. The idea that the federal government is disparaging Quebec's values and interests and imposing its own, serves to emphasize the fact that Quebec is a separate nation with its own interests and identities. Marois' statement, for instance, pins Quebec's values against the rest of Canada's.

The analysis of parliamentary discussions surrounding the tuition issue reveals that references to national identity were not limited to the discourse of the PQ representatives. While perceived by the PQ as denying the flourishing of Quebec nationalism, PLQ representatives also evoked the important link between national identity and higher education in their arguments supporting the tuition hike. As stated by Lehouillier,

> [I]t must be said and I am affirming it here, it is now well known by everyone that the liberal government, since in power, is a government which continuously increases investment in education. Why? Because men and women with a quality level education are necessary for us to take our place in this new world, **assume our identity in the international sphere, which is unique in America**, M. President ... Quebec universities are thus in a North-American environment, let's not forget this. And I am surprised

that people wishing to form a country tomorrow, ok do not question themselves on the strong added value our universities will need if **we want to assert our identity in the world, and especially to maintain and propel it**, M. President, and this is extremely important (National Assembly of Quebec, 19 April 2012, my emphasis).

Discussed as important markers of Quebec's international identity, universities are prescribed a crucial role in the province's image-producing process. Yet the tuition subsidy argument is turned on its head here: for Quebec to assume its distinct identity through its universities – these must acquire the resources to gain an added value. The tuition fee issue in Quebec has long been the focus of debate and is a prime case of contrasting party positions. Indeed, party positions and policy decisions are not consistent between the different political parties engaged in these discussions. Noteworthy is that the visions of what Quebec's nationalism entails, and what it needs to flourish, are also inconsistent.

Societal Choices: An Affront to Quebec's Higher Education Model

Ultimately, the earlier excerpts highlight Quebec's distinct values vis-à-vis the rest of Canada, as they relate to the higher education domain. This corresponds with Henderson and McEwen's (2005) research in which they argue that reference to shared values is a commonly used tactic by Québécois politicians to strengthen the notion of Quebec representing a distinct society. As the authors note, "[t]he idea of shared values can serve to emphasise the commonality of one nation and its distinctiveness from another, nurturing the view that distinctive values require distinctive national institutions in which they may be expressed and preserved" (189).

The notion of distinctiveness runs deep in Quebec, with its distinct society status inherent to the Québécois psyche. An underlying assumption in the discourse on tuition fees is that Quebec's distinctiveness is partly attributed to its higher education system and specifically its low tuition rates. Indeed, Quebec's low tuition fees have been an important marker of its *distinctiveness*. The permeation of discourses of nationalism and distinctiveness in discussions over tuition fees lends weight to the notion that policy ownership for minority nations provides a stepping stone towards policy distinctiveness (Béland and Lecours 2008; McEwen 2005; Moscovitz 2020). During the Quiet Revolution era, Quebec sought control over the education policy domain (among others) to promote itself as the provider of its citizens' needs, as well as ensure its policies were congruent with its distinct aspirations as a minority nation within Canada. The subsidized tuition fees are part and parcel of the *modèle Québécois*, based on an appreciation for the public character of higher education and the state's responsibility towards maintaining it. The linking of tuition fees to nationalism is also indicative of the role of nationalism in seemingly unrelated policy questions. While the relationship between nationalism and (higher) education is commonly related to questions of language policy, culture, and the teaching of national histories, here decisions over what might be perceived as detached from nationalist ideals, take on strong nationalist connotations. Tuition policy itself might not align with issues typically associated with nation building, yet for Quebec, holding control over decisions in this sphere and determining its distinct policy choices, are part of its nation-building process. This is yet another example of the banal ways nationalism and higher education interact in the Quebec case.

The contrasting of two visions for higher education and its implications for societal choices, in general, are also evidenced within Quebec itself. With an anglophone minority, Quebec's university landscape includes both francophone and anglophone universities. As Quebec's cultural metropole and home to the province's largest English-speaking minority, the city of Montreal represents a valuable lens for assessing these relations in the university sphere. Anglophone universities (notably McGill, Concordia) and Montreal's English-language Cégeps found themselves in a delicate position regarding the Maple Spring events. At the collegial level, it was reported that while twenty-eight out of forty-three francophone Cégeps participated in the strike, none of the five anglophone colleges participated (Freed 2012). While students at both McGill and Concordia participated in the protests, they did so to a much lower degree than their francophone counterparts. This was evidenced by the fact that while classes in francophone universities were to a large degree disrupted throughout the demonstrations, only a small proportion of classes were disrupted at the two anglophone institutions (Freed 2012). Hence, while the *modèle Québécois* of higher education is conceived as a reflection of the Quebec nation, a collective "societal choice," the society in question is itself not homogeneous. As will be substantiated further in the next chapter, Quebec's francophone and anglophone universities are often at odds in the higher education/nationalism discussion.

The Tuition Issue in Quebec's Party Politics

The Maple Spring events are a clear illustration of the intersection between higher education and nationalism in Quebec. Not only did the protests take on a nationalist character, but their eventual success can also be explained in nationalist terms. The protests ultimately led to early elections and to a PQ victory under the leadership of Pauline Marois. The PQ's return to power after over ten years of Liberal Party rule is partly accredited to its position in the Maple Spring protests. One of its very first acts was to repeal the tuition hike proposal. While the government was short-lived (it lost power eighteen months later), its electoral victory in 2012 attests to the strong nationalist currents permeating questions of higher education in the province. The protests are also indicative of the sustained role of higher education for nationalism in Quebec and the perceived value in maintaining the distinct Quebec model for higher education. To date, the idea of raising university tuition domestically has been largely abandoned by the whole spectrum of political parties in Quebec. As discussed at length in chapter 5, however, proposals to raise tuition fees for international students have emerged since the Maple Spring events. The issue of international student fees is a major source of contention between francophone and anglophone universities. Ultimately, substantial changes to domestic tuition rates in Quebec come up against arguments around Quebec's distinctiveness within Canada and as a minority nation in the world. This aligns with what Carpentier and Courtois (2022) find in the French case where the notion of the university as a public good is highlighted for domestic students but not international students.

Tracing the policy discussions around tuition fees in Quebec reveals a power struggle and ideological divergence between political parties, namely, the PQ and the PLQ, between which power fluctuated in the years under analysis. As outlined throughout this chapter, changes in tuition fee policy often coincided with or prompted electoral shifts. This finding supports the need to scrutinize party dynamics in the study of higher education (Jungblut 2015). Understanding the role of political parties in higher education politics "broadens the scope of analysis as it goes beyond the assumption that countries have put in place similar policy objectives with variations in reforms being mainly due to the countries' politico-administrative system and rather focuses on the partisan characteristics of higher education policy" (Jungblut 2015, 879).

Not only did policy choices diverge from one party to the next, so, too, did their interpretations of Quebec nationalism. Both sides of the tuition fee debate relied on nationalist discourse to make their case (to varying degrees). Ultimately, the higher education sphere became a discursive site for the promotion of nationalist values irrespective of the policy decisions made.

4 McGill University and Quebec's Nationalist Politics

Internationally renowned, McGill University is one of Canada's most recognizable academic institutions. Consistently ranked in the top forty in world university rankings, and among the top universities in Canada, McGill is a staple of the country's higher education system. Located in Montreal, Quebec's most populated city and its cultural metropole, the anglophone university has for decades been entangled in the province's linguistic tensions, becoming a focus of nationalist concerns over the status of the French language in Quebec. This chapter investigates the political discourse surrounding McGill University and its place in Quebec's socio-political landscape, between 1968 and 2022. Situating McGill within broader debates on Quebec's nation-building agenda, the chapter uncovers its positionality vis-à-vis Quebec's ambition to promote a distinct francophone identity within Canada and around the world.

The story of McGill offers a valuable vantage point to understand the role of language in Quebec's nationalist endeavours. By placing a spotlight on one university and considering its unique position within Quebec society, this chapter provides a more focused account of some of the major themes promoted in this book. Highlighted in this discussion are the tensions arising between the desire to maintain a francophone identity and the need to ensure competitiveness in the international higher education sphere given the superseding role of the English language. Debates surrounding McGill University's place in Quebec echo broader discussions over the significance of French as a distinguishing and critical marker of Quebec identity and nationalism.

Montreal, the City of "Two Solitudes"

A discussion of McGill University as a microcosm of Quebec's linguistic tensions should be contextualized against the backdrop of Montreal as a city of "two solitudes." Famously coined by Canadian author Hugh MacLennan in his 1945 novel, the term came to epitomize Montreal's linguistic tensions and "uneasy communication" between its anglophone and francophone populations. While the city has long held a francophone demographic majority, prior to the Quiet Revolution, "it's linguistic *character* was undeniably English" (Levine 1991, 7). The predominance of English, despite its minority status in Quebec, was attributed to its command in Montreal's (and Quebec's) economic affairs. With the British rule over Canada in the eighteenth century, an alliance was formed between the anglophone merchant class and the governing elite, cementing the anglophone dominance over economic matters in Canada.

As outlined by McLeod Arnopolous and Clift in their 1984 book, *The English Fact in Quebec*, a stark distinction between the roles of English Canadians versus those of French Canadians was established as far back as the 1774 Quebec Act enacted by the British. The former became the managers of economic affairs in Quebec, with the latter consigned with overseeing the social organization of the territory. Although the English dominance over the economy in Canada is expected, the allocation of economic power to the anglophone community in Quebec is less clear-cut. Despite its minority status in Quebec, the anglophone community assumed the role of the province's commercial elite. Montreal was the epicentre of Quebec's commercial industry and the breeding ground for its economic leaders. English became the language of Montreal's industrial activity, and the city emerged as Canada's financial and commercial centre (Levine 1991).

While Toronto eventually superseded Montreal as the country's financial core, Montreal has maintained its status as the commercial stronghold of Quebec, providing business, public services, and communications to the rest of the province (Germain and Rose 2000). This economic sphere was governed primarily by the anglophone elite, and with time, Montreal's workforce became increasingly divided along linguistic lines, with anglophones representing the majority in managerial positions, and francophones taking up the majority of "working class" jobs (Levine 1991). While the economic asymmetry between the two language communities narrowed, particularly in the years following the Quiet Revolution, linguistic tensions continue to come to a head in Montreal, where the "clash of mentalities and ideologies" between the two language communities is at its peak (McLeod Arnopolous and Clift 1984, xv). While the changing immigration patterns of recent decades and the increasingly multi-ethnic character of Montreal have nuanced the strict anglophone–francophone binary so often used to describe the city (Germain and Rose 2000), language battles between French and English speakers have far from receded. More so, the increasingly multi-ethnic character of the city has revived some old tensions around language.

The two language communities have long held separate visions of Montreal's role in Quebec society. For the English-speaking community, to be effectively inoculated into the society of "world cities" (McLeod Arnopolous and Clift 1984) or "international metropolis" (Germain and Rose 2000), it would have to embrace English as the international language of commerce or, at the very least, flaunt its bilingual character. For the nationalist French-speaking community, the embedding of Montreal into the international economic arena risks its dissociation from the rest of the province and, ultimately, the demise of French culture (McLeod Arnopolous and Clift 1984). This binary picture of language in Montreal comes to the fore in the investigation of McGill University within Quebec's nationalist politics. As this chapter reveals, the university is considered both a threat to the preservation of French culture and identity in Quebec and a prized possession to be harnessed towards Quebec's international image and prestige.

Situating McGill in Montreal's Linguistic Landscape

Founded in 1821, McGill University was named after James McGill, a prominent fur trader of Scottish origin, thought to have arrived in Montreal around 1774. Alongside his business dealings, McGill took on various political roles, representing Montreal in the Legislature of Lower Canada and eventually taking up a position on the Executive Council. Having cemented a place among Montreal's economic elite, James McGill would have a profound impact on the city's economic landscape. As outlined by McLeod Arnopolous and Clift (1984), McGill had a hand in "consolidat[ing] the economic vocation of the English-speaking population" (3). Upon his death in 1813, McGill endowed 46 acres of land and £10,000 to the Royal Institute for the Advancement of Science to establish an academic institution which would bear his name. The institute would eventually become the governing body for McGill College, established in 1821. It would take almost a decade for the college to officially welcome its first students, following years of litigation on McGill's will. Since its establishment, the university has cultivated a strong reputation. McGill's legacy for Montreal and Canada more broadly is complex, with its founding associated to nineteenth-century slave trade and settler-colonial logics of the time.[1]

McGill University eventually became the learning ground of Montreal's anglophone elite and business community. Its anchoring above Mont Royal, overlooking the city, and in the Golden Square Mile, home to its anglophone elite, consolidated its role in sustaining the domination of the English protestant community. McGill College expanded with the help of private donations from this community, and a strong "proprietary pride" in the institution was cultivated among Montreal's anglophones (Frost cited in Hampton 2020). While this chapter focuses on McGill's entanglement in Montreal's and Quebec's linguistic tensions, an understanding of other inequalities and tensions attached to it, most notably along class and racial lines, is important to consider. Indeed, as described by Hampton (2020), McGill's establishment among the primarily English (Scottish) elite "above the hill" in contrast to the population of Irish Catholic and newly arrived black communities "below the hill," was an explicit signifier of the university's role in the racial and class divisions of Montreal, unrelated to language.

The university also gained prestige and recognition internationally. McGill eventually took on the persona of "the Harvard of Canada" or "Harvard of the North." The growing prominence of global higher education rankings in recent decades has provided further impetus to the university's image and reputation aspirations. As a "representation of the relative prestige and influence of postsecondary institutions" (Pusser and Marginson 2013, 551), global university rankings like the Times Higher Education, QS, and Shanghai systems are a source of power for the institutions themselves as well as the territories in which they operate. McGill's place on the global rankings is commonly referenced in its institutional promotional materials, as a marker of the quality of its teaching and research excellence. The university's status in the international rankings is also of value to Quebec as a territory looking to enhance its profile on the international scene. It is perceived as an important marker of Quebec's external identity. Accordingly, McGill is often portrayed as an institution capable of bridging Montreal's linguistic divide, or its "two solitudes". Yet the university's potential to serve as a unifying force between the two linguistic communities is not without its challenges. As this chapter demonstrates, McGill has long been at the centre of nationalist concerns over the status of the French language in Quebec. As an anglophone institution in a francophone city, McGill's place in Quebec society is not straightforward.

If we consider, as this book does, that universities are institutions deeply engrained in their surrounding territorial and socio-political environments, McGill's connection to Quebec and Montreal offers a unique lens to advance understandings of their role in multinational federations, and bilingual cities specifically. In what follows, three vignettes of linguistic tensions around McGill are presented: the Opération McGill français movement (1969), the decision to establish a medical campus in the Outaouais region (2014), and the decision to finance an expansion and refurbishment project for McGill (2021). Each policy event reveals the political spotlight placed on McGill in Quebec's language debate and highlights both the symbolic and manifest ways in which this institution is leveraged by political actors on opposing sides of the spectrum.

Opération McGill français

The Quiet Revolution and Quebec's national "awakening" put a spotlight on McGill University, which was increasingly viewed as a symbol of British imperialism and a marker of the disproportionate advantage of the English language in Montreal (Levine 1991). In 1969, McGill was at the centre of Quebec's national awakening with the Opération McGill français protest movement calling for the university to shift to French-language teaching and research. Bringing together the province's labour, socialist, and nationalist movements, the protests constituted the largest manifestation in Quebec since the Second World War (Levine 1991). The movement's diverse composition saw the consolidation of alliances between anglophone socialists concerned with workers' rights and Quebec nationalists concerned with the state of the French language in the province (Mills 2010). In an account of the 1960s' linguistic struggles in Montreal, Mills (2010) notes that "the linguistic explosions of the late 1960s were characterized by a mixing of people and ideas, of issues and analyses which defy the classification in which they have so often been understood" (140).

Against the backdrop of the massification of higher education and the Parent Report's call for wider accessibility, there was a heightened sensitivity to the need for university spaces, and particularly for francophone students. Reports of a lack of spaces in francophone universities for the upcoming cohort of Cégep graduates sparked a large-scale protest among pre-university students in the fall of 1968. Inspired by the May 1968 student protests in France, Cégep students declared a strike, occupying buildings in almost three-quarters of the province's Cégeps, denouncing the continued inaccessibility of the system and the government's lack of planning amid the increasing levels of university participation (Radio Canada 27 March 2019). Echoing the Parent Report's discourse around the critical societal role of an education system, the student activists in the summer of 1968 described Quebec's education system as a "reflection of society," noting that "if you attack the system, you are attacking this reflection as well" (Radio Canada 27 March 2019). Among their demands was the establishment of a second French-language university in Montreal, alongside l'Université de Montreal, to resolve the lack of spaces. Adjacent to this call was the aspiration of turning McGill University itself into a French-language institution.

The 1968 Cégep strike would serve as an important precursor to the Opération McGill français movement, culminating in a massive protest on 28 March 1969, with more than ten thousand marching in the streets of Montreal. Led by student and faculty activists, the movement's demands included a call for a gradual move to a full French teaching and learning environment at McGill; the reduction of tuition fees on par with those of the city's only French-language university, l'Université de Montreal; and the acceptance of part of the Cégep students graduating that year. Ultimately, the movement sought to see the university reflect Quebec society and its predominantly francophone character. McGill as an institution was perceived by the movement's leaders as a symbol of British imperialism and power in Quebec (Mills 2010). Its very existence was thought of as misaligned with the interests of Quebec's majority (francophone) population. One of the movement's leaders, Raymond Lemieux, summarized its claims in a March 1969 Radio Canada interview:

> McGill is an institution which is not at all integrated in Quebec society, which does not provide the services which a university is meant to provide to the population of Quebec in light of the subsidies it receives from it ... Today's university is becoming an increasingly central decision maker in the wider society, of course in terms of language but also on the economic and social fronts. With regards to research at McGill, it is not at all conducted in the interest of the population, rather there are projects for the Pentagon for example, or for the United States or federal government, and private companies. For everyone except the population of Quebec (Radio Canada 27 March 2019).

A week prior to the 28 March protest, the university's daily newspaper the McGill Daily, published a special edition titled *Bienvenu à McGill*, written entirely in French. One hundred thousand copies (a sizeable difference from the fourteen thousand usually printed) were widely distributed throughout the province (Warren 2008). The edition's editorial was drafted as an endorsement of the movement's demands and in support of the protest:

Knowing, from personal experience, that McGill is at the service of the Anglo-American monopolies and that these work against the interests of the Quebec people, we are publishing this issue to share with the Quebec people what we know about the actual role of McGill. We are publishing it in support of the protest on March 28, the Operation McGill, and we join the demands of the students and workers. *McGill français, McGill aux Québécois* (*McGill Daily*, 3 March 1969).

McGill français, McGill aux Québécois

The discursive connection made between the notion of a French McGill and the idea of a McGill for *Québécois* is indicative of the intricate link between language and nationalism in Quebec. The interchangeability between the two slogans reflects the underlying demand of the initiative: promoting the awareness of Quebec as the society of French speakers as opposed to a French-speaking society. Laurier Lapierre, director of the Canadian studies centre at McGill at the time, summarized this argument in the following phrase: "McGill needs to stop being simply *in* Quebec, to being *of* Quebec" (Laurier Lapierre, speech 24 March 1969, my italics). Turning McGill into a French-language institution, or at the very least creating a bilingual institution, would help the university reflect the *true* society it represents and rupture its attachment to the Anglo-American context.

While the movement took on a nationalist character, it was never adopted by "mainstream nationalist politics" (Mills 2010). The newly formed Parti Québécois steered clear, fearing its support for what was considered a radical group would alienate voters at a crucial time for the party. The ruling PLQ for its part, responded firmly, sending in police forces against protestors. Ultimately, the movement remained a largely fringe grouping with little political support. The reported engagement of the Front de libération du Quebec, a militant independentist movement, is demonstrative of the radical persona attributed to the movement and its supporters. Nor can the McGill français movement be reduced to a clash between French and English. Indeed, Stanley Grey, an anglophone faculty member, led the movement's demands and many of its supporters were anglophone students, including the editors and staff of the McGill Daily. As noted in a *McGill Daily* report in the aftermath of the 28 March protest, "as it turned out, the true division of forces was not on lines of language or race; there were English and French on both sides. It was a division between oppressor and oppressed. One side has people, the other side had money and guns"

(*McGill Daily* 2 April 1969). The McGill français movement was entangled in the broader anti-colonial and anti-imperialist thought propagated during the 1960s around the world (Mills 2010). Activists drew from de-colonial ideas interlacing the language issue with the "political economy of empire" (Mills 2010, 140).

Between McGill français and McGill "International"

The opposing side of the *McGill Français* debate claimed that a shift to French-language teaching would have serious repercussions for the university's international standing and prestige. This, in turn, would deteriorate the positive image of Quebec fostered by the university's reputation. In an editorial titled "McGill and its Future" (*McGill et son avenir*), published a few days before the 28 March protest, Claude Ryan, a journalist who would later become head of the PLQ (1978) and minister of education (1984), pointed to the importance of finding the appropriate balance between the need for McGill to integrate more profusely in Quebec (francophone) society and the need to maintain its global reputation. While acknowledging that its location in a predominantly francophone territory makes it difficult for McGill to "act as if it was located in Toronto or Montreal," Ryan also highlights the importance of the university's anglophone character for the province:

> The maintenance of McGill's anglophone character is needed in the name of equality. It is also important in terms of the advantages it brings to francophones to have a highly renowned English language institution of learning located in Montreal. None of these considerations should however replace the necessity for McGill to integrate more profusely in Quebec society, to participate more intensely to its life and concerns, to collaborate more closely in the realization of its projects (*Le Devoir*, 26 March 1969).

Similar ideas were expressed by Marie-Claire Kirkland-Casgrain, PLQ member and the first woman to be elected to Quebec's legislative assembly. During an event for McGill's Graduate Society in May 1969, Kirkland-Casgrain spoke on the McGill français movement and its implications for the university and Quebec society. Recurring in her speech are nods to McGill's international standing and "vocation":

> Still Cambridge and Oxford can be said to have made England what it is ... The university not only takes on the colour of the community, it forms its own environment by the actions of its graduates. And in the case of international universities, such as McGill, its outward-oriented action,

embraces the world (Marie-Claire Kirkland-Casgrain, speech to McGill graduates' society 11 May 1969, McGill University archives).

Juxtaposing McGill to Cambridge and Oxford, Kirkland-Casgrain underscores the unique standing McGill has as an institution. While recognizing that the strengthening of French in the university could very well enhance its international persona by emphasizing "another great culture," the McGill français movement is described in Kirkland-Casgrain's speech as risking the downgrading of the international role that the University has played for over a century.

> How and why one can object to this role, I cannot understand. Because surely it seems to me that this remains a source of pride for every Québécois citizen, when we think of the number of young boys and girls who come from all over the world in order to receive an education. And when they leave us, they take with them an image of our community and become our ambassadors around the world.

Kirkland-Casgrain's statement relates to McGill as a source of pride for Québécois as well as a lever of international influence. In another excerpt from the speech, McGill is described as one of the "glories of the province": "[o]ne of Quebec's glories will be that in Central America, South America, Switzerland, Germany, Holland, Norway in England and even France, Quebec's McGill is considered one of the great universities, one of the glories of our Province!"

McGill's international reputation reflects Quebec's own reputation and image. If the McGill français movement was geared towards anchoring McGill University more deeply within Quebec society, the voices supporting the status quo prioritized the importance of anchoring it within global society. A tension is thus observed between the national and international functions of the university. While not limited to the Quebec case, this balance between *nationalizing* and *internationalizing* takes a different tone in a minority nation like Quebec. The minority status of the French language and the global hegemony of English are at the core of this dilemma. This is a theme that will be revisited in subsequent chapters of this book as it is recurring in Quebec's higher education policy decisions and challenges.

Opération McGill left an important mark on Montreal's oppositional politics, as Mills (2010) describes, it led the way for "the beginning of a new era in which linguistic struggles would be played out on the streets of Montreal" (138). Yet, its demands were left largely unanswered,[2] and to this day, the movement is in many ways remembered as a fringe initiative. In the years following the event, the linguistic tensions underpinning it were also described as dissipating. In a 1985 press conference following his election as prime minister replacing René Levesque, Pierre Marc Johnson discussed his vision for the anglophone community of Quebec in contrast to his predecessor:

> I think a certain climate has changed in Quebec in the past ten years. I mean, we have been in power now for nine years. You know, I remember being at "l'Opération *McGill français*" in the sixties. Do you really see an "opération *McGill français*" for next month? Things have very profoundly changed in terms of relationships between the English and French Communities in Quebec (P-M Johnson press conference, 3 October 1985).

Opération McGill is often discussed *en passant* in the literature on Quebec politics and society as an example of the language battles permeating the 1960s and 1970s and the appeals for the preservation of the French language. In most accounts, it is also described as a short-lived and ultimately failed project. Yet as outlined in the remainder of this chapter, McGill University continues to be embroiled in the linguistic tensions and nationalist concerns of Montreal and Quebec more broadly. In what follows, two more recent policy decisions in which the nationalist sensitivities around McGill University emerge, will be discussed: the 2014 PLQ decision to establish a McGill satellite campus in the Outaouais region and the 2020 CAQ decision to fund the expansion of McGill University and Dawson College, Quebec's largest Cégep.

A Medical Campus in the Outaouais: *Anglicizing* Quebec or a *Francization* of McGill?

In 2016, Prime Minister Phillip Couillard (PLQ) announced the government's plan to establish a satellite campus of McGill's medical school in Quebec's Outaouais region.[3] The Ministry of Health and Social Services was set to finance the CAN$23 million project and coordinate it jointly with the Ministry of Education. Underpinning the initiative was the need to retain doctors in the Outaouais region, where one-third of residents did not have a family doctor. In his announcement, Couillard noted the importance of where medical staff are trained in determining where they will end up working. The initiative was well received in the Outaouais, viewed not only as a solution to the lack of doctors in the region but also as an opportunity to provide first-class training in the community. While Couillard did not reference language in his announcement, it soon became a focal point for debate. The announcement was followed by questions about the language of instruction this campus would adhere to. Following the backlash to reports that close to a quarter of teaching would be conducted in English (*Le Droit*, 17 March 2014), the PLQ was quick to assure critics that its plans for the campus called for only 8 per cent of teaching to be conducted in English and that these classes would concern mainly first-year compulsory courses.

The four years of planning and construction for the campus were followed by turbulent debates, rehashing some of the core issues of the McGill français movement. Opposition to the project from members of the PQ and CAQ was swift. Their challenges were based on the fear of instilling an anglophone academic institution in a francophone region. Both parties called on the PLQ to ensure that the program be taught entirely in French. For Jean-François Lisée (PQ), "[i]n Quebec, when we want to become a doctor in a francophone society, we should be able to study in French from start to finish. It is simply inconceivable that we would not be able to offer this to students in the Outaouais" (Radio Canada, 3 February 2017).

In an interview with Le Droit, Claire Samson, opposition party CAQ spokesperson for the promotion of the French language, rebuked the PLQ decision:

> The Liberal Party always downplays the defense and primacy of French. The CAQ demands that the government correct the situation and offer courses in French at the medical faculty's inauguration in 2020. They have three years to do it, it is a reasonable timeframe, a reasonable and legitimate effort which demonstrates the primacy of French ... The medical faculty in the Outaouais will only be accessible to Québécois who are fully bilingual. I don't want us to train doctors for Ontario, I want to train them for Quebec, and for this it must be possible for the training to be conducted in French (*Le Droit*, 22 September 2016).

For Samson, ensuring the campus has the capacity to teach fully in French was a "non-negotiable." The opposing side of the debate also focused on language as a basis for support of the project, with PLQ representatives noting the significance of enhancing French-language teaching at McGill. According to their logic, the establishment of the campus was not a case of *anglicizing* Quebec as the opposition saw it, rather it was an example of the *francization* of McGill. As argued by PLQ minister of education at the time, Hélène David:

> I would say that in fact, this new medical training offered by McGill University in the Outaouais, in fact, we are not anglicizing the Outaouais, we are francizing McGill University. ... I remember in the 60s and

70s, the McGill français protests. Well, I swear to you that now we are turning McGill into an institution which in the Outaouais, commits itself to conduct studies entirely in French (National Assembly of Quebec, 4 May 2017).

Reassuring colleagues that by 2020 the teaching will be conducted entirely in French, David further stated, "We are not talking about *McGill Anglais*, we are talking about *McGill Français* here" (National Assembly of Quebec, 4 May 2017). Evoking the McGill français events, David implies that this decision answers some of the movement's calls for heightened French-language teaching. David alludes to a full circle moment linking the aspirations of the 1960s' movement to the PLQ's actions decades later.

In 2018, a report by the daily Le Droit revealed that Cégep students preparing to enroll in McGill's Outaouais program would be obliged to complete a prerequisite year of studies in Montreal, conducted entirely in English. Sceptics of the plan were quick to challenge the government's failure to avoid an *anglicization* of the teaching program. L'impératif francais, an organization working for the protection of the French language in Quebec, was among the project's fiercest critics. Confiding to an anglophone university the task of training future doctors in "a francophone region, in a French Quebec" was described by the organization as absurd (*Le Devoir*, 9 November 2016). The government plans were seen as reflective of a broader policy that contributes to the relegation of francophones as a "minority in the only North American territory in which we are a majority."

Politicians also denounced the plans. Mathieu Lacombe, CAQ representative for the Outaouais, noted the importance of investing in the project to ensure it can provide French language teaching; "it is a lot of money to uphold a principle, but the principle is important" (Radio Canada, 2 November 2018). The controversy surrounding McGill's satellite campus in the Outaouais reflects once again the unique challenge faced by Quebec as a minority nation, in its elaboration of higher education policy. In his statement, Lacombe depicts a tension between financial needs and the upholding of the "principle" of ensuring that a university campus in the Outaouais region could provide teaching in French. This principle is ultimately related to the importance of having academic institutions reflect the societies in which they operate. In this scenario, the McGill campus in the Outaouais was meant to increase the number of doctors in the community – a predominantly French-speaking community.

The pressures brought on the government by political opponents and university activists ultimately led to a reversal of the initial plan for the campus. In 2020, the Ministry of Education announced its decision to ensure that the first year of study would be conducted fully in French. Explaining the policy shift, Jean-François Roberge, minister of education at the time, stated:

> We have made education and higher education our top priority and today's announcement confirms our commitment to this. By taking this step, we are ensuring that we can offer identical quality training on the two teaching sites and allow hundreds of doctors and future health professionals to benefit from unprecedented accessibility to this internationally renowned establishment. Training can evidently meet many regional needs. This is why we must invest and ensure that this training is adapted to the reality of the environment by offering quality education in French (Newswire, 10 February 2020).

2020: Bill 66 for the Expansion of McGill University

McGill University's entanglement in Quebec's language battles, resurfaced in a 2020 debate over government-supported plans for its expansion. A CAQ proposal to fast-track certain infrastructure projects was introduced in the National Assembly in September 2020. The timing of the bill coincided with the second wave of the COVID-19 pandemic in Quebec and the province's economic recovery efforts. The initiative was described as a way to "accelerate projects of importance to the government as well as all Québécois" (National Assembly of Quebec, 23 September 2020). Beyond its role in stimulating the economy, the bill was also described as one that would "provide Quebec with modern infrastructure which meet the expectations of its citizens" (ibid.). Several provisions are set to accelerate these projects, including the laxing of environmental protocols, exemptions from required environmental authorizations, and simplified municipal authorization processes.

"An act respecting the acceleration of certain infrastructure projects" (Bill 66) was adopted on 11 December 2020, following months of controversy and resistance voiced by members of the opposition, most notably the PQ and Québec Solidaire (QS). While the PLQ supported the CAQ's plans, the two self-described nationalist opposition parties opposed. Alongside environmental concerns raised by opposition leaders, disapproval of the initiative was focused on three of the 188 expansion projects outlined in the bill: the "expansion of Dawson College" project, the "development on part of the site of McGill University Health Centre's Royal Victoria Hospital," and "the expansion and modernization of the McGill University Health Centre's Lachine Hospital" (National

Assembly of Quebec, 23 September 2020). The three projects are tied to two institutional pillars of Montreal's anglophone community: McGill University and Quebec's largest Cégep, Dawson College.

Plans for McGill included the financing of the university's refurbishing and modernization project of the historic Royal Victoria Hospital and the development of a state-of-the-art research and learning space with a particular consideration of the "balance between functionality, nature, heritage and recognition of the Indigenous history of the land" (*McGill Reporter*, 17 September 2020). With the iconic building empty since 2015, McGill had conducted feasibility plans for developing the site along with the Société québécoise des infrastructures. In the last decade, Dawson College has seen enrolment numbers rise above the Ministry of Education's set capacity, leading it to plan for the development of a new pavilion to accommodate the growing student numbers. The plan, which was estimated to cost CAN$100 million, was included in Bill 66, viewed by the government as a necessary investment to resolve the years-long space shortages in the institution. The inclusion of the McGill and Dawson College expansion projects in Bill 66 is rationalized as a response to the natural growth of these institutions and the need to adapt their infrastructure needs accordingly. In other words, for the CAQ government, the inclusion of these projects in its infrastructure is logistically justified. Yet, for those opposing the inclusion of these projects in Bill 66, arguments ran along cultural-linguistic lines. The bill was described as one that "finances and accelerates the anglicization of Montreal" (National Assembly of Quebec, 21 October 2020).

In its efforts to prevent the go-ahead of these projects, the PQ introduced a motion to the National Assembly calling for the removal of the McGill and Dawson projects from the bill and the transfer of the CAN$750 million earmarked for these projects to francophone academic institutions. Introducing the motion, PQ member Pascal Bérubé reflects on its significance for the preservation of Quebec's distinctiveness: "Quebec's destiny is not to become another American State or another Canadian province. Quebec's destiny, its originality for the world is to be a French nation ... If we didn't have French, I don't know what would distinguish us from other Canadian provinces" (National Assembly of Quebec, 21 October 2020).

By facilitating the propagation of the English language in Quebec's institutions, the projects were seen as threatening its very existence as a "French nation." The decision to include McGill and Dawson College in the infrastructure bill was also perceived by the PQ as an affront to Quebec nationalism and a failure of a self-proclaimed "nationalist" government. According to Berubé, "this is a tipping point for a government which defines itself as nationalist" (National Assembly of Quebec, 21 October 2020)."

Opposition to the plan is also linked to the perceived existential threat it poses on Quebec. The expansion of the anglophone higher education institutions is viewed as a step towards the *anglicization* of Montreal and of the decline of French as the common language in Quebec. The backlash against the projects is set against the backdrop of the proven decline of the French language in Quebec and particularly in Montreal. A 2021 Statistics Canada study, commissioned by the Office québécois de la langue française, projected a decline in the usage of French at home by Québécois from 82 per cent in 2011 to 75 per cent in 2036 (l'office québécois de la langue française 2021). The risk of decline in Montreal is even greater as it continues to develop towards "world city" status. Ultimately, the opposition to these projects was tied to nationalist discourses of maintaining Quebec's status as a French-speaking nation. For Paul St-Pierre Plamondon (PQ),

> and hence the importance that the education system, first and foremost, send the signal that the common language is French. Otherwise, a century-old survival of the French language won't be possible, as our current data estimates ... This is a critical question for the future, a question of social cohesion as well. We will have a better feeling of being in the same boat and having a common destiny and will have a better feeling of fraternity if we share a common language, as opposed to being completely divided in two universes (National Assembly of Quebec, 15 October 2020).

Plamondon's recurring reliance on metaphors of community including notions of "being in the same boat," "common destiny," and "fraternity" is indicative of a homogenized view of society, based on a francophone majority culture and language. In many ways, the discourse surrounding Bill 66 echoes that of the McGill in Outaouais debate taking place a few years earlier. Quebec's distinctiveness is referenced as an important justification behind the opposition to the bill, with the understanding that the growth of anglophone institutions comes at the expense of Quebec's francophone flourishing.

On the other side of the debate, CAQ representatives described the opposition's petition as a "scorched earth" exercise (National Assembly of Quebec, 21 October 2020). McGill's place in the international rankings is noted as an important source of pride for Quebec and the fight against its expansion is described as hindering Quebec's reputation and development. CAQ representative Mario Laframboise lamented the opposition to the bill, referencing the importance of being "proud of what Quebec is doing, no matter what." Laframboise further stated, "We should not be following a scorched earth policy, rather we should be able to develop our educational institutions in Quebec so that our children can be among the best in the world" (National Assembly of Quebec, 21 October 2020).

Once again, the tension between the acknowledgment of McGill's international reputation and its implications for the French character of Quebec is brought to the fore. Contrary to its political opponents representing the PQ and QS, the CAQ is not vocal about the project's potential for hindering Quebec's francophone character. Yet the decline of French in Quebec is of chief concern to the CAQ, and the party has introduced stringent measures to protect it. In May 2021, the government introduced Bill 96 to the National Assembly, calling for revisions to Bill 101, Quebec's landmark language policy. The bill "on the official and common language of Quebec – the French language" affirmed that "Quebec's only official language is French" and that "French is the common language of the Québécois nation" (National Assembly of Quebec, 13 May 2021).

Among its provisions, the bill calls for a cap on the number of students in English Cégeps to not surpass 17.5 per cent of the total student population. Bill 96 is the most comprehensive legislation on language to be introduced in Quebec since Bill 101 in 1977. Given CAQ's strong legislative push towards defending the French language in Quebec, its position on the McGill and Dawson projects is noteworthy. By going forward with these initiatives, the CAQ is accused by political opponents of betraying its pledge to ensure the vitality of French in Quebec. What this discrepancy suggests is that in its quest to balance the preservation of Quebec's francophone character with the desire to uphold Montreal's status as a "world city," the latter might be prioritized.

The CAQ's ambiguous position corresponds to Graefe and Rioux's (2020) assessment of the party in what they deem a "post-liberal" Quebec. The authors suggest the CAQ government elected in 2018 – the first not headed by the PLQ or PQ in over fifty years – "has ideas about budgeting and the public sector that depart at times from the neoliberal mantras usually adopted by conservative parties" (305). The CAQ government's legacy for Quebec, according to Graefe and Rioux, will depend on "whether its nationalist inclinations with regard to the autonomy and strength of the Quebec state and Quebec businesses take precedence over its fiscally conservative proclivities" (305).

McGill in Quebec Society: Implications for Minority Nationalism

The intersection of language and national identity in discussions surrounding McGill University echoes a larger issue within Quebec society. In many ways, McGill represents a symbol of anglophone power in Quebec. As such, it is not surprising that it has been at the centre of linguistic tensions over the years. The conflicts around McGill University explored in this chapter are associated with broader power imbalances between the linguistic communities in Montreal. The city's universities reflect the linguistic communities themselves, as two separate spaces in the "city of two solitudes." This comes to substantiate the critical societal function of the university as an institution and the idea that it is deeply embedded in the values and character of the territory in which it operates. It also lends weight to the discussions of the university as constituting a "political institution" (Pusser 2018; Weimer and Nokkala 2020). Particularly disheartening to those voicing their concerns about the perceived prioritization of anglophone institutions is the idea that the imbalance is being sustained and perpetuated at the political level. The university is seen as an agent of the nation-building agenda and one which the political leadership is meant to support. Political parties and elected officials pursuing these projects are called out as doing so against the interests of Quebec nationalism.

What makes Quebec unique as a minority French-speaking nation is that it is the French-speaking universities specifically that are described as allies in the nation-building objectives of the state. Building on state-theoretical approaches to understanding the politics of higher education as promoted by Pusser (2018), the case of minority nations is particularly intriguing. The university is understood as nested in both civil society and state institutions, at times, coming together and, at times, putting the two in conflict. Universities are "sites, instruments and actors in broader political contests" (Pusser 2018, 24). In this case, however, political contests are themselves divided between linguistic communities and their institutions.

5 Higher Education as a Catalyst to Quebec's "Identity Paradiplomacy": The French Connection

This chapter takes readers back to the Quiet Revolution and highlights the catalysing role of higher education for the development of Quebec's international relations. In the last six decades, Quebec has cemented a strong international presence and profile. Having established bilateral relations with more than thirty states and regions across the globe, as well as signing hundreds of *ententes* and currently boasting thirty-three foreign offices in eighteen countries (Quebec Ministry of International Relations and La Francophonie 2024), Quebec is a quintessential paradiplomatic actor. Quebec also represents a clear case of "identity paradiplomacy" (Bélanger 2002; Paquin 2004), as its international relations are closely intertwined with the pursuit of its national identity interests and nation-building agendas. There is, as Kirkey et al. (2016) observe, "a strong correlation between the acceleration and intensification of Quebec's international engagement since the 1960s and the evolution of nationalism and political life in Quebec" (141).

While currently spanning a host of policy arenas, Quebec's international engagements were spearheaded by developments in the higher education sphere and, specifically, its 1965 education cooperation agreement with France. It follows that there is a critical link between international relations and higher education in Quebec going back decades. This chapter seeks to decipher this link and consider the role of nationalism therein. At the core of this discussion are the relations between France and Quebec and their significance for nationalism. Through an investigation of Quebec's international education activities and focusing on bilateral schemes with France, this chapter advances an understanding of how higher education, international relations, and nationalism interact in Quebec. The findings presented in this chapter point to the use of international education for "identity paradiplomacy" over time. Yet tension is also observed between Quebec's nationalist interests and its economic considerations.

Higher Education as a Precursor to Quebec's Paradiplomacy

Quebec's international relations are grounded in the 1965 Gérin-Lajoie Doctrine, which was laid out in two seminal speeches by Quebec's first minister of education and deputy prime minister at the time, Paul Gérin-Lajoie. The first speech was delivered to a group of consular servants in Montreal on 12 April 1965, and the second a week later (22 April) to an audience of French and Swiss university students. The speeches outlined Quebec's intentions to be received as a legitimate actor in the international arena. In the 12 April speech, Gérin-Lajoie advocated for more effective control by Quebec of its international affairs. In line with the *maîtres chez nous* ethos epitomizing the 1960s, the speech called for the Quebec government to take on its rightful jurisdictional role as the political entity responsible for the work of its consular actors and international engagements. The pinnacle of the speech was Gérin-Lajoie's contention that "[i]n all areas which are completely or partially under its authority, Quebec from here-on-in intends to play a direct role, according to its personality and the extent of its rights" (Gérin-Lajoie 12 April 1965). To this day, this statement constitutes the basis of Quebec's actions in the international arena. Gérin-Lajoie also associated the need for stronger control over international affairs with Quebec's identity turn:

> I spoke to you about them [the constitutional issues] mainly to show you how Quebec foresees its future and how it intends to fully represent and serve a people who is acquiring a growing consciousness of its cultural and social identity and which manifests a growing desire to follow its own destiny in the contemporary world (Gérin-Lajoie 12 April 1965).

Gérin-Lajoie attributed the need for Quebec's control over its international relations to its distinct status and character within North America. Quebec is described as "the political expression of a people which distinguishes itself in many ways from the anglophone communities living in North America" and as "the political instrument of a distinct and unique cultural group in the wider North America." In his 22 April speech, Gérin-Lajoie reiterated his position on the constitutional arrangements around international relations outlined the week prior. Here, Quebec's distinctiveness within the Canadian federation is highlighted, supporting the need for enhanced authority over international affairs:

> Quebec in fact is not just a province among others, and Québécois plan to behave like a people master of its own destiny: French-speaking Canadians consider the government of Quebec as the rightful instrument of their collective fulfilment, the guarantor of their sustainability and the symbol of their unity. In short, they agreed to assign it the role of the political expression of their society (Gérin-Lajoie, 22 April 1965, cited in Michaud and Simard 2018, 311-316).

According to the logic outlined in the doctrine, where Quebec holds authority domestically, any activity pertaining to the international dimensions of said policy sphere should also be relegated to the Quebec government. This doctrine has provided the basis of government policy in international relations since its proclamation, with governments of various parties unanimously supporting and invigorating it (Bélanger 2002; Paquin 2006). The ideals and values of Quebec's newfound political personality emanating from the Quiet Revolution were critical to the development of its international relations (Balthazar 2003). It was precisely the *maîtres chez nous* agenda that Gérin-Lajoie promoted in his speeches. The call for increased policy control was in this case geared towards the external. It was taking the *maîtres chez nous* ideal a step further to encompass Quebec's engagement on the international scene. If the Quiet Revolution provided the necessary conditions for Quebec to take control of its international relations, one specific policy initiative could be seen as catalyst: the 1965 Franco-Quebec Education Cooperation Agreement.

The Franco-Quebec Education Cooperation Agreement: Precursor to the Gérin-Lajoie Doctrine

With the opening of Quebec's delegation in Paris in the fall of 1961, Quebec's bilateral relations with France flourished. While its first official representation abroad was the New York office established in 1940, the Paris delegation was the first to take on an official diplomacy function. During his trip for the inauguration of the office, Quebec prime minister Jean Lesage was welcomed by French government officials with honours usually reserved for heads of state. The work of the *Maison du Quebec* was considered on par with that of its Canadian counterpart in Paris.

Supportive of Quebec's newfound ambitions in the international sphere, French president Charles de Gaulle granted it diplomatic status, which would turn out to be instrumental in consolidating Quebec's early paradiplomacy (Balthazar 2003). Educational and cultural matters were at the core of the Franco-Quebec cooperative initiatives stemming from this partnership largely because they were competencies over which Quebec had authority. It was also tied to Quebec's needs as it developed and revamped its education system in the years following the Parent Report. A partnership with France was considered valuable for gaining the expertise and insight for this modernization (Balthazar 2003). As discussed by Balthazar, the work and thought processes surrounding the Parent Commission motivated the Quebec government to look outside its borders for inspiration.

France was the ideal partner for such an endeavour. In February 1965, the Quebec government signed the Franco-Quebec Cooperation Agreement on Educational Matters. The bilateral scheme set an ambitious agenda for education cooperation and exchange, the provision of scholarships, as well as the initiation of cooperation for teacher-training programs between Quebec and France (Mesli 2009). The tremendous feat of this agreement extends far beyond its content. This was Quebec's very first international agreement and the very first time its representatives put their signatures on an international cooperation scheme. It held strong symbolic significance.

The agreement with France was not without contention. The federal government challenged Quebec's authority to engage with foreign governments independently from its own foreign affairs framework. The federal government, under Prime Minister Lester B. Pearson, saw itself as the sole representative of Canada abroad. As such, it alone was authorized to assume international engagements and appoint diplomats. Underlying this position was the notion that the federal government was responsible for representing the voice of Canada abroad (Bélanger 2002). The Quebec government offered a different interpretation of the constitutional arrangement whereby as legal entities within Canada, provinces could engage in international affairs pertaining to their domestic interests and competencies. Responding to Quebec's growing diplomatic efforts vis-à-vis France, the federal government insisted that the agreement between them be supported by an exchange of letters between French representatives and the federal government. That way, it would be clear that it was the federal level that permitted such an arrangement and that it was ultimately under the ambit of Canada–France relations (Bélanger 2002; Mesli 2009). As remarked by Fitzgerald (1966) in an international law journal published the year after the agreement: "[t]he exchange of notes was a type of umbrella agreement between the two Governments under which international effect was given to an arrangement which otherwise would have had no standing in international law" (532).

On 27 February 1965, while Paul-Gérin Lajoie and Claude Morin signed the Franco-Quebec education cooperation agreement with their counterparts in Paris; the exchange of letters between the federal government and French government was signed in Ottawa (Fitzgerald 1966). While this exchange of letters took place, the final agreement between France and Quebec made no mention of it. More so, the Quebec government made the best of the practice imposed by Ottawa by referring to this arrangement as an *entente*. By so doing, the government was able to institute "a practice of ratification and presenting these agreements as having autonomous legal value" (Bélanger 2002, 204). From the Quebec government's perspective, these forms of agreements would facilitate its international presence and cultivation of an international personality, even though they were not considered to hold official legal value by the federal government (Bélanger 2002).

The federal government put forth the tripartite model for ratification of agreements in its Cultural Exchange Agreement with France, signed in November 1965 (Fitzgerald 1966). The arrangement for provinces seeking to collaborate with France was outlined as follows:

Within the framework of the said Agreement exchanges with France in the field of education and of cultural, scientific, technical, and artistic relations may be subject of ententes entered into with Provinces of Canada. In such a case the French Government will inform the Canadian Government.

The authority for the provinces to enter into such ententes will stem either from the fact that they have indicated that they are proceeding under the Cultural Agreement and the exchange of letters of today's date or from the assent given them by the Federal Government (Government of Canada 1965, Section II).

For the Quebec government, the provision set out by the federal government was inadequate for Quebec to effectively fulfil its role in the international arena and to advance its international affairs. During a reading of Quebec's Bill 33 for the establishment of a ministry of intergovernmental affairs,[1] Gérin-Lajoie denounced the federal government's rigid position on the matter:

In my opinion, there is no reason why the right to implement an international agreement should be dissociated from the right to conclude this agreement. These are two essential steps of a single operation.

An agreement is concluded with the primary aim of being applied, it is up to those who will implement it to specify its terms. (National Assembly of Quebec, 13 April 1967).

The 1965 agreement served as a springboard for additional *ententes* signed by Quebec in the years to come (Barbarič 2020). The agreement and the tensions it engendered were the catalyst to Gérin-Lajoie's famous speeches pronounced a few months later. This is evidenced by the recurring references to these events in both the 12 April and 22 April speeches. In the latter, Gérin-Lajoie discusses the "need to establish exchanges with brethren countries and with which (Quebec) shares a common heritage" (22 April 1965, cited in Michaud and Simard 2018, 311–316). The agreement is described as a reflection of "Quebec's determination to take the place it deserves in the contemporary world and to ensure it has the means, both internally and externally to realize the aspirations of the society it represents." The education cooperation initiative with France is tied to "Quebec's determination to collaborate with members of the French cultural community and to show its true image to the world." Forging a relationship with France through the conduit of educational affairs was a necessary condition for Quebec's true image to be projected. It is of course no coincidence that Quebec's very first international agreement was signed with France, a country with which it shares deep historical and cultural ties.

The events around the Franco-Quebec educational agreement were also instrumental to the decision to establish a ministry of intergovernmental affairs, promulgated in Bill 33 (1967). It was described by Quebec prime minister Daniel Johnson as necessary to solve the "Canadian constitutional problem while at the same time widen the horizons of Quebec in its spheres of competency" (National Assembly of Quebec, 13 April 1967). For Gérin-Lajoie, the federal government's insistence on having sole authority over international relations places it in an "ambiguous and embarrassing situation both internally and externally" (National Assembly of Quebec, 13 April 1967). Johnson also cited the strengthening of cultural and educational relations with France as an important motivating factor behind the bill:

[O]n the subject of relations with France which continue to develop. This is a source of deep satisfaction for the government of Quebec. France's attachment towards us, the loyal and active friendship of its President and our strong desire to strengthen the bond that unites us every day, make me very optimistic for our cultural and economic relations (National Assembly of Quebec, 13 April 1967).

Education was a strong precursor to Quebec's impressive international relations. Quebec's authority over the education policy arena facilitated its engagement in international relations otherwise relegated to the federal jurisdiction. Alongside the critical role of education in facilitating Quebec's early paradiplomacy, the fact that this agreement was signed with France of all countries, also had an easing effect. Quebec's perceptions of France, especially after the Quiet Revolution, were based on ideals of cultural solidarity and an acknowledgment that Quebec was very much a product of French civilization (Meren 2012). The political desire to amplify cultural relations with France was also aimed at alleviating the perils of *Americanization* and the fear of a decline in Quebec's francophone character (Meren 2012). France and particularly Charles de Gaulle's willingness to treat Quebec as a diplomatic partner in its own right were instrumental in the early development of Quebec's paradiplomacy.

The 1978 Mobility Agreement: Solidifying the Franco-Quebec Education Cooperation

In 1978, the Quebec government announced plans to raise tuition fees for international students which had up to that point matched those paid by Quebec residents. The decision prompted concerns from the French consul general citing the potential repercussions for Quebec's and France's "special relationship" consolidated through student exchanges between the two and supported by the 1965 education cooperation agreement. In an exchange of letters between the consul general and Quebec's minister of intergovernmental relations and minister of education, the latter noted the need to "consider the privileged links between Quebec and the francophonie" in developing its tuition policy vis-à-vis international students (letter to Marcel Beaux from Jacques-Yvan Morin, 1 June 1978). The discussions led the two parties to sign the Agreement on Matters of Student Mobility at the University Level (1978).

The agreement's preamble states: "[R]ecalling that Quebec and France have maintained for over fifty years a direct and privileged relationship ... [the agreement] aims to encourage and favour student mobility between France and Quebec (entente France-Québec 1978)". To this end, the agreement established reciprocal tuition fee rates between Québécois and French students pursuing exchanges. Paying the same tuition rates as Quebec natives, French citizens studying in a Quebec higher education institution held a considerable advantage over international students from other countries and even over Canadian students from other provinces. As per the agreement, a student from Toronto would pay twice as much as a student from Paris to study in Quebec. This paradox is indicative of Quebec's paradiplomatic objectives, namely, to promote its distinct francophone identity by prioritizing relations with France. Strengthening relations with France was a stepping stone to Quebec's identity paradiplomacy. Quebec's prioritization of relations with France in its burgeoning international relations was rationalized in its first official international relations strategy as follows:

> The highly privileged status of the relationship between France and Quebec renders Franco-Quebec relations exceptionally significant and uniquely positioned in the framework of Quebec's international policy. The government confirms the fundamental strategic decision at the root of Franco-Quebec relations, that is the creation of a true community of interests which works to strengthen Quebec's identity in North America and the world in the long term (Quebec Ministry of International Relations 1985, 78).

Quebec's approach to France is described in the report as a "strategic decision". While relations with France were prioritized, particularly in the years following the 1978 mobility agreement, the agreement would also serve as the impetus for additional bilateral initiatives for boosting student exchange with other countries and "enriching Quebec's relations with its partners, most notably francophone ones" (Quebec Ministry of International Affairs 1991, 98). Since 1978, Quebec has signed an additional forty bilateral agreements providing a tuition exemption – the most recent being in 2018 with Belgium's Francophone community. Of note is that among the forty countries with which Quebec has signed bilateral agreements on student mobility, 62 per cent can be considered either part of the francophonie, or as having francophone colonial heritage (Quebec Ministry of Higher Education 2017). Indeed, research on Quebec's international education activities has tied them to its ambitions in the francophonie (Barbarič 2020; Moscovitz 2022).

The privileged status granted to French students through the 1978 agreement had an undeniable impact on the international student landscape in Quebec for the ensuing decades. The number of French students choosing Quebec as a study destination grew exponentially over the years, reaching more than twelve thousand in 2013. This represented 38 per cent of the total number of international students in Quebec at the time. Alongside the tuition subsidies, French students are drawn to Montreal's reputation as the "world's best student city" (Coughlan 15 February 2017), its high quality of life and vibrant student life. The presence of French students in Quebec (and primarily Montreal) was a symbolic attribution of the privileged relationship between France and Quebec and the affinities between their peoples. It reflects the early discourse around Quebec's international relations outlined in the Quebec government's first international policy rolled out in 1985. The language used to describe the burgeoning relations extends beyond that of two governments establishing cooperation, to incorporate a discussion of two "communities" coming together:

> On a cultural level, Quebec society recognized the vital need to reconnect with France, with whom it shares an obvious community of interest. The government's first initiative set forth concrete achievements, with the two governments recognizing their shared interests and the positive effects of their cooperation for the two communities (Quebec Ministry of International Relations 1985, 3).

The value of educational exchanges for cultivating ties between the people of France and Quebec is worth elaborating on. The fact that the Quebec government held authority over the sphere of education provided it with the ability to conduct international affairs pertaining to education cooperation, as outlined in the Gérin-Lajoie Doctrine. It also facilitates the "people to people" feature of student exchanges, so crucial for the establishment of positive interstate relations. The cross-border movement of students is key to promoting Franco-Quebec relations. During an official visit as part of the Franco-Quebec biannual meetings, René Lévesque associates the coming together of Quebec's and France's education systems and the strengthening of their foreign relations:

> For only a century and a half – enough to create a sustainable common wavelength between us – Quebec's history and culture were intertwined with yours. We then had to create our own expressions and destiny, but without ever breaking these essential links. It is thus with unsurprising satisfaction that we can now add to these links forged in the past, the ones being constantly reinforced between experts at the Sorbonne and our academics and researchers, between our two education systems, as well as between our two countries.
>
> Between French and Québécois academics, there are hundreds of cooperation agreements ... this large network of governmental or private exchanges, this multifaceted collaboration, is even stronger as it is founded on equality and friendship and a recognition and respect for differences (R. Lévesque, Sorbonne University speech, 15 December 1980).

The value of French international students for Quebec was also tied to immigration. A look at discussions on immigration taking place around the 1965 Franco-Quebec agreement on education cooperation reveals the government's preoccupation with promoting francophone immigration to Quebec. Coinciding with the legislative proposals aimed at establishing a ministry of international relations were similar proposals for taking on a more pronounced role in immigration policy through a ministry of immigration separate from the federal apparatus (Legislative Assembly of Quebec, 10 February 1965). Introducing the motion, member of the opposition parti *l'union nationale*, Gabriel Loubier remarks:

> In its immigration policy vis à vis the province of Quebec, Ottawa has never considered the bi-ethnic and bi-cultural character of the country. Once again, the central government has betrayed its mission to recognize the co-existence of two distinct peoples, in their origins, culture and language and to promote the fulfilment of these two nations in all aspects of our national life (Legislative Assembly of Quebec, 10 February 1965).

The need for more effective control over immigration is tied in the motion to Quebec's very "existence and national survival" (ibid.). Loubier further notes that "for Quebec, due to its unique characteristics and in light of its geographic location on an Anglo-Saxon continent, the issue of immigration, is of even more vital importance." The immigration of French nationals (and French-speaking populations more broadly) is highlighted as critical to ensuring Quebec's collective development. In 1978, the ministers of immigration for the federal and Quebec governments signed the Collen–Couture agreement, providing Quebec with a determining power over immigration to Quebec, including the immigration routes proposed to international students (Kostov 2008). Quebec's appeal for policy control over immigration has been attributed to its nation-building agenda and, specifically, its desire to differentiate itself within Canada (see Barker 2010).

While international students are not explicitly referenced in the 1965 motion on immigration, this connection would become even stronger in the following decades. The Ministry of Immigration began to take a more pronounced role in the sphere of international student recruitment in the mid-2000s. This timing reflects global trends towards the appreciation of international students as potential "high skilled" labour. Viewed as a linchpin for the development of knowledge-based economies, higher education around the world became increasingly entangled in domestic economic issues, perceived as offering solutions to labour shortages and demographic deficits. While similar tendencies are identified in the Quebec case, the immigration–higher education nexus is also discursively connected to national identity issues and, specifically, the desire to maintain and strengthen Quebec's francophone character.

International Students as "Prime Candidates" for Immigration

The link between international students and immigration in Quebec gains significance in the new millennium. Beyond the financial benefits of hosting international students, the importance of recruitment efforts is also tied to demographic goals. Quebec, like the rest of Canada, has since the mid-2000s suffered from a demographic deficit. Low birth rates and an aging population are considered significant challenges. This immigration issue is commonly evoked in discussions on international student recruitment. This is certainly not anomalous among countries pursuing international education activities. What is noteworthy in the Quebec case, however, is the inferences to national identity in these discussions. As discussed later, a strong identity discourse is embedded in the wider immigration motivation, specifically through a discussion of the potential integration of international students as future citizens of Quebec.

The desire to persuade international students to immigrate to Quebec reflects the global trend towards "managed migration" (Kofman 2005). Around the world, governments are increasingly concerned with filtering immigration and prioritizing the arrival of immigrants that would have the highest socio-economic benefit to the host society (Kofman 2005; Cheong et al. 2007). Managed migration is also related to the conditions of integration of migrants into a society (Kofman 2005) as "immigration policies are directed towards selecting those who will be most advantageous to the economy, will fit into the existing national culture and not disrupt a supposed social and community cohesion" (463).

For Quebec, the ideal of "managed migration" aligns with its minority nation status and its ambition to maintain its cultural and linguistic distinctiveness within the wider North American continent. In the decades following the 1965 discussions over immigration policy control, international students, considered to be "favoured" candidates for immigration became a target of Quebec's managed migration. Quebec's first immigration policy strategy published in 1990, notes the importance of "temporary immigrants," including temporary workers and international students, as "susceptible to provide a good guarantee for integration and contribution to Quebec's economic and social life" (Quebec Ministry of Cultural Communities and Immigration 1990, 38). Although evoked earlier, it would take until 2009 for the Quebec government to cement this into a policy orientation, with the rolling out of the Programme de l'éxperience québécoise (PEQ) providing fast-track immigration routes to international students graduating in Quebec. Describing the initiative, Quebec prime minister Jean Charest notes:

> Each year, Quebec welcomes about 22,000 foreign students. They are young, they are brilliant, they are talented. The whole world is fighting over them ... Less than 1 in 10 stays in Quebec. While many of them have learned a new language, while many have learned our values ... We are aiming to triple the number who choose to stay in Quebec (National Assembly of Quebec, Charest Inaugural Speech, 10 March 2009).

The PEQ was launched in 2009 as an immigration program geared towards international students and temporary workers. The program established a fast-track route to permanent residency status for foreigners graduating from a higher education institution in Quebec or who have worked in Quebec full-time for at least 24 months. Among its stated objectives, the PEQ seeks to benefit from the immigration of individuals who are already on the territory – "who know and share the values of Quebec and whose integration process is already well underway" (Quebec Ministry of Immigration Diversity and Inclusion 2010, 1). The program is viewed as coinciding with Quebec's integration policy because it is offered to individuals "who are already integrated" (Quebec Ministry of Immigration Diversity and Inclusion 2010, 16). When they apply for the PEQ, they "choose a society that they already know and to which they want to join ... these are prime candidates" (ibid.). International students feature prominently in the 2015 Immigration Policy document rolled out by the PLQ "Together, we are Quebec." The document advances the government's aim to prioritize the integration of international students as they are "already an integral part of society" (Quebec Ministry of Immigration Diversity and Inclusion 2015, 19) and allow them to "continue to participate in community life" (ibid.). The document further notes:

> International students with a Quebec diploma hold a strong potential for transition towards permanent status. They are young, and their diploma is recognized. They already have a considerable understanding of Quebec life and many have acquired work experience (Quebec Ministry of Immigration Diversity and Inclusion 2015, 22).

As the literature on managed migration attests to, the desire to attract and retain international students is commonplace in today's global economy. The world's strongest economies are competing for high-skilled immigration to fill labour shortages and demographic deficits. For Quebec, however, the potential of international students for immigration extends beyond their "high-skilled" status. The integration of international students into Quebec society is also tied to their potential for maintaining social cohesion and specifically the francophone character of the territory. Underlying the discussions on the PEQ is the notion that international students will have an eased integration into Quebec society. The concept of shared values is also recurring in these discussions. During a parliamentary debate on international students, the minister of immigration at the time, Michelle Courchesne discussed the international student/immigration connection in the following terms:

> And you know that we hope to attract international students because we would like to keep them, you know. We believe an international student who comes here for a few years, who settles here, who develops ties and who gets to know Quebec, to know its values, to know its population, who develops a network too, possibly professional inside his/her courses, could very certainly be interested in settling in Quebec (National Assembly of Quebec, 22 April 2009).

A 2011 Immigration Planning document made similar connections:

> International students graduating from a Quebec academic institution and temporary workers can contribute greatly to Quebec society. Indeed, these individuals are already on the territory for a while, know and share the values of Quebec and their integration process has already begun ... Moreover, temporary workers as well as a large proportion of international students have acquired a Québécois work experience, which facilitates their integration (Quebec Ministry of Immigration and of Cultural Communities, 2011, 8).

Having spent several years in Quebec academic institutions, international students are deemed to have already established roots in Quebec and, most importantly, to have an understanding and appreciation of the values that make up Quebec society. The discussion of shared values and facilitated integration reflects the link made in the literature between immigration, social cohesion, and national identity. As explained by (Cheong et al. 2007), "social cohesion is taken to mean a common national identity built via the development of common values, shared symbols, shared ceremonies and so on" (39). Immigrants who are most likely to adhere to the host country's values and symbols are prioritized, as they are also most likely to adopt the collective identity framework. According to this logic, international students are perceived as valuable immigrants since they have already come to know Quebec's values through their study experiences.

Politicians also commonly reference the notion that international students already hold positive perceptions of Quebec and that these can be harnessed towards a stronger integration into society. In the following statement, the minister of immigration and cultural communities at the time, Kathleen Weil, reflects on the affinity of international students towards Quebec:

> So, these are people who want to immigrate because they know Quebec, they love Quebec, they speak French, they know our values. There are also more and more French here, so ... or from other countries who understand Quebec and know its values (National Assembly of Quebec, 20 April 2016).

When Identity Paradiplomacy Meets Economic Rationales

The 2015 Reform of the Franco-Quebec Mobility Agreement

Notwithstanding its important legacy for Quebec's international relations, the Franco-Quebec agreement on student mobility has been met with increased scrutiny over the years. The 2012 Maple Spring protest and subsequent cancellation of the proposed tuition fee hike led to a need to balance the higher education budget through other means. As outlined in chapter 3, Quebec's higher education financing went through turbulent years in the 2000s, with the government intensifying efforts to diversify its financing system and support the development of quality higher education in the province. Among the avenues proposed for addressing the financial deficit of institutions was a hike in the tuition fees paid by French students in Quebec. Discussions in Quebec political circles on the need to renegotiate the 1978 mobility agreement with France ensued. The idea first surfaced in the aftermath of the Maple Spring and the election of the PQ under Pauline Marois. The newly elected government's 2014 budget referred to a need to revise certain tuition exemption schemes. In the official speech on the budget, the government noted:

> While acknowledging the undeniable value of international students for Quebec society, the government plans to revise measures pertaining to

exemptions on tuition fees, all the while ensuring that they continue to benefit from one of the lowest tuition rates in North America (Finances Québéc, Budget Speech, 20 February 2014, 33).

While not directly referencing the 1978 mobility agreement with France, the budget speech alarmed French counterparts, who worried about its implications for the French students in Quebec. In a communication to the media, France's consul general noted France's "high concern" with the remarks (AFP, 30 March 2014). With the PQ reign short-lived and the PLQ taking power in April 2014, the former's plans were never realized. They would resurface under the new government, and this time with a much for explicit call for revising the tuition rates of French students.

Underpinning the PLQ's rationale behind the renegotiation was the fact that while the number of French students in Quebec proliferated in the decades following the signing of the 1978 agreement, the number of Québécois students taking advantage of the tuition subsidies in France was ten times lower (Comité consultatif sur l'accessibilité financière aux études 2015, 10). Practical and mainly financial implications placed the mobility agreement under increased pressure in Quebec. Responding to the need to balance the higher education budget, a plan to renegotiate the 1978 agreement was put forth. On 12 February 2014, Prime Minister Philippe Couillard (PLQ) announced the government's decision to amend the tuition-fee exemption scheme for French students. From the following September, undergraduate French students in Quebec would pay a tuition rate equivalent to Canadian students from outside Quebec.

While remaining lower than other international students, the tuition for French students would henceforth be three times higher than the rate outlined in the original agreement. According to the government, the amendment would save the government close to CAN$10 million in the transitional 2015–2016 year, and CAN$30 million annually in the years to follow (Comité consultatif sur l'accessibilité financière aux études 2015). The rationales behind the renegotiation of the 1978 agreement were purely financial. The amount saved from the higher tuition rates for French students would be invested back into Quebec's universities to alleviate the budget crisis of recent decades (Finances Québec 2014).

The agreement was at the centre of French president François Hollande's visit to Quebec in 2014, the first state visit of a French president to Canada in twenty-five years, calling for the status quo and noting in parliament that "the specificity [of the scheme] is not a privilege, it is a recognition of our friendship" (National Assembly of Quebec, 4 November 2014). In Quebec, universities, and student unions called on the Couillard government to revert its decision, noting the expected loss of French students as a result. The head of the Federation of Quebec Students accused the government of considering French students as a "budgetary problem" as opposed to recognizing "the positive economic, demographic and cultural benefits these students bring" (Oti 24 November 2014). Coinciding with the fiftieth anniversary of Franco-Quebec relations, spearheaded by the 1965 education cooperation agreement, the PLQ announcement became embroiled in a wider debate on Quebec's commitments to France and to the francophonie.

Reforming the PEQ

In the lead-up to the publication of its 2020 Immigration Policy, the CAQ government announced an impending rescaling of the PEQ. The announcement signalled a significant reduction of the eligibility criteria under the previous arrangement set out by the PLQ a decade prior. In the revised scheme, only graduates of specific programs (218 in total) would be eligible for fast-track immigration. The decision was described as necessary to respond to labour market needs. During a debate in the National Assembly following the announcement, Prime Minister François Legault and Minister of Immigration Simon Jolin-Barette defended the decision before members of the opposition. Responding to calls to explain the decision, Jolin-Barette declared, "We are making sure we respond to the needs of the labour market ... to ensure that Quebec's economy is competitive" (National Assembly of Quebec, 5 November 2019). Similarly, Legault stated, "For the wellbeing of the economy, for the sake of economic immigration, we should focus on people who respond to labour market needs" (National Assembly of Quebec, 5 November 2019).

Resistance to the decision was strong with representatives of the three opposition parties voicing their discontent during the 5 November Plenary. PQ member Pascal Bérubé warned that the revision to the PEQ would be "costly for Quebec's economy and for the image of our nation" (National Assembly of Quebec, 5 November 2019). Referring to international students, Bérubé further contends that "they are already in Quebec, they are educated, they are integrated, and often in the regions. They speak French. They are one of us." PLQ representative Carlos J. Leitao made similar remarks about the international students already in Quebec who had been "promised" a fast-tracked immigration. According to Leitao,

The people who are here, they are working, they pay their taxes, and we are going to send them back to their home. They are integrated; they speak French as well as other languages. They are at home here. Why should we deprive ourselves of these talents? A little bit of humanity please (National Assembly of Quebec, 5 November 2019).

Gabriel Nadeau-Dubois, leader of Quebec Solidaire, accused the minister of immigration of treating immigration as a commodity, calling on the government to consider that these decisions are about "peoples' lives" and not about statistics:

> With its decision to modify the Quebec Experience Program, the people he is throwing into distress are our neighbours, these are people who live in Quebec, who study in Quebec, who speak French, who settle in Quebec and who see their future in Quebec. These are people we went to get. We made them promises. Today the CAQ government is slamming the door in their face. It's bad for the economy of course, but it is also breaking a promise that we made to human beings, people that are here in this building today.

While the debate did not provoke a backtracking by the government on its decision, it did lead the CAQ to incorporate a "grandfather clause" to ensure that the international students who were already in Quebec would retain their right to an eased immigration as per the previous PEQ iteration. For upcoming cohorts of international students, more stringent criteria for eligibility to the PEQ were introduced including the requirement that graduates have a minimum of twelve-month work experience in Quebec before applying. New criteria around language acquisition were also introduced according to which both applicants and their spouses are required to show evidence of a certain level of French-language knowledge. Hence, while the PEQ reforms are indicative of the prioritization of labour market needs, stricter language requirements also reflect a desire to ensure the vitality of the French language in Quebec. It is another indication of the CAQ's unusual ideological stance – between a nationalist vision and the precedence of neoliberal and austerity measures (Graefe and Rioux 2020).[2]

A Minority Nation between "Identity Paradiplomacy" and Economic Competitiveness

The findings outlined in this chapter point to a strong connection between domestic and foreign policy goals and policies. The support of international student exchanges serves Quebec's foreign policy endeavours by promoting its international engagements and spearheading its bilateral agreements. These also have important domestic implications as they help Quebec advance cultural, linguistic, and labour market needs. This dual domestic–foreign function echoes the literature on paradiplomacy, which describes how minority nations harness their foreign policy activities towards their internal nation-building agendas and distinguish themselves from the central state apparatus (Lecours and Moreno 2003; Rioux Ouimet 2015). The scholarship on paradiplomacy of minority nations tends to highlight it as a positive force for these territories to take their place in the global economy and assert their distinctiveness both within and outside their borders. This conception is supported by the research conducted here.

Yet the preceding discussion also showcases how Quebec's identity paradiplomacy can come at a cost. The recent reforms to the Franco-Quebec mobility agreement and PEQ are indicative of a broader tension for Quebec: the balance between economic imperatives and nationalist aims. The precarity of these programs reflects the challenge Quebec faces in maintaining the "identity" dimension of its paradiplomacy without causing financial strains. This predicament corresponds with the scholarship citing the challenges of minority nations within the globalized economic system (Gagnon 2014; Rioux 2020). As a minority nation, Quebec finds itself balancing its desired status as a "competition state" externally (Cerny 1997) and the maintenance of its cultural and linguistic distinctiveness internally. While these two goals can under certain conditions be mutually reinforcing, they can also clash. Prioritizing French students in its international education programs served a cultural function, cementing Quebec's international actorness and exemplifying its close connection to the French nation, people, and the francophonie. more broadly.

Quebec does hold an advantage in comparison to other minority nations given the widespread use of French worldwide. It can (and does) prioritize linkages with francophone-speaking countries in its international affairs. Not all minority nations have this luxury. More so, for minority nations like Scotland, where English is dominant, language is not an impediment to economic competitiveness. As a minority nation, Quebec strikes a balance between its economic imperatives and nationalist ambitions. It does so, however, under specific circumstances and conditions – in this case, a French-speaking nation with aspirations and connections to the wider francophonie. The specificities of the Quebec case lend weight to the need for context-sensitive approaches to minority nationalism.

6 Branding Minority Nations: Marketing and Promoting Quebec as an International Study Destination

The recruitment of international students has become a top policy concern for governments around the world looking to compete in the "international student market." In countries like the United Kingdom, Australia, and New Zealand, "education exports" are among their top export earnings, with international students generating immense returns for their economies. International students in the United Kingdom, for instance, generate close to £30 billion annually (Hillman 2021). In today's increasingly competitive international environment, attracting and recruiting international students becomes yet another arena where economies jostle for status and appeal on the world stage. In recent years, national governments have devised strategies for promoting their territories as worthy study destinations within their broader international education strategies. To this end, there is a recognition that to attract international students, cultivating and promoting images of the territory (in most cases the country) in question is imperative. Governments are increasingly relying on marketing and branding strategies to promote their countries and higher education systems among potential international students. Initiatives for cultivating and disseminating images of "nation" are among the tools in the policy toolbox that are used to advance international education strategies. While on the surface aimed at projecting images of higher education systems, these tend to encompass a broader portrayal of the territory itself or of the "nation" in which universities operate. In this way, international student recruitment policies have been described as promoting a nation branding function.

While the study of international education branding has gained traction in recent years (Lomer, Papatsiba and Naidoo 2018; Moscovitz 2022; Potter 2008; Sataoen 2015; Stein 2018), most of these remain focused on national governments with little attention paid to how minority nations promote themselves as study destinations (for a discussion on the case of Quebec, see Moscovitz 2022). This chapter addresses this gap by exploring how Quebec promotes its international image through its international student marketing campaigns. It takes Quebec's unique position as a minority nation within a multinational federation as a backdrop to investigate how nation branding practices are realized in contexts in which nationalisms coincide and even compete. The chapter addresses how Quebec's education marketing rationales reflect the majority–minority tensions vis-à-vis the federal level. It also considers how Quebec juggles its desire to project a distinct, national (francophone) image with its need to remain competitive and appeal to a wide "market" of potential international students. In this way, the chapter provides further indication of the precarious position held by minority nations in the global economic landscape.

Nation Branding

Nation branding practices have become ubiquitous in the contemporary global economic system as states compete to attract foreign investments, tourists, "high-skilled" migrants, and international students. With economic competitiveness a key priority in what has been deemed the "competition state" (Cerny 1997), governments are turning to branding and marketing techniques to cultivate and project their territorial images. Described as a form of "commercial nationalism" (Volcic and Adrejevic 2011) and as a process that "reinterprets national identity in markets terms" (Jansen 2008, 122), the notion of nation branding presupposes a certain convergence between economic interests and nationalism. Akin to commercial branding strategies, nation branding entails the highlighting of specific features that set a country apart. These features are commonly inspired by the narratives around a country's national identity, including nods to its history, culture, and values.

According to Szondi (2008), nation branding entails the "strategic self-presentation of a country with the aim of creating reputational capital through economic, political and social interest promotion at home and abroad" (5). Aronczyk (2013) discusses nation branding as the result of an "interpenetration of commercial and public-sector interests" (16). Hence, akin to traditional commercial marketing strategies, nation branding initiatives entail the selection of specific features identified as the most valuable to presenting a positive image. As outlined by Wang (2013) commercial brands and nation brands share the need for "differentiation through identity and communication" (36). A chief objective of nation branding is to highlight what makes nations unique and elucidate how they stand out in an increasingly competitive global environment. As such, differentiation is a crucial marker of a nation's brand. As outlined by Dinnie (2015), "[m]any contemporary discussions of international competition stress global homogenization and a diminished role for nations. But, in truth, national differences are at the heart of competitive success" (5).

While on the surface an "'externally' oriented strategy," nation branding also serves an "inner-oriented" function, mobilizing citizens domestically and promoting internal nation-building goals (Varga 2013, 829). In an account of Canada's nation branding strategy, Potter (2008) contends that "when a country's citizens see themselves reflected in the mirror of others' perceptions, that reflection can either strengthen or weaken national identity and citizenship; it can reinforce or challenge prevailing values by providing new perspectives on them" (4).

Marketing International Education in Quebec: Early Beginnings

As outlined in the previous chapter, the recruitment of international students has constituted a central component of Quebec's international relations since it catapulted onto the international scene in the mid-1960s. Long before the prevalence of international education marketing and branding trends, the Quebec government had been promoting Quebec as a study destination through its foreign diplomatic missions. Throughout the 1990s, Quebec delegations abroad were taking part in student fairs with the aim of recruiting international students. Asia was an important target for these missions, including campaigns in South Korea, Japan, and Hong Kong (Quebec Ministry of International Relations 1991, 1993). During this time, the promotion of Quebec universities abroad was largely uncoordinated, with universities and embassies working in parallel towards attracting international students. In 2002, Quebec published its first international education strategy, titled "To Succeed in Internationalizing Quebec Education: A Mutually Advantageous Strategy." With it, Quebec was more than a decade ahead of the federal government in terms of strategizing for education internationalization (the federal strategy for international education, detailed below came in 2014). The strategy refers to a need to "position" Quebec as an "influential player in internationalization" (Quebec Ministry of Education 2002, 9) and to "exercise and affirm Quebec's jurisdiction in educational matters"(8). Affirming Quebec's jurisdiction in educational affairs, the strategy makes the case for Quebec carving a space for itself in the marketization of education.

And indeed, with the rising competitiveness of an international student "market" in the mid-2000s, the Quebec government began to call for a more integrated approach to international education marketing. In a 2005 Action Plan, the Ministry of International Relations described this aim as follows:

> Around the world, competition is fierce between academic institutions, cities and even states for attracting high value students and researchers. Quebec, attracting 20 000 international students annually, especially in its universities, must intensify its efforts to sustain, even reinforce its recruitment capabilities among international students ... At this time, the promotion of studies in Quebec are conducted by different actors working on isolated promotional initiatives (Quebec Ministry of International Relations 2006, 50).

The Action Plan also noted the need to "combine the efforts and work of institutions in order to develop an integral marketing strategy which positions Quebec as the centre of education excellence" (51). This specific target was aligned with the broader goal of "promoting Quebec's growth and prosperity." Recognizant of the economic benefits of international education promotion, the Quebec Ministries of Education and International Relations intensified their marketing efforts in this sphere. In 2009, they jointly initiated the development of an online portal to "position Quebec as a destination of choice for international students" (Quebec Ministry of International Relations 2011, 19). The "Study in Quebec" webpage was integrated into the international section of the government services online portal and would act as a reference point for promoting Quebec as a study destination. Describing the initiative in the National Assembly, Minister of Education Michelle Courchesne (PLQ) noted the importance of a brand promotion:

> It is very much related to the investment in promotion. Other countries do a large amount of promotion, they invest budgets to attract foreign students. We have therefore decided with our partners to pretty much do the same thing. And in this sense, we need to develop a brand, we need to develop it as a study destination. We did it in tourism, we did it in the business sphere, and have now understood that we need to do the same thing in terms of study destination (National Assembly of Quebec, 22 April 2009).

Equating Quebec's need for an international education brand to the fact that "other countries" are pursuing similar promotional measures,

Courchesne promotes an essential paradiplomacy ideal: that sub-state entities act like nation states on the international scene (Lecours and Moreno 2003). Courchesne further described the need for the government to take on a coordinating function in branding Quebec as a study destination:

> Universities do it but they do it individually because they are sort of in a context of competition. We are saying: why not do missions abroad in target countries, that is in countries with which we already have relations, those we were talking about earlier, to improve what we have to offer? So this is what is being done now (National Assembly of Quebec, 22 April 2009).

While universities compete for international students, for Quebec as a whole, the recruitment of international students serves a common purpose. In this way, Quebec's universities are on the same team in promoting the territory as a valuable place to study and live. Here, the rationales behind the need for an education brand are tied to the desire to foster a coordinated effort to increase the number of international students choosing Quebec. As described later, however, a strong push factor for these efforts was exerted from above as a reaction to developments occurring at the federal level and Quebec's desire to demarcate itself from these.

Consolidating a Coordinated Marketing Effort: Reactions to the Federal Marketing Initiatives

Although Quebec's efforts in international student recruitment can be traced back decades, it would take until the late 2000s for a concerted discussion of a coordinated and sustained marketing effort in this regard. In its 2017 strategy, the Ministry of International Relations outlined the need for a "new strategy to attract international students towards Quebec's academic institutions" including a "promotional strategy for Quebec universities" (Quebec Ministry of International Relations and La Francophonie 2017, 28). The development of an impending international education strategy is described as "in line with the government's priorities aimed at economic prosperity, in a world where the internationalization of economies, increased movement of people and demographic changes are having a constant impact on Quebec society" (Quebec Ministry of Education and Higher Education 2018a, 5). This follows global trends and ideas on the perceived significance of international student recruitment for enhancing economic competitiveness in the global arena. In this way, Quebec's aspirations and rationales for pursuing a promotional strategy are on par with those of national governments working towards similar goals.

Yet, as a minority nation within Canada, Quebec's rationales and opportunities in this domain are also somewhat distinct. As outlined below, the political discussions on the need for an education brand to represent Quebec's universities abroad are tied to Quebec's unique status as a minority nation within a larger multinational federal state. Any discussion of education nation branding in Quebec requires an understanding of how it fits into the broader context of Canada's international education strategies and education branding projects.

In 2007, the Department of Foreign Affairs and International Trade (DFAIT), today referred to as Global Affairs Canada, launched the Edu Canada initiative, aimed at increasing Canada's international education capacities, with a particular focus on strengthening the country's recruitment of international students. Following these efforts, in 2014, the Department rolled out its first official international education strategy. The policy document titled "Harnessing Our Knowledge Advantage to Drive Innovation and Prosperity" outlines the federal government's plan to utilize the international education sphere to strengthen Canada's economic capacity in the global economy. In the opening remarks of the document, Minister of International Trade Ed Fast states:

> International education is critical to Canada's success. In a highly competitive, knowledge-based global economy, ideas and innovation go hand in hand with job creation and economic growth. In short, international education is at the very heart of our current and future prosperity (Department of Foreign Affairs, Trade and International Development Canada 2014, 4).

While the international education strategy is clearly led by economic incentives, its associated policy documents also reflect an identity-related outcome. In the Department's advisory panel document outlining key recommendations for Canada's international education strategy, the term "diplomacy of knowledge" (viii) is used to describe the value of international education for the country. It notes that "[i]nternational alumni of Canadian institutions can go on to become leaders around the world. Their experience of Canada's culture, values and opportunities will form the foundation for meaningful bilateral relations between Canada and their home countries" (Department of Foreign Affairs and International Trade 2012, 49). The strategy further states that "[i]nternational education is a key vehicle to engage with other countries and to share our Canadian values worldwide. International education makes an important contribution to Canada's culture, diplomacy and prosperity" (50).

International students are perceived as important for spreading Canadian values in their home countries, assigning to international education an important image-promoting role. Image promotion has, in fact, been a major focus of the federal government's international education strategy, through the development of a Canadian education brand to promote the country as a study destination abroad. The idea to produce an education brand for Canada was initiated in a 2007 DFAIT pilot, through which extensive consultations took place in an effort to formulate a common marketing image for Canada's universities. The brand was developed by the DFAIT, together with the Council of Ministers of Education, Canada (CMEC), through large consultations between government representatives both at federal and provincial levels (via the CMEC), as well as relevant stakeholders in the Canadian higher education landscape, including the Canadian Bureau for International Education (CBIE).

The consultations culminated in the launching of the Imagine Education au/in Canada brand, visually represented by the maple leaf, "the most recognizable symbol for Canada" (Department of Foreign Affairs, Trade and Development 2014, 50). The slogan "imagine" was intended to reflect "a personal proposition inviting students to interpret what they will read and see." The slogan also alludes to Canada's bilingual character by using both *au* and *in*. A discussion of the decision to highlight bilingualism and its challenges was referenced in the advisory panel's report: "opinions varied on the effectiveness of the *Imagine Education au/in Canada* name. For example, several discussions raised concerns about the user 'unfriendliness' of 'au/in' (which was a compromise reached to reflect Canada's bilingualism)" (Department of Foreign Affairs and International Trade 2012, 50).

With the 2014 International Education Strategy, and the branding initiatives preceding it, as well as the 2019 international education strategy "Building on Success" (Global Affairs Canada 2019), the federal government cemented its role in devising and implementing policies pertaining to international education and international student recruitment specifically. Yet Canada's engagement in this policy domain is not clear-cut. The distribution of competencies set out in the 1867 BNAA placed higher education under the authority of provinces and territories. At the federal level, Canada lacks any official role in determining higher education policy in the country. This is exemplified by the fact that there is no federal ministry responsible for education. Yet, as outlined by Trilokekar and Jones (2020), international education "falls between the cracks of jurisdictional divides" (30). While education is beyond the scope of its competencies, the federal government retains authority over foreign affairs and trade, two areas closely related to international student recruitment. It is through the guise of these policy spheres that the federal government has been able to insert itself in an otherwise provincial competency.

Quebec's Reaction to the Federal Initiatives: A Call for Policy Ownership

For the Quebec government, the education branding initiatives pursued at the federal level were perceived as an infringement on a provincial sphere of competence. The PQ officials in power at the time described the 2014 federal international education strategy as "illegal" (*Le Devoir*, 22 January 2014). Alexandre Cloutier, minister of inter-governmental relations at the time, made the following claim, nodding to the Gérin-Lajoie Doctrine: "Quebec is not just a partner when it comes to education. It has control over its decisions in the sphere of higher education, as much inside its borders as outside them" (*Le Devoir*, 23 January 2014). Cloutier also noted the constitutional arrangement, calling on the federal government to "respect" it, arguing that "if they want to undergo a process of constitutional amendment, that will be their decision, but as long as we are in the current regime, we demand that Quebec's competencies be respected."

The PQ government demanded compensation from the federal government, according to which the funds earmarked for the Edu Canada initiative be invested instead in Quebec's own branding project. The example of the Millennium Scholarship fund was cited as a precedent for the compensation (*Le Devoir*, 23 January 2014). As argued by Pierre Duchesne, minister of higher education, research, science and technology:

> Quebec must be able to invest according to its needs and priorities in education, not according to the interests of the government of Canada. This is why Quebec must receive these funds in the form of a transfer rather than in the form of various programmes established by Ottawa (Secrétariat du Québec aux relations Canadiennes, Press release 22 January 2014).

In 2018, the Quebec Ministry of Education and Higher Education produced a parliamentary report making the case for developing a separate international education strategy. Quebec's "exclusive competency over education" and its need to "position itself strategically and to strengthen its actions if it wants to gain leadership in terms of internationalization of education" (Quebec Ministry of Education and Higher Education 2018a, 2) were touted as motivations for a Quebec strategy on international education. The discussion included reference to the need for Quebec to invest the proper resources to market and promote itself as a competitive and attractive study destination to "strengthen Quebec's international reputation as a popular destination for students from around the world" (Quebec Ministry of Education and Higher Education 2018a, 4). A separate strategy and marketing initiative is also described as imperative in a context in which "the federal government promotes an image of Canada as a study destination and solicits Quebec universities to use it in their international activities" (2).

Distinctiveness as an Underlying Rationale

On par with policy ownership discussions outlined in previous chapters, the appeals for Quebec to ensure its competency over international education be respected are discursively tied to ideals of *distinctiveness*. The significance of policy ownership is strongly connected to the need to recognize and maintain Quebec's distinctiveness within Canada. The demand for financial compensation from the federal government for the 2014 international education strategy was supported by the PQ's claim that the federal government did not take into consideration the "specificities of Quebec." As outlined by Jean-François Lisée, minister of international relations at the time:

> We are once again faced with a Canadian strategy which does not take into consideration the Québécois specificity. Attracting international students in a francophone nation necessitates a different strategy than that of an anglophone nation. The application of the Gérin-Lajoie Doctrine, the constitution and common sense should make Ottawa respect Quebec's competence (Parti Québécois press release, 22 January 2014).

Concerns of the sort predated the federal government's 2014 international education strategy. Already in 2008, as the Edu Canada branding pilot was underway, the PQ challenged the federal involvement in this sphere. At this time, Marie Malavoy, PQ spokesperson for higher education, noted her discontent with the branding initiative:

> Quebec must be wary of embarking on such an adventure ... We must develop our own Quebec brand. It must be clear for foreign students that

Quebec is a Francophone state and not a bilingual province. This [brand] reflects an image of a bilingual country. This is a clear case where Quebec should have distanced itself (*Le Devoir*, September 29, 2008).

Quebec's desire to maintain control over its international education promotion is consistent with its paradiplomatic endeavours since the Quiet Revolution. Intentions in this sphere are not only discussed in terms of putting in place an independent or parallel strategy but also a distinct and even competing one. As an international actor in its own right, Quebec should also be able to present itself as a worthy study destination, separate from Canada. In this way, in its efforts to recruit international students, Quebec is not only competing with other countries and territories around the world but also with Canada itself. By promoting the image of a bilingual and multicultural country, the Canadian brand is seen as neglecting the *multinational* character of the country and subsequently disregarding Quebec's status as a founding nation (Moscovitz 2022).

Promoting a Distinct Nation Abroad

The distinctiveness rationale attached to Quebec's international education projects is twofold. First, consistent with the discussions in previous chapters, the demand for policy ownership is attached to a need to demarcate Quebec from the federal scale and ensure that its distinct needs and interests are considered in policy design around higher education. This supports previous studies linking policy ownership with distinctiveness (Béland and Lecours 2008; McEwen 2005; Moscovitz 2020, 2022). There is in this case, however, another dimension at play. The discussions around international student recruitment and marketing/branding of Quebec as a study destination are also tied to the need to ensure a fair representation of Quebec abroad. The federal government's perceived intrusion in Quebec's sphere of competency through its branding initiative and international education strategy was problematic on a purely structural level, in that it called into question constitutional arrangements in place since 1867. Yet it was also problematic at a symbolic level, through the image of Canada, which was represented.

As argued by Malavoy in the previously cited quote, portraying Canada as a bilingual country, the Edu Canada brand misrepresented Quebec by disregarding its status as a francophone territory. Malavoy's statement echoes a long-standing position of consecutive Quebec governments (most explicitly supported by PQ). When the federal government produced its first foreign policy strategy in 1995, Quebec officials were alarmed as to its constitutional implications, and the federal government's right to represent Quebec on an international level. Of particular concern for Quebec, was the federal government's appeal for the "projection of Canada's culture and values internationally" (1) through the promotion of Canadian industry, culture and education (Department of Foreign Affairs Canada 1995).

Citing Quebec's competencies in culture and education in its 2001 foreign policy strategy, the Quebec government argued that this federal foreign policy objective "once again ignores the fact that Quebec is a society with its own culture" (Quebec Ministry of International Relations 2001, 23). Hence, the image of Canada projected by the federal government whether through broader foreign policy strategies or the Edu Canada brand specifically, is seen as misrepresenting Quebec and circumventing its ability to project its distinct image internationally. The challenges Quebec faced in projecting its image were also attributed to the lack of French-language media covering Quebec and the reliance of foreign journalists based in Montreal on media from "English Canada." The action plan also noted that the "ministry of international relations, has for these reasons, a duty to intervene so that an accurate image of Quebec's realities are reflected across the world" (Quebec Ministry of International Relations 2001, 52).

International education activities and the recruitment of international students specifically were among the areas in which the Quebec government sought to promote an accurate and attractive image of its territory. Recent plans (outlined in the 2018 international strategy) to create a coordinated Quebec brand between different ministries and target different "audiences," including international students, are described by the Ministry of International Relations as necessary to distinguish Quebec on the international scene. A brand strategy will "raise Quebec's power of attraction abroad by presenting a unified and coherent identity. It faithfully reflects what Quebec is, its culture, its values, its distinct features, its economic dynamism, all that it has to offer the world" (Quebec Ministry of International Relations and La Francophonie 2022, 7). Of note, the development of a brand strategy is described as necessary to distinguish Quebec both internationally and within Canada. The impending branding strategy is discussed as a "reflection of Quebec identity and culture, its values, the vision which our nation holds of itself, its distinctive traits, and its contribution to the world" (Quebec Ministry of International Relations and La Francophonie 2021, 7).

The Cultivation of Quebec's Distinct Image as a Study Destination

In lieu of an official international education branding strategy, over the years, Quebec has promoted itself as a study destination in different promotional materials and recruitment endeavours. Within the "Study in Quebec" pamphlets produced by the Ministry of Education (starting in 2001, with the latest version produced in 2021), Quebec is characterized using a common set of traits and characteristics of its territory, culture, and people. As described in the introduction to the 2001 brochure intended for potential international students, "[p]eople wanting to pursue their studies abroad first want to have information about the host country and its education system" (Quebec Ministry of Education 2001). Indeed, this is well understood by governments today and is the basis of international education branding strategies. Arguably, these branding initiatives are much more about the host country than the universities or higher education systems themselves.

An overarching feature found in these materials is Quebec's distinctiveness. This is, of course, not surprising, any branding exercise, whether to promote a product or country, involves a certain differentiation element. It is about identifying what makes this place/item unique and positioning it in such a way to demarcate it from its competition (Dinnie 2015). Yet, as this book aims to substantiate, Quebec's endeavours, including its branding ambitions, should not be understood as simply another example of nation branding in the global arena. This speaks to a broader argument about nation branding and the need for context-specific readings of the trend. The very need for a separate and distinct brand is tied to Quebec's desire to assert and command its distinctiveness within Canada. There is an internal dynamic at play whereby through promoting an externally geared, distinct Quebec brand, Quebec is able to support its domestic appeal for distinctiveness within Canada. The domestic implications of nation branding in Quebec are significant as it becomes entangled in broader tensions between majority and minority nationalisms in Canada.

Americanité as a Marker of Distinctiveness

Articulations of distinctiveness in the promotional materials examined are tied to Quebec's status as a francophone minority within North America. Quebec's *américanité* consistently appears as a marker of its distinctiveness with Quebec described as "the beacon of the francophonie in the heart of the Americas" (Quebec Ministry of Education and Higher Education 2018b, 31), "the francophone space in the heart of the Americas" (Quebec Ministry of Education 2011). Materials also relate to the fact that Quebec "distinguishes itself with the richness and uniqueness of its francophone culture in the Americas" (Quebec Ministry of Education and Higher Education 2018b, 13). The Ministry of Education and Higher Education notes that Quebec holds tremendous potential to be considered a top study destination citing among others its "francophone character" and its "belonging to the Americas" (Quebec Ministry of Education and Higher Education 2018b).

The reliance on *américanité* as a feature of Quebec's identity is mirrored in its wider international policy. Indeed, the discursive embedding of Quebec in a wider American hemisphere is commonly observed in different international policy documents published by consecutive Quebec governments over decades. In the international policy document produced by the PLQ in 2006, Quebec's North American attachment is described as follows: "As an integral part of the North American landscape, Québec must make a place for itself in this new world context by asserting its identity, prospering economically, and preserving its values" (Jean Charest opening statement, Quebec Ministry of International Relations 2006, VII). The 2019 international policy describes Quebec as "the locus of the French fact in North America" (Quebec Ministry of International Relations and La Francophonie 2019, 82).

This supports existing literature on Quebec's américanité which discusses the leveraging of Quebec's continental belonging to the Americas, its identity discourse as well as in its strategic positioning in the international arena (Oakes and Warren 2007). Quebec's américanité is described as "a way to differentiate Quebec from the rest of Canada and to reaffirm its national status within and outside the Canadian federation" (Dupont 1995, 1). Américanité becomes one of Quebec's distinguishing traits thereby facilitating a branding process that differentiates it from other territories competing for international students but, importantly, also from the Canadian brand being promoted by the federal government. It is not simply Quebec's francophonie which is emphasized, as this is a trait Canada can (and does) also claim. Quebec's historical and cultural ties to the American hemisphere and its unique position as the only francophone majority in this space are leveraged in its marketing initiatives.

For Quebec, asserting its place within the larger American hemisphere provides a much-needed springboard for promoting distinctiveness within Canada. While its attachment to Canada's federal structure is viewed as posing a threat to the maintenance of its distinct culture and language, its attachment to the Americas supports this endeavour. The emphasis on Quebec's special status as the only francophone majority in the Americas serves to strengthen its appeal for policy ownership of international education and international student recruitment. Quebec has a distinct image to promote than the one disseminated at the federal level, and it strives to demarcate itself through its image-projecting efforts.

Between Internationalization and Nationalism: Tensions and Paradoxes

Consistent with the discussions in previous chapters, Quebec's unique position as a minority nation with global ambitions is apparent in its international education branding efforts. Once again, a tension is observed between Quebec's need to pursue nationalist interests on the one hand, and its desire to remain globally competitive on the other. Although throughout these promotional materials, Quebec's affiliation to the francophonie is emphasized, another pivotal feature is, paradoxically, bilingualism. On par with the federal government's promotion of Canada, the "possibility of pursuing studies in French and English" is reiterated throughout Quebec's promotion of itself as a destination for international students. The competitive edge attributed to Quebec's potential as a study destination is, in part, associated with the "presence on its territory of both anglophone and francophone institutions" (Quebec Ministry of Higher Education 2021, 4). The possibility of teaching in French and English enables the recruitment "of a large and diverse pool of international students" (Quebec Ministry of International Relations and La Francophonie 2017, 26). Indeed, there are increasing calls in Quebec to diversify the "pool" of international students to raise the number of students coming from non-francophone countries. During a press conference presenting a 2018 university financing plan, the minister of education and higher education Hélène David discussed the government priorities for international student recruitment in the following terms:

> I think that what we started in the 80s with the French students ... This was like a natural clientele, our French cousins. And in the current geopolitics, now we are jumping 50 years later, I think we are, with the quality of our university system, in an extremely favorable position, whether it be for our francophone or anglophone universities (Press Conference of the Minister of Education and Higher Education, National Assembly of Quebec, 17 May 2018).

Evidently, to ensure its competitiveness in the international student market, Quebec will need to look beyond French-speaking countries for the recruitment of international students. While a key feature of its distinctiveness, Quebec's francophone character is also described as an impediment to its international competitiveness in the international student market. As outlined by a representative of the Association of Rectors of Quebec during a parliamentary debate on the matter,

> In a globalized world, where English dominates, attracting international students to pursue studies in French is a major challenge. Quebec's linguistic reality requires the development of approaches which target a francophone or *francophiles* clientele, which requires a lot of more effort and resources, than those aimed towards the anglophone market which has a natural growth (National Assembly of Quebec, 13 September 2011).

The presence of anglophone higher education institutions, notably Montreal's two English-language universities, McGill, and Concordia, is considered an asset to the recruitment of international students. The discussions around McGill University outlined in chapter 4 attest to this as the university is caught in the crosswinds between the ideal of a francophone Quebec and the vision of a globally competitive Quebec, and Montreal as a so-called world city. In the marketing and branding discussions too, a difficult balance is upheld between the two visions. However, there is an appeal to focus Quebec's international education marketing efforts in francophone countries. This aligns with the discussions and debates on the tuition fee exemptions for French students outlined in chapter 5. Among the potential solutions cited to address the decline of French in Quebec (and Montreal specifically) was the prioritization of francophone markets in recruiting international students to Quebec.

In a 2014 op-ed published in *Le Devoir*, PQ member Jean-François Lisée made a case for re-organizing and strengthening the international student recruitment capabilities of Quebec, with a focus on prioritizing francophone students and their potential immigration to Quebec postgraduation. The fact that Quebec lacks a coordinated brand to market itself as a study destination is viewed as a significant impediment to its recruitment possibilities. Yet, for Lisée, this marketing should be geared primarily towards francophone students or at the very least, students willing to study in French: "Quebec should launch a program aimed at all those who want to study in French, from whichever nation, France, Canada outside Quebec, Africa or otherwise" (*Le Devoir*, 6 November 2014). Lisée also noted his vision that Quebec become a recognized hub for francophone students from around the world looking for an international education experience and hopefully an immigration experience long term. As described in his op-ed: "Starting from scratch, we could aim to attract francophone students and researchers and make Quebec a centre of excellence of higher education in the Francophonie." Ultimately, for Lisée, such an approach would mean that Quebec's strengths as a study destination will be widely recognized throughout the francophonie (*Le Devoir*, 6 November 2014).

Similar appeals for the prioritization of francophone students in marketing and recruiting efforts have more recently been made by the CAQ-led government, first elected in 2018. In 2022, Quebec's minister of immigration, Jean Boulet, announced the decision to reduce the tuition fees for international students planning to study in francophone institutions outside of Quebec's main urban centres. The plan was motivated by a need to address the labour shortages in primarily French-speaking peripheral regions of Quebec, and to counterweigh the decline of French by incentivizing francophone students to choose Quebec as a study destination. It was described by Boulet as a winning formula to "promote the learning of French and consequently ensure a lasting integration to the values of society" (Radio Canada, 19 May 2022).

These discussions were accompanied by challenges to the federal government and calls for policy ownership over immigration policy. The federal government was accused by members of the Bloc Québécois at the federal level, and members of the PQ and the CAQ, of discriminating against francophone international students in the provision of visas (Bloc Québécois Communiqué, 25 August 2022). While the Quebec government could prioritize francophone students in its marketing and recruitment efforts, their arrival remains dependent on the federal government that, despite Quebec's growing input in international student immigration, retains control over immigration for the country. A federal parliamentary report commissioned by the Permanent Committee on Immigration and Citizenship outlined a significant discrepancy in the number of visa refusals for international student applicants from francophone-speaking countries versus those from anglophone-speaking countries (House of Commons Canada. Report of the Permanent Committee on Citizenship and Immigration, May 2022).

Bloc Québécois representative at the federal level, Alexis Brunelle-Duceppe called this a "systematic discrimination," further stating,

> It is completely ridiculous. In Quebec, the government is providing scholarships to attract these students because we need them, we need their labour. But the federal government refuses them, this is nonsense and a dual vision. It is really time to give this competency over to the provinces

who manages education ... The government of Canada keeps saying it wants to do more for the French language, but here is proof that this is false (Rainville, le Quotidien, 18 August 2022).

Quebec's distinct policy interests in the field of international student recruitment are once again relied upon to justify a need for greater policy ownership – in this case over immigration. Brunelle-Duceppe's statement also highlights the fact that the federal government does not share Quebec's interests and therefore should not be responsible for decisions over student visas in Quebec.

The discussions around the recruitment of international students are also tied to questions about tuition fees in Quebec. Debates around whether Quebec should deregulate tuition fees for international students brought to the surface the perceived unfair advantage of Quebec's anglophone universities. In a 2018 National Assembly debate, Québéc Solidaire member Gabriel Nadeau-Dubois described this issue as follows:

> The problem, Mr. Chairman, is that we already know, we can already predict who will win this race for clientele: it won't be the francophone universities in the regions, it won't be the francophone universities in the cities. The universities who will win in this fierce competition, in this race for clientele are the anglophone universities, and one in particular, McGill University. And if universities like McGill win this race for clientele, it is not because they are the best universities, it is not because they provide a better education, it is for structural reasons. It is because anglophone universities in Quebec, Mr. Chairman, have access to a completely different market than the one which francophone universities have access to (National Assembly of Quebec, 27 November 2018).

Allowing universities to charge higher tuition fees for international students will according to Nadeau-Dubois perpetuate a "structural imbalance" between francophone and anglophone universities. And "for a government that proclaims to be a government of the francophone majority, and who wants to defend the regions of Quebec, it is even more troubling that they are continuing to defend this decision."

Evidently, elected officials and political actors in Quebec do not all share this view of a need to target francophone international students for the preservation of the French language in Quebec. On the other side of the debate are those who contend that the successful recruitment of international students benefits Quebec regardless of whether they attend its francophone or anglophone institutions. PLQ member

Jean-François Roberge stated, "[A]nd I think that at the end of the day it is all of Quebec which will get richer" (National Assembly of Quebec, 2 May 2019). Roberge continued: "[I]n my view, there is something interesting in welcoming international students whose fees are deregulated. It brings in international students. It enriches Quebec. For me, that is non-negotiable. It also increases funds to our universities." Roberge also notes how Quebec's university sector is a space where the linguistic communities come together: "there are not two solitudes. Especially in the university network, there is less and less solitude, there is increasingly one network."

Education Branding in Minority Nations

Reflecting global trends, Quebec has in recent years intensified its efforts to market itself as a worthy study destination. While the marketing of Quebec as a potential host territory for international students is not new, coordinated efforts to enact a branding effort to this effect began in 2017. Quebec's desire to promote itself as a competitive candidate in the global market for international students is on par with its broader paradiplomatic goals – notably to promote its interests and identity on the world stage. Its engagement in the policy sphere of international education requires stronger consideration of the role of substate actors in this domain. Indeed, studies on government international student recruitment policies tend to focus on the nation-state scale. Yet this neglects the fact that states come in different configurations, and, as a result, policymaking and the rationales behind it, do not follow a one-size-fits-all paradigm.

Canada's multinational federal system requires consideration of the provincial government's policies as well. This is of relevance for Quebec, where policy and nation building are strongly connected. As outlined throughout this chapter, Quebec pursues its own marketing and branding efforts when it comes to international student recruitment, in parallel (and at times in competition) with federal initiatives. In this way, Quebec should be considered a study destination separate from Canada, with its distinct image to project and distinct interests to address. Quebec's efforts in this domain are comparable to any country pursuing marketing and branding in international education. At the same time, as a minority nation, Quebec should also be viewed as a unique actor with distinct needs and policy interests. This challenges the scholarship on nation branding that tends to view it as a following a "homogenized approach" (Aronczyk 2013, 31). Such perspective obscures the differentiated rationales and challenges faced by minority nations in promoting these practices. While the techniques and strategies for cultivating and disseminating nation brands might be consistent, the very reasoning behind them is not. In branding its nation, Quebec's aspirations are not solely outward-looking, this branding exercise also plays a critical domestic role, clarifying its distinctiveness not only globally but also within Canada.

7 Promoting the Quebec Nation through Education Diplomacy

This chapter explores the public diplomacy function of Quebec's higher education policy and how it intersects with its nation-building agenda. The discussion centres on education-oriented government initiatives aimed at promoting Quebec internationally. The chapter opens with an investigation of the Quebec studies programs developed internationally and traces these from the very first Quebec studies centres in Europe (1971) to more recent budget challenges faced by these initiatives (2018). The promotion of Quebec studies has long been viewed as central to Quebec's public diplomacy efforts, advancing an "understanding and appreciation of Quebec" (Association internationale des études québécoises 2016,1) among foreign publics. Since its creation in 1967, the Quebec Ministry of International Relations has supported and encouraged the establishment of research, study and teaching on Quebec history, culture, society, and politics in different corners of the world, as part of its broader cultural diplomacy initiatives. The promotion of Quebec studies beyond Quebec and Canada is a key component of Quebec's education diplomacy. These efforts are aimed at projecting a positive image of Quebec internationally and, as the analysis reveals, demonstrating its distinctiveness from the image of Canada propagated by the federal government.[1]

The chapter then moves on to outline the education diplomacy efforts specific to Quebec's regional ambitions in the Americas. It considers the role of the Centre de la francophonie des Amériques inaugurated in 2008 by the PLQ government to promote the French language in the Americas and foster ties between its francophone communities. Education-oriented activities feature prominently among the centre's initiatives, providing a valuable lens to delve deeper into Quebec's education diplomacy and consider the implications of its role in the francophonie, as well as its sense of attachment to the wider American space, or *its americanité*.

Public Diplomacy, Soft Power, and Image: Unpacking the Triad

Public diplomacy is defined as the attempts by governments to "direct communication with foreign peoples, with the aim of affecting their thinking and ultimately that of their governments" (Malone 1985, 199). It encapsulates "efforts to manage the international environment through engagement with a foreign public" (Cull 2009, 12). The notion of public diplomacy has evolved to reflect the post–Cold War dynamic of international relations and importantly, the shift away from state-centred perspectives (Gilboa 2008). As outlined by Gilboa (2008), in line with the proliferation of non-state actors in international relations, these are also increasingly engaged in public diplomacy efforts traditionally confined to national governments. Describing the "new" public diplomacy, Melissen (2005) points to the fact that the "ordinary individual is increasingly visible in the practice of diplomacy" (23). This shift is partly attributed to the advent of the information age, which provides citizens with a participatory role in international politics (Melissen 2005). The recognition of new public diplomacy actors and their interaction with government/state actors in this field is critical to advance the understanding of public diplomacy as it is pursued today. While the goal of public diplomacy, namely, the management of the international environment, remains unchanged, the actors involved, and mechanisms utilized are transformed (Cull 2009).

Public diplomacy takes on myriad forms with actors harnessing different types of activities to engage with their targeted publics. In his taxonomy of public diplomacy efforts, Cull (2009) outlines five spheres of activity: listening, advocacy, cultural diplomacy, exchange diplomacy, and international broadcasting. Public diplomacy efforts studied in this chapter fall between the cultural diplomacy and exchange diplomacy mentioned by Cull. Indeed, education has long served as a central public diplomacy tool, relied on by governments to cultivate strong relationships with foreign publics. Educational exchanges are undoubtedly the most cited form of "education diplomacy" with prominent examples including the American Fulbright exchange program and the UK's Rhoades scholarship program. Government-sponsored or government-sanctioned exchanges are described as ideal forms of public diplomacy given their reliance on people-to-people contacts and the potential for cultivating long-term relationships with foreign publics (De Lima 2007; Metzgar 2016; Scott-Smith 2020).

A lesser-studied site for education diplomacy, and one, which is at the centre of inquiry in this chapter, involves the creation of study and research centres aimed at disseminating knowledge on the country or territory in question and its history, culture, and language. This form of education diplomacy is commonly associated with the Chinese government's Confucian Institutes and their broader cultural diplomacy goals, aimed at "spreading the teaching of Chinese and Mandarin language and culture worldwide" (Yang 2010). By supporting the creation of centres anchored within universities around the world, the Chinese government can promote its national culture and values, in turn projecting a positive image on the international scene. Similar initiatives are promoted through the French Alliance française and UK's British Council, both of which promote language teaching and the projecting of their respective cultures internationally. A small number of studies have explored similar initiatives, notably the promotion of Canadian studies internationally, pursued by the Canadian government (Brooks 2018A; Hoerder 2010; Potter 2009). The promotion of Canadian studies abroad is discussed in part as a cultural diplomacy effort by the federal government and as a vehicle to promote Canada's soft power internationally (Brooks 2019).

As the discussion on the Canadian context substantiates, education diplomacy activities have a strong soft power potential, in that they allow for the promotion of "the attractiveness of a country's culture, political ideals and policies" (Nye 2004, 4). In Nye's (2008) view,

> in international politics, the resources that produce soft power arise in large part from the values an organization or country expresses in its culture, in the examples it sets by its internal practices and policies and in the way it handles its relation to others (95).

By disseminating knowledge on Quebec through research and study programs, Quebec's education diplomacy does just this. Exploring the education diplomacy rationales and approaches of Quebec, this chapter seeks to contribute to the understanding of this specific form of public diplomacy and generate knowledge on how it is manifested in minority nations.

For Quebec, the reliance on education to advance its public diplomacy goals was a natural and straightforward project. As laid out in the previous chapters, Quebec's education system and its international relations framework are intricately connected. As public diplomacy is inherently about soft power and the projection of external image, there is value in examining how it is manifested in a minority nation. Identity paradiplomacy is itself an exercise of soft power, as it is used by minority nations to project and promote their distinct images and identities on the international scene.

Quebec Studies Abroad: A Genesis

On the heels of the Quiet Revolution and the spearheading of its international relations framework, the Quebec government was preoccupied with promoting Quebec abroad through cultural and, germane to this study, education diplomacy efforts. Among them were initiatives and projects aimed at promoting Quebec studies in universities abroad. The establishment and trajectory of Quebec studies outside Quebec (and outside Canada) should be understood against the backdrop of the Canadian federal government's own experience and interest in promoting Canadian studies abroad.

The Canadian studies program developed by the federal government in the late 1970s is the outcome of the Commission on Canadian Studies (Symons Commission) and its deliberations. The commission was mandated to make recommendations on the state of teaching and research relating to Canada. The commission's report, titled "To Know Ourselves," included a section dedicated to the question of Canadian studies abroad. The report outlines the importance of promoting the study of Canada in foreign universities to promote a better and, importantly, *clearer* image of Canada internationally:

> It is little wonder, then, that our image abroad is vague, when it is not a complete distortion. Canada is literally viewed abroad as a distinct country and society whose history, politics and literature merit serious intellectual examination. A few of the old "ice and snow" myths linger on and the epithet of the "unknown country" may have acquired new meaning (Symons Commission Report Vol. II, 3).

The Symons Commission report was met with significant opposition by the newly elected sovereigntist PQ (Harvey 2001). The report's recommendations for promoting Canadian studies were construed as a federal government plan to cultivate an "intellectual basis" for Canadian nationalism (Quebec Ministry of Cultural Development 1978, 23). The foreign policy dimension of Canadian studies was of particular concern with the view that the "federal government is presenting itself as the government of all Canadians. On the international level it is the only voice which is meant to represent the voice of Canadians" (Quebec Ministry of Cultural Development 1978, 25). The importance of being recognized as "more than a province like all others" underlined much of Quebec's early paradiplomacy objectives. As a people "conscious of its national identity, (35)" Quebec had a distinct cultural identity to promote, necessitating a distinct cultural development policy. These arguments were consistent with the policy ownership discourse at the time and, specifically, the discussions around the Gérin-Lajoie Doctrine.

It comes as no surprise that during these years, the Quebec government was also preoccupied with its cultural diplomacy appeal and potential. In 1979, the PQ government rolled out Quebec's very first cultural policy strategy, one deemed "true to its own culture" (Quebec Ministry of Cultural Development 1978, 17). The development of a pan-Canadian cultural policy was described as resulting in the "provincialization of Quebec culture" (18), hence the need to establish a clearly defined and clearly distinct policy on cultural matters representative of Quebec and its people. While the contents of the 1978 cultural policy relate primarily to domestic cultural initiatives and issues, it also includes a discussion of the international dimension of Quebec's cultural policy. The document describes culture as a "space of dialogue between countries," further noting its significance for "national prestige" (142).

Quebec's cultural policy has, since its inception, been closely linked to its international relations framework. The Gérin-Lajoie Doctrine principles are reflected in the cultural policy, which states that

[t]he Canadian federation, officially bilingual and multicultural, cannot claim to represent a national culture, and can only represent itself: a whole made up of the superposition of the disparate elements which it brings together. At the beginning of the 1960s through the voice of its prime minister Mr. Jean Lesage, Quebec came to terms with its responsibility vis à vis francophones of North America: experience still prompts us today to agree that only the state of Quebec is able to act as a necessary and effective springboard to enable us to access the network of international cultural relations (Quebec Ministry of Cultural Development 1978, 146).

Cultural diplomacy was a linchpin to Quebec's flourishing international relations and a gateway to promoting a positive image vis-à-vis international partners. It is within this broader discussion of Quebec's cultural policy/diplomacy that the idea to promote Quebec studies abroad emerged. Quebec could promote its culture and language beyond its borders by supporting initiatives for teaching, research, and study on Quebec in universities around the world. With this objective in mind, the Ministry of International Relations provided financial support to establish the very first Quebec studies centres abroad, in Treves, Germany (1976), and Liège, Belgium (1977). It was the American context, however, that saw targeted efforts by the Quebec government to support Quebec studies.

Opération Amérique and the Establishment of Quebec Studies in the United States

The United States has long been one of Quebec's most important bilateral partners sharing deep historical and economic ties. The very fact that Quebec's first representative office abroad was established in New York City attests to the strength of the Quebec–US relationship. Second to France, the United States became a key ally of Quebec's paradiplomatic efforts early on. It has even been suggested that Quebec's policy vis-à-vis the United States has been prioritized over its policy with France since the 2000s (Paquin 2024).

As it consolidated its international relations, the Quebec government under Jean Lesage understood the importance of ensuring a strong relationship with its neighbour to the south. In the early 1960s, Lesage made several visits to the United States to promote the Quiet Revolution and the image of a modern Quebec ready to take its place in the world (Balthazar and Hero 1999). Economic interests were a critical motivating factor behind Lesage's policy vis-à-vis the United States. As Quebec was working towards nationalizing its electricity apparatus, securing financing for the project became a priority. The search for private investments in Quebec's burgeoning hydroelectricity program (Hydro-Quebec) was oriented towards Wall Street. In his dealings with the State Department, Lesage aspired to cultivate a similar diplomatic relationship Quebec had secured with France, that is, one independent from the Canadian federal government apparatus. Yet, unlike de Gaulle's openness towards Quebec as a separate actor from the Canadian federal government, the US State Department was reluctant to offer special status to Quebec. Instead, US relations with Quebec were to be conducted under the ambit of the former's relationship with Canada. Through this "three-way" relationship, the US government would deal directly with Ottawa in matters pertaining to Quebec (Paquin 2016).

On the heels of the PQ's electoral victory in 1976 and its growing sovereigntist appeals, Quebec's image in the United States began to waver. The burgeoning Quebec independence movement and subsequent contentious politics within Canada led to significant backlash with American businesses projecting risks in their commercial dealings with Quebec (Couture Gagnon and Chapelle 2019). On a political level, the image of a radical government in Quebec was growing in the United States prompting Lévesque to reassure Americans that Quebec was a reliable and worthy partner (Balthazar and Hero 1999). Once independent, Quebec would need to be on good terms with the United States.

Reassuring American counterparts of Quebec's intentions as an international partner became an important mission for Lévesque.

In March 1977, Lévesque delivered a speech at the Economic Club of New York titled "Quebec: a Good Neighbour in Transition," in which he drew parallels between Quebec's sovereigntist movement and the American Civil War, presenting a picture of the Québécois as "a tenacious people, true to itself, loving continuity (Lévesque 1977)." In his speech, Lévesque sought to shift the perception of the changes occurring in Quebec as one of chaos and extremism to one of careful transition towards what would become a "quiet independence." The speech did not achieve its intended objectives, with Americans left skeptical of the independence movement, including potential investors who worried about the security of their financial investments in Quebec (Paquin and Chaloux 2010). Undoubtedly, a speech alone would not suffice to alter the negative image of Quebec in the United States. Reverting this perception of Quebec and securing American business ties became a priority for the Lévesque government. As a result, Quebec's policy vis-à-vis the United States developed more profusely during the PQ reign than it had during previous administrations (Paquin and Chaloux 2010).

Lévesque's strategy sought to propagate a positive image of Quebec among American political, economic, and public spheres – through Opération Amérique. The operation aimed to "improve Quebec's image in the United States and its relations with various American communities" (National Assembly of Quebec, 25 May 1979). The initiative spearheaded new activities and intensified existing ones, which promoted Quebec among the American public as well as the political elite. Seeking to promote "a complete image of the Quebec reality… the political, economic and social" and avoid a limited government to government approach (National Assembly of Quebec, 25 May 1979), Opération Amérique took on the core elements of a public diplomacy effort. Germane to the premise of this book, education diplomacy was at the heart of the program, with activities related to the promotion of Quebec studies in the United States and the promotion of teaching on Quebec through French-language university programs.

Asked in parliament how the government intends to ensure a positive presentation of Quebec in the United States through Opération Amérique, Claude Morin, minister of inter-governmental affairs at the time, cited the government's initiatives in supporting French-language teaching in the United States, as well as its support of Quebec study centers in various American universities (National Assembly of Quebec, 25 May 1979). These were considered crucial springboards for Quebec to have its culture, language and identity propagated among American students and teachers. Beyond their direct impact on education stakeholders was an understanding that these activities would have a trickle-up effect reaching the American economic and political elite.

Opération Amérique ultimately lasted eighteen months. Within this short timeframe, the initiative led the way for a series of long-lasting ties between Quebec and the United States. Chief among them is the American Council for Quebec Studies (ACQS), established in 1984 to promote the study of Quebec history, culture, and society in the United States. The ACQS was the offshoot of the Northeast Council on Quebec Studies (NECQS), established by a group of American professors in 1981 interested in French Canadian literature, culture, and history. These professors had been teaching courses on topics related to Quebec literature and culture in universities across the American Northeast, including in Plattsburgh, New York; Vermont; and Maine. The regional focus was a testament to the historical ties between Quebec and New England (Gould 2003). Seeking to open the organization to more universities and regions across the United States, the council broadened its scope and changed its name to the ACQS in 1984. Aligning with its Opération Amérique, Quebec's Ministry of International Relations "assisted" in the transformation of the NECQS to the ACQS (Quebec Ministry of International Relations 1985, 48). The ministry also lent its support to individual university centres and Quebec studies programs as well as granted a postdoctoral fellowship for research on Quebec pursued in the United States (ibid.).

Described by the Quebec Ministry of International Affairs (1991) as a means to "enhance knowledge of Quebec's character as a democratic and modern society, open to world and to American decision-makers" (144), the establishment of Quebec studies centres in American universities proliferated during these years. Following the creation of the ACQS, approximately 150 American institutions had a Quebec-oriented study program, partially financed by the Quebec government (Quebec Ministry of International Relations 1985). The importance of Quebec studies in the United States for promoting Quebec's image was cited in its 1991 foreign policy strategy:

> Quebec will also pursue its efforts to make sure American decision-makers, at both national and regional levels, have a better understanding of its character as a democratic, open society, open to the world, where private and public stakeholders are dynamic partners. ... It will continue to promote the development of Quebec studies in certain American institutions as well as stimulate the study of American realities in Quebec institutions (Quebec Ministry of International Affairs 1991, 144).

The notion that teaching and research activities on Quebec have a direct role to play in the dissemination of Quebec's image as well as the strengthening of its international visibility and attractiveness are recurring in policy documents over the decades. In its 2010 strategy vis-à-vis the United States the Ministry of International Relations notes:

> The Minister also recognizes the contribution of research chairs and centres of Quebec studies in the United States which allow it to reach opinion leaders in political, economic and social spheres and which will be able to establish networks of influence, as well as the contribution of Quebec studies south of the border which improve the credibility and stability of perceptions vis à vis Quebec (Quebec Ministry of International Relations 2010, 11).

Economic rationales are also central to Quebec's education diplomacy efforts in the United States. In fact, the Quebec–US relationship has always been first and foremost based on economic imperatives. Yet an important cultural component is viewed as a precondition to ensuring strong commercial relations. Of particular importance is the cultivation and projection of a positive image of Quebec as a means to strengthen its commercial ties with the United States. The 1991 white paper on Quebec's international relations noted the significance of image for economic relations through the analogy of marketing products:

> The growth of resources intended for public affairs and marketing is a prime example of the importance which companies – and countries put towards activities aiming to promote their identity and products. The best product at the best price in the world will not sell if it remains unknown ... To be known and appreciated is not a given, especially in the context of today's international competitiveness. This is why one of the main areas of Quebec's international action includes the activities which aim to contribute to the attractiveness of Quebec, that is to make Quebec's most important features known and appreciated abroad (Quebec Ministry of International Affairs 1991, 117).

The role of soft power in achieving economic goals is not uncommon. Yet Quebec, as a minority nation, needs to work twice as hard to cultivate its international persona that is difficult to disentangle from the image of "Canada" promoted by the federal government. Circumvented by its status within the Canadian federal system, Quebec lacks a direct political relationship with the United States. Education diplomacy efforts take on a particularly valuable function for Quebec, as a minority nation. These provide opportunities to engage with foreign governments in a way which might otherwise be impossible. The potential of education diplomacy to serve as a gateway to reaching American political figures is also underscored:

> The ministry has for a number of years now directly intervened to encourage publications and conferences of these Quebec study centers and Quebec study associations functioning in the United States. You know that in many countries around the world, think-tanks, researchers and experts are those who are consulted by governments as they design their policies vis à vis these experts countries ... In the United States this is common phenomenon. This is true in many countries, hence Quebec's interest to be engaged in this domain (National Assembly of Quebec, 7 May 1998).

Promoting Quebec Studies around the World: Towards the AIEQ

As centres and programs for Quebec studies proliferated in the United States, a similar trend was occurring in Europe. In fact, the first Quebec studies centres were established in Europe; at the University of Liège (1976) and the University of Treves (1978). Over half of the world's Quebec studies centres are in European universities, making it an epicentre for students, teachers, and researchers interested in the study of Quebec. The growing number of Quebec studies centres across Europe along with the success of the ACQS, created the impetus for establishing an international network bringing together the world's *Québécists*. The International Association for Quebec Studies (Association internationale des études québécoises) was created in 1997, with the goal of "encouraging and supporting the development of a better understanding, comprehension and appreciation of Quebec around the world" (Association internationale des études québécoises 2017 1).

The significance of the AIEQ was also linked to Quebec's distinctiveness and the need to redirect the federal government's role in promoting Quebec through Canadian studies. Discussing the establishment of the AIEQ, Quebec's minister of international relations at the time, Sylvain Simard noted:

> I always regretted the fact that Quebec, after having promoted, I must pay homage here to a previous administration, at the end of the sixties and beginning of the seventies, after having been very present in Quebec studies abroad, in university networks, researchers, professors, students, has slowly given up this space to the Canadian government, who has occupied it very well, often neglecting in fact Quebec's specificity (National Assembly of Quebec, 18 April 1997).

Simard also attributes an important public diplomacy rationale to the AIEQ, stating that "by informing more and more on Quebec, in these university networks, it is the governments we are informing indirectly" (National Assembly of Quebec, 18 April 1997).

At the first European Conference on Quebec Studies, taking place in Paris in 2003, the AIEQ was described by its standing president at the time as "a universal community which reflects on and diffuses the specificity of North-American francophonie of which the principal pillar remains Quebec" (Kolbloom in Laliberté and Monière 2004, 12). He further described members of the AIEQ as "a community of multipliers and mediators of knowledge on Quebec" and the "linchpin to Quebec's openness to the world." At the same conference, Quebec's minister of international relations under the PLQ Charest government also delivered a speech in which she revered the AIEQ's role in promoting a better understanding of Quebec around the world (Monique Gagnon-Tremblay in Laliberté and Monière 2004, 361). In her speech, Monique Gagnon-Tremblay relayed Prime Minister Charest's pledge to promote Quebec diplomacy, paraphrasing his argument that "[s]ocieties like Quebec, who lack a numerical advantage, have a bold duty. Our economy and our culture depend on our ability to make ourselves known on all continents." While Quebec endeavours to promote public diplomacy efforts on par with those conducted by nation-states, there is a recognition that as a minority nation, it faces different challenges in pursuing these goals. Having Quebec known and understood becomes even more important under these circumstances.

The AIEQ plays a key role in this regard, supporting Quebec studies abroad, funding research on Quebec and promoting the mobility of *Québécists*, among other activities. Viewed as an important instrument in "promoting Quebec, its realities, specificities, its culture and institutions" (Quebec Ministry of International Relations 2007, 17), the association has long been described as a valued partner of Quebec's Ministry of International Relations. The ministry's interest in the AIEQ and its work is evidenced by the pivotal role it played in its establishment, having provided CAN$40,000 in start-up financing and CAN$130,000 to support its operations (National Assembly of Quebec 7 May 1998). For the Quebec government, the AIEQ was a vector for "promoting an accurate perception of Quebec" and for ensuring its "increased influence" (Quebec Ministry of International Relations 2003, 74). International researchers pursuing studies on Quebec are attributed a contributory role to the projection of Quebec's distinctiveness and enabling Québécois to "take our place in the world" (Quebec Ministry of Higher Education, Research, Science and Technology, 2013, 15).

Challenges to AIEQ Funding

While the AIEQ has long been perceived as an asset to Quebec's public diplomacy efforts, it has in recent years been subject to significant budget cuts by the Ministry of International Relations. Towards the end of 2014, under PLQ leadership, Quebec's Treasury Council announced plans to end the ministry's funding to the AIEQ, which would effectively compel it to shut its doors by the first quarter of 2015 (Gervais, 24 December 2014). For the political opposition, the decision was an affront to Quebec's distinctiveness within Canada. Voicing concern over the move, PQ representative Carole Poirier notes that "[t]he liberals are using austerity measures to justify cuts aiming to minimize Quebec's influence abroad. For [Prime Minister] Philippe Couillard, Quebec should simply be a Canadian province like the others" (PQ 2015). The implication here is that as a minority nation, Quebec requires public diplomacy tools which the other provinces can do without. André Gaulin, former PQ member and professor at Université Laval, called on the government to reconsider the budget cuts:

> Could we explain to senior decision-makers in your government who thrive on economic consideration, that we have better commercial relations with states when we know their history, their culture, their literature. Cutting a small promotion budget, supported free of charge by dozens of academics across five continents, reflects a miscalculation! ... we are abolishing a whole network of individuals who are themselves disseminators of our existence and our identity in the world (Gaulin, *Le Devoir*, 31 December 2014).

The elimination of the AIEQ's budget was ultimately walked back, with the minister of international relations, assuring the organization that the MRI has advocated for the importance of its continued support to the promotion of Quebec studies. While the AIEQ's budget line from the Ministry of International Relations was saved, it was reduced by 20 per cent that same year, leading to a significant reduction in activities (Association internationale des études québécoises 2016). In 2018, the AIEQ was at risk again when the PLQ announced its decision to cut funding by an additional 40 per cent. Opposition leaders and academics were once again quick to defend the organization and its pivotal role for Quebec's international influence. The pressure exerted on the government led it to double down on its decision to cut funding. This time, it put forth what it deemed to be a more sustainable solution to the budget difficulties. To ensure consistent financing for AIEQ, in 2018, the Ministry of International Relations established a partnership with the National Research Fund, through which the AIEQ's funding would from then on be managed (National Assembly of Quebec, 26 April 2018).

Noteworthy here is that cuts to the federal Canadian studies abroad program – titled "Understanding Canada" – were conducted around the same time as the discussions around the AIEQ funding. In 2012, DFAIT announced the "phasing out" of the federal government program, citing "the current fiscal context" as the reasoning behind the decision (*Globe and Mail*, 19 June 2012). The decision was challenged by Canadian scholars who viewed the program as indispensable to promoting the study and understanding of Canada around the world. Yet, the decision stood and continues to be a point of contention. Quebec's continued (albeit threatened) support for its Quebec studies programs is contrasted to the federal government's decision in appeals for its reversal. In a 2019 speech delivered at the American Council for Canadian Studies in Montreal, a former director of the Academic Affairs Committee of the federal government's external affairs service in the 1970s, John W. Graham noted the following:

> However, it is essential to note that the glitter of success masks a major problem: a seriously weakened infrastructure that is the direct consequence of the loss of Canadian Government support. The absence of key research, travel grants and other financial assistance has made it increasingly difficult (often impossible) to recruit new staff and thereby control attrition. Meanwhile the Government of Quebec maintains support for its extensive network of Quebec Studies abroad (Graham, ACSUS conference speech, November 2019).

In this quote, Quebec's unique position and separate decision regarding funding its studies abroad networks are the source of envy by those opposing the closure of the Understanding Canada program.

Centre de la francophonie des Amériques: Education Diplomacy for International Leadership in the Francophonie

In 2008, the Charest government inaugurated the Centre de la francophonie des amériques (CFA) to support and encourage the promotion of the French language across the Americas and foster links between francophone communities in the American continental space. The idea was introduced by Charest in 2003 during the National Assembly inaugural speech and confirmed by decree in 2006. The organization was established to reinforce and enrich relations and complementary action between francophones and *francophiles* in Quebec, Canada and elsewhere in the Americas in order to contribute to the promotion and highlighting of a francophonie bearer of the future for the French language (National Assembly of Quebec, 28 November 2006).

The centre's establishment was also predicated on the need to protect the French language and ensure its sustainability within Quebec's continental vicinity. "Specific measures" were deemed necessary to "counterbalance the cultural uniformity resulting from the omnipresence of English and the cultures it conveys" (Sécrétariat du Québec aux relations canadiennes 2006, 2). Language and culture are intractably linked in these discussions. As noted by PQ member Daniel Turp during a reading of the bill in the national assembly,

> because the battle here, for the francophonie, is not only a fight for the future of the French language, it is a fight for the sustainability of the cultures which express themselves in the French language (National Assembly of Quebec, 28 November 2006).

Alongside the importance of protecting the French language, underpinning the centre's ethos was a reckoning that as the only "majority francophone" territory in the Americas, Quebec has a responsibility and an opportunity to assume a leadership role in this space. This became a priority for the Charest government, which accused the previous PQ administration of ignoring its responsibility vis-à-vis francophone communities outside Quebec (National Assembly of Quebec, 4 June 2003). The government budget for the project included CAN$2.25 million in financing for infrastructure and an initial annual budget of CAN$2 million (Sécrétariat du Québec aux relations canadiennes 2006).

To promote ties between francophone communities, the CFA incorporates a broad scope of activities and initiatives including youth movements, the creation of an online catalogue of literary works by francophone authors from the Americas and the financing of mobility programs between researchers and students across the hemisphere. While wide-ranging, a significant portion of the centre's activities is geared towards "research and the university environment" (Centre de la francophonie des Amériques webpage). In fact, the centre's very first activity in its inaugural year was an academic conference on Louisiana's French history and present (Centre de la francophonie des Amériques 2008) Permanent education-oriented activities include the program for mobility in the Americas, aimed at facilitating the exchange of expertise and best practices through cooperation between students, French-language educators, and academics (Centre de la francophonie des Amériques 2009); the annual summer school for francophonie in the Americas, providing an intensive course described as a "privileged space for the development of knowledge on the francophonie of the Americas" (Centre de la francophonie des Amériques 2009); and the provision of fellowships and scholarships to researchers working on themes related to the francophonie in the Americas. Through these activities, the CFA acts as a provider of Quebec's education diplomacy. Exploring the CFA's diplomacy role allows for a deepening of the public diplomacy/nationalism discussion to incorporate Quebec's américanité as part of its distinctiveness and national identity.

Universities as "Valued Partners" in Promoting la Francophonie des Amériques

Universities and research centres are described by the CFA as "valued partners" in the effort to foster ties among francophones in the Americas (Centre de la francophonie des Amériques 2009). As stated in its 2009 report,

> [the centre] believes in the importance of research and the diffusion of knowledge to gain a better understanding of the history and lived experiences of francophones across the Americas. The development of a sense of belonging, solidarity, and the pooling of resources to promote the French language necessitates a mutual understanding of different francophone spaces (Centre de la francophonie des Amériques 2009, 26).

Supporting the mobility of researchers across borders and encouraging collaboration between them is an important way to leverage the potential for mutual understanding in the wide space that is the American continent. The centre describes its activities as fundamental to "building bridges between the university sphere and the community" and "making research accessible" (Centre de la francophonie des Amériques webpage). Universities, research centres, and their communities are thus attributed an important role in the consolidation of a shared sense of belonging in the Americas made possible by the mutual connection to the French language. As one of the centre's flagship programs, the "researchers' mobility programme in the Americas" seeks to "support the development and radiance of francophone spaces in the Americas" by "encouraging the creation of strong links through collaboration between the university sphere, local communities, and organizations working towards the development of the francophonie" (Centre de la francophonie des Amériques 2023).

Supporting the movement of researchers across borders is also described as promoting "knowledge at the service of the francophonie" (Centre de la francophonie des Amériques webpage). In this way, the education activities pursued by the center follow the underlying logic of education diplomacy. Bringing communities together to exchange, develop and stimulate knowledge on francophone culture in the Americas is perceived as a springboard to cultivate a sense of mutual belonging and collective mobilization.

Conceptualising the centre's activities and driving forces as examples of education diplomacy requires a reflection on how these specific endeavours align or depart from traditional education diplomacy efforts as pursued by the Quebec studies centres examined earlier. A first notable distinction relates to the fact that through this diplomacy, Quebec is reaching out to communities sharing a common heritage, culture, and, importantly, language. There is a strong discourse of collective mobilization permeating the discussion on the centre's goals and initiatives. Quebec's ambitions in this sphere are connected to the recognition of its place within North America and the Americas as a whole. This aligns with Quebec's student mobility efforts towards France outlined in chapter 5. These, too, were predicated on a certain level of shared culture and language. Both initiatives are indicative of Quebec's identity paradiplomacy, aiming to promote the image of a francophone nation on the world stage. In a parliamentary debate introducing the motion to establish the centre, PQ representative Marie Malavoy noted its significance for Quebec's anchoring in the Americas as a space: "I think that we see ourselves in Quebec as being part of this wider space constituting the Americas. The creation of this *Centre de la francophonie des Amériques*, I think it's a way for us to recognise that we are anchored in this reality" (National Assembly of Quebec, 23 November 2006).

Educational exchanges are often discussed in terms of promoting mutual understanding between communities, cultures, and peoples of diverse backgrounds. Undoubtedly, the American hemisphere is home to a diverse set of cultures and communities and among the centre's goals is to promote this cultural diversity. Yet, unlike educational exchanges and diplomacy programs pursued by national governments as part of their new public diplomacy efforts, those advanced by the centre are seeking to bring together communities sharing a language, and to a certain degree sharing a francophone culture. This sets the activities of the CFA apart from the AIEQ's, which is looking to promote an understanding of Quebec to peoples and territories with less affinity and knowledge of its culture, history, and language. The CFA's audience is anchored in the American hemisphere and bonded by a common language. Among its stated objectives, the CFA aims to produce "a deeper sense of attachment to the francophonie of the Americas" (Centre de la francophonie des Amériques 2019, 14).

Promoting a (Minority) Nation's Leadership through Public Diplomacy

While the perceived role of the AIEQ is explicitly geared towards promoting a positive image of Quebec by disseminating its values, culture, and history across borders, the case of the CFA presents a more implicit public diplomacy role. Indeed, as previously mentioned, the activities are seemingly aimed at promoting people-to-people contacts and fostering collective mobilization among francophones, rather than overtly aimed at promoting a positive image of Quebec on the world stage. Yet, on closer investigation, the dissemination of Quebec's image is uncovered. Quebec is actively promoting a positive image and consequently wielding soft power by cultivating a leadership role for itself within the francophonie of the Americas. Hence, it is not simply about promoting an image of Quebec but, rather, about promoting the image of Quebec as a leader in a particular field and territorial context as well.

The notions of leadership and responsibility are recurring in the analysis of Quebec's political discourse around the CFA. The centre's web page describes its rationale as linked to the fact that "Quebec recognises its responsibility towards francophone communities as well as affirms its desire to take on a mobilising leadership role" (Centre de la francophonie des Amériques web page, "About Us"). Coinciding with Quebec City's four-hundredth-year celebrations in 2008, and located in a heritage building in the "national capital's" historic old city, the centre's establishment reflected a desire to promote Quebec as the "main pole" of francophonie in the Americas (Secrétariat du Quebec aux relations canadiennes 2006, 5). It is about allowing Quebec to "be strongly identified with the francophonie of the Americas" (5). The idea that Quebec is the only majority francophone entity within North America is relied on to make the case for its leadership role:

> As the only majority francophone state in North America and the main locus of the French fact in the Americas, it is up to Quebec to exert a unifying leadership within Canadian francophonie and the francophonie of the Americas, against the backdrop of a recognition of cultural diversity (Société du Québec aux relations Canadiennes 2006, 2).

During a reading of the bill to establish the centre, PLQ member Benoît Pelletier highlights the critical role of Quebec in safeguarding the French language in the Americas:

> We will never be able to increase the influence of our language in the world without solidarity and leadership. In the Americas, it is incumbent upon Quebec to take on this leadership and to encourage the emergence of such a solidarity. It must continue to develop strong ties with all components of the francophonie of the Americas. The Centre de la francophonie des Amériques is one of the tools through which Quebec seeks to reach its objectives because the French language concerns us all, because the French language needs us all, and because the French language is and must remain a public treasure (National Assembly of Quebec, 28 November 2006).

It is not only Quebec's self-awareness of its leadership role which is highlighted but also the external perceptions around it. In the following statement, Michel Matté (PLQ) notes the significance of how other Canadian provinces view Quebec:

> I have had the pleasure to experience certain situations in recent years, concerning the role of Quebec in matters related to the francophonie, and I was pleasantly surprised to find how our counterparts from other provinces recognize us as leaders of the francophonie. They are extremely appreciative of our role and the steps we are taking ...We want Quebec, the Quebec state to be able to play and reinforce an active role and influence ... It [the Quebec state] has always played a role in promoting Quebec's cultural identity on an international scale and contributing to solidarity efforts ... And they are unanimous in telling us that Quebec plays a role and that without Quebec, I think the francophonie of the world would not be as strong as we say it is (National Assembly of Quebec, 16 April 2012).

A similar argument is evoked by PLQ representative and Minister of Inter-Governmental Affairs Yvon Vallières:

> It is important for Quebec to play a leadership role in Canadian *francophonie*, because of Quebec's strategic position and because of the francophone majority we have here, which as we know is drowning in an anglophone sea in North America. And we have brothers and sisters of the *francophonie* who are elsewhere in Canada and who need Quebec to become an essential leader in the realm of the francophonie. (National Assembly of Quebec, 16 April 2012).

The soft power potential of Quebec's engagement in the Americas is strengthened by this gateway to leadership, one that is less readily available in other public diplomacy missions. This adds an intriguing dynamic to the Centre's role in promoting Quebec. Through these activities, it is not only Quebec that is being promoted but also its role and potential as a leader in a particular region. Here, Quebec's status as a minority nation, and specifically its status as holder of a minority language within Canada, also provides it with a competitive edge in terms of wielding its soft power. Quebec's proven resilience in protecting the French language within its borders is cited as a valuable attribute to undertaking the role of language protector throughout the Americas. Hence, Quebec's resilience not only is a marker of distinctiveness within Canada but also provides it with a unique international status. This recognition can be leveraged to promote a positive image and in turn to advance an underlying paradiplomacy ideal, that is, to carve a distinct path as an international actor separate from the federal government.

Higher Education for Quebec's Paradiplomacy

Quebec's education diplomacy initiatives explored throughout this chapter provide further indication of the key role of education in the pursuit of its paradiplomacy. While the previous two chapters focused on the hosting of international students in Quebec and the marketing of Quebec as a study destination, the discussion here rests on how Quebec promotes itself and its image through educational programs outside its borders. As a public diplomacy endeavour, the promotion of Quebec studies and education outreach activities pursued around the world, arguably have a wider reach in terms of potential audiences. In other words, Quebec does not need to rely on the presence of a foreign audience on its territory to promote its image and raise its profile. This is at the very foundation of public diplomacy as a government strategy. On par with the activities pertaining to international student recruitment, Quebec's education diplomacy is also relied on as a marker of national distinctiveness and is not immune to the power dynamics and tensions between Canada's majority nation and Quebec's minority nation. While geared towards foreign publics, much like the branding example explored in chapter 6, these efforts also hold important domestic implications. Indeed, public diplomacy is a "Janus-faced" exercise (Potter 2009) informing both the foreign and the domestic.

Conclusion: What Implications for the Study of Minority Nationalism?

As substantiated throughout the seven chapters of *The Politics of Higher Education in Minority Nations*, the consolidation of Quebec nationalism over the last six decades is intricately connected to developments in the higher education policy sphere. Inquiring into Quebec's higher education policy discussions and decisions since the Quiet Revolution provides a unique vantage point to study minority nationalism in a particular context. At the same time, the investigation of the nationalist politics around higher education in Quebec presented here also sought to contribute to a wider theorization of minority nationalism. Unearthing the relationship between higher education policy and Québécois nationalism, the book adds empirical support to the role of policymaking for the pursuit of minority nationalism by considering the role of higher education policy, which remains understudied.

If the case of Quebec advanced throughout this book tells us anything, it is that higher education and nationalism are intricately connected and mutually reinforcing. From the Quiet Revolution to today, political discussions and decisions pertaining to higher education in Quebec are strongly permeated by nationalist ideals and discourses. Given the palpable and long-standing connection between higher education and nationalism in Quebec, it is somewhat surprising that more studies on Quebec nationalism have not focused on its entanglement with this policy sphere. While the focus here was on Quebec, and recognizant of the importance of promoting context-sensitive approaches to any study of nationalism, this connection could arguably also be identified in other cases of minority nationalism around the world. In this concluding section, several overarching themes of the book are summarized and discussed. It also delves into how these themes inform a better understanding of minority nationalism, on one hand, and the politics of higher education, on the other.

The Value of the Domestic–Foreign Analytical Framework

As a domain straddling between domestic and foreign policy decisions and interests, higher education as a policy context provides a valuable lens to explore the connection to nationalism all the while avoiding the "territorial trap" of a siloed vision of domestic and foreign policy (Agnew 1994). Although the chapters of this book are neatly divided between "domestic" (2–4) and "foreign" (5–7) policy discussions, the demarcation between these two spheres of analysis is not always clear-cut. While dividing the book in this way served a useful analytical purpose, in each chapter, domestic and foreign policy interests intertwine, at times in a complementary fashion and at times in more conflicting arrangements. This lends further support to Agnew's (1994) contention that the foreign and domestic should not be viewed in binary terms but, rather, in "conjunction." It also provides a useful lens to explore the imbrication of nationalism and national identity in both domestic and foreign policy spheres.

While the Quiet Revolution was on the surface a domestic endeavour aimed at modernizing Quebec, it is difficult to ignore its implications for Quebec's foreign policy initiatives. As argued by Balthazar (2003), the Quiet Revolution was the precursor to Quebec's international relations. Domestically, the *maîtres chez nous* slogan was used to justify greater control by the Quebec government over higher education policy; externally, it was also calling for greater control over its international relations. Plans to reform Quebec's education system prompted a look to the external, and specifically to France for inspiration (Balthazar 2003). For Balthazar, "Quebec could not affirm itself as a distinct society, as the 'political expression of French Canada,' according to the expression often used by Jean Lesage, or even as a national state, without looking to showcase this image abroad" (Balthazar 2003, 8, translated from French). The consolidation of Quebec's newfound national identity was dependent on how it would be received by the international community. The promotion of Quebec's international image is tied to its domestic nation-building ambitions and collective mobilization efforts of the Québécois people. The higher education policy sphere provides a useful lens to explore the domestic/foreign connection as it is geared towards both. Today, higher education policy is of concern to ministries of education and higher education, immigration, and economic development, as well as ministries and officials responsible for international trade, foreign affairs, and public diplomacy. The interests vested in higher education policy development are wide-ranging and not necessarily aligned between the different policy actors involved.

The case of McGill University (chapter 4) exemplifies the dual role of the university and the potential contradiction between them. The contestations around McGill and its place in Quebec society are predicated on the valuation of its domestic function versus that of its role in promoting Quebec's international image and engagement. The perception of the university posing a threat to Quebec's national distinctiveness is rooted in the idea that higher education institutions represent the Quebec nation and its primarily francophone character. However, McGill is valued for its role in promoting Quebec's global image and recognition, regardless of (and perhaps thanks to) its language of instruction being English.

Moreover, Quebec's international student recruitment policies, and its marketing as a study destination (chapters 5 and 6), serve an external purpose, that is, to promote Quebec's interests and image internationally. Yet, they also fulfil domestic functions, as the presence of international students is viewed as a potential solution to addressing labour market and demographic shortages, as well as maintaining a French-speaking majority in the territory. A handful of government agencies and state ministries are engaged in negotiations around international student recruitment policies, including those concerned with foreign affairs, as well as those working on immigration, labour, and economic policy. The example of Quebec's education diplomacy efforts outlined in chapter 7 provides further evidence of the domestic/foreign connection. While on the surface, the AIEQ and the CFA both serve a public diplomacy function, that is, to promote Quebec among foreign audiences, they should also be seen as pursuing important domestic objectives. By promoting itself and its image as separate from the one promoted by the Canadian federal government, and highlighting its leadership role in the francophonie, Quebec is also making a statement within the context of Canada's multinational federation. This imbrication of foreign and domestic policy goals illustrates the view set out in the critical geopolitics literature that foreign policy is as much about the "outside" as it is a space where the "domestic self is evoked and realized" (Tuathail and Dalby 1998, 2).

This is especially relevant to minority nations and is echoed in the literature on paradiplomacy that emphasizes the significance of nationalism for international relations and vice versa. In Quebec, as noted by Kirkey et al. (2016), "[t]he achievement by the late 1960s of a distinct – albeit circumscribed – international personality was a major accomplishment of Quebec nationalism" (136). Paradiplomacy provides minority national governments and leaders with legitimacy both outside and inside their borders. Through "identity paradiplomacy" (Paquin 2018), minority nations cultivate and promote their national identity by pursuing international affairs in line with their nation-building agendas. Identity paradiplomacy is a prime manifestation of the domestic/foreign convergence described by Agnew and a testament to the importance of disrupting their binary view.

The Gérin-Lajoie Doctrine itself conflates between domestic and foreign policy ambitions. In his famous 1965 speeches, Gérin-Lajoie made a case for Quebec to consolidate its international role based on its nationalist appeal, a desire to be seen and treated as a nation in its own right, and to promote its international affairs in line with its domestic nationalist ambitions. Ultimately, Gérin-Lajoie promoted the contention Agnew would make decades later on the difficulty of detaching foreign and domestic policy. The difficulty in separating these two policy domains along strict lines is used by Gérin-Lajoie as justification for his appeal for Quebec to pursue its own course of action in the international arena. Quebec could not effectively pursue its own education policy course if it lacked authority to conduct international policy.

By showcasing the close connection between higher education and Québécois nationalism in both domestic and foreign policy spheres, the evidence laid out throughout the book lends weight to the importance of considering the domestic and foreign as intertwined. It also supports the scholarly discussion on the relation between nationalism and foreign policy, or paradiplomacy specifically. By bridging the scholarship on minority nationalism's connection to domestic policy (social policy, welfare policy) and that on its connection to foreign policy (identity paradiplomacy), the book provides a useful framework which can potentially be applied to additional studies. This could entail the investigation of different minority nations, and/or the investigation of different policy fields.

Minority Nations in a Globalized Economy: Between Opportunities and Challenges

The plight of minority nations in the globalized economic landscape is a recurring theme throughout the book. In deciphering how nationalism and higher education policy interact in Quebec, a significant and long-standing tension is identified between preserving Quebec's needs and interests as a minority nation and promoting Quebec as a viable and competitive counterpart in the global arena. This tension has been discussed by scholars of minority nationalism arguing that these specific political entities are particularly vulnerable to the fast-paced transformations of globalization. As noted by Gagnon (2014), "[i]n and of itself, one phenomenon-globalization-has markedly contributed to the uncertain future of minority nations. Indeed, globalization is one of the foremost threats to the continued existence and growth of minority nations" (34). With international competition a key priority in the current global economy, economic calculations often come at the expense of cultural interests with "potentially destructive impact on the social fabric of a polity" (Gagnon 2014, 38). Yet, as rightfully pointed out by Gagnon, globalization has served both as an impediment to the preservation of minority nations and as a springboard for the attainment of their political claims.

By enhancing interdependence between the world's economies and reducing the nation state's hold on domestic economic processes, globalization has also provided minority nations with new opportunities to engage in international affairs. As described by Paquin and Lachapelle (2005), "globalization is expanding the set of actions undertaken by substate nationalist movements to ensure their survival as a nation" (81). In this way, the paradiplomacy of minority nations could be said to have been facilitated by the intensification of globalization processes from the 1990s onwards. And, as the literature linking paradiplomacy to nationalism attests to, minority nations use their international relations to promote their distinct interests and images on the world stage, as well as strengthen a sense of nation building domestically. In other words, through their engagement in the international arena, minority nations gain prestige and power both externally and internally.

The different vignettes showcasing the relationship between nationalism and higher education in this book point to this dual opportunity/constraint view of globalization. On one hand, engagement in the global economy serves to promote and strengthen nationalism. It provides Quebec with a venue to promote its national image and distinctiveness internationally and the opportunity to make strides as a player in the global economy. On the other hand, the desire to engage globally can also challenge the preservation of minority cultures and languages. Quebec's higher education system and institutions were shown to be at the centre of this dilemma. Two features of this tension are worth elaborating on here: the issue of language, and implications for the understanding of how economy and nationalism interact.

On Globalization and Language

As substantiated throughout the book, Quebec's minority nationalism is intricately connected to French as a minority language within Canada and the desire to protect its use within Quebec. The debate between preserving national distinctiveness and engaging more profusely in the global economy is heavily grounded on language and specifically, the status of French. This tension is identifiable going back to the 1960s. The debates around the McGill français movement in 1969 saw McGill University serve as both a target of nationalist ideals around the preservation of the French language in Quebec and an example of Quebec's emersion into the global higher education landscape. Montreal was seen as holding high potential to be regarded as a "world city," in part thanks to its anglophone institutions. However, as an anglophone university in a predominantly francophone culture, McGill University was seen as a threat to Quebec's linguistic and cultural heritage and landscape. This contrasting view of the university's status in Quebec society would endure over decades, most recently coming to the fore over the decision to fund the revamping of the institution's infrastructure in 2021.

Recruiting international students from francophone countries is deemed necessary to maintaining Quebec's national character, and uniqueness within Canada. It is also, however, perceived as limiting its possibilities on the international student market that is increasingly reliant on emerging economies such as China, India, and Brazil for students. English is the language of international student mobility, rendering the existence of English-language programs indispensable to the recruitment of international students to any country. In the "global hierarchy" of international education English holds a competitive advantage and English-language universities a "special power" (Marginson 2006, 25). Accordingly, anglophone universities and anglophone countries come out on top in the global competition for international students. It is no surprise that the top destinations for international students globally are primarily English-speaking countries (Australia, the United States, the United Kingdom, Canada). The recognition that English is a key resource for the recruitment of international students has led non-English-speaking countries to establish English-language programs to attract international students to their universities (Saarinen and Nikula 2013). For countries or territories home to minority languages, the decision to offer courses in English is not made without trepidation as it has implications for the state of the minority language in the territory in question.

For Quebec's higher education system, promoting English programs and institutions is both a cost and a benefit. It benefits Quebec by enhancing its international attractiveness and placing its higher education institutions among the top echelons of the global higher education space. Yet, it also comes at a cost to the preservation of Quebec's national distinctiveness within Canada, the Americas, and the world, as it is seen as posing a threat to the continued protection of French in Quebec. The literature on minority language rights provides a valuable lens to discuss this cost-benefit dilemma of language for Quebec. As pointed out by May (2012), there is a significant difference in the way minority languages are perceived compared to majority or dominant languages in society. While the latter are viewed as instrumental and providing an opportunity for individuals and communities, the former are generally viewed as "carriers of tradition" or of "historical identity" (May 2012, 216). English, as the global *lingua franca*, "has come to be linked inextricably with modernity and modernization" (208).

If English "functions as a gatekeeper to positions of prestige within societies" (May 2012, 217), the same can be said for English as a gatekeeper for a heightened standing in global society and the global economy. The use of English has become instrumental for economies to perform and compete on the global stage. Marketing campaigns aimed at attracting foreign investments, tourists, and international students are often conducted in English to reach a wider audience. Importantly, however, while French is a minority language within Canada, it is not a minority language globally. Put differently, widely spoken around the world, French is not necessarily under threat of decline in the global sphere. This places Quebec in a somewhat advantaged position among minority nations striving to enhance their status and visibility in the global arena.

As discussed in chapters 5 and 6, in its efforts to recruit international students and market itself as a study destination, Quebec can direct its efforts towards la francophonie, carving an alternative linguistic network to the English-dominated global arena (Oakes and Warren 2007). This is also achieved to a certain degree through the activities of the Centre de la francophonie des Amériques (chapter 7). Ultimately, however, by promoting itself in the *Francophonie*, Quebec solidifies its leadership position within the francophone-speaking world, as supporting the maintenance of a French-speaking demography domestically. Moreover, by fostering collective mobilization and *rapprochement* between francophone communities in the Americas, Quebec can also be seen as engaging in a counter-project to the hegemonic English-dominant global higher education arena. This points to the importance of considering not only the challenges faced by minority nations in the context of economic globalization but also their resistance and resilience in the face of these challenges.

The strategic connections made with the francophone world in the higher education policy sphere lend weight to the idea that globalization does not a priori pose a threat to minority languages like French in Quebec. As noted by Oakes and Warren (2007),

> far from either being caught in or choosing heroically to wage a constant fight against the global, Quebec is able to take advantage of the opportunities that globalisation throws up to "act locally" through global cooperation in order to further its own linguistic and cultural ends (63).

Hence, Quebec finds ways to protect and promote its minority language within the confines of the globalized system. Not all minority nations have this luxury, as their languages might not be spoken as widely. This supports the need for context-sensitive approaches to studying (minority) nationalism.

On the Link between Economy and Nationalism

Beyond language, a broader tension is observed between Quebec's economic interests and its nationalist ambitions. In many of the policy events examined, the preservation of nationalist interests required a degree of financial investment by the Québécois government. The debate over tuition fees (chapter 3) saw a clash between a desire to maintain Quebec's national character and values and a perceived threat to its economic stability and the quality of its higher education system. The tuition freeze, put in place during the Quiet Revolution, was emblematic of the values of democratization and accessibility outlined in the Parent Commission's report. As pointed out by Graefe (2005), "[c]oming out of the 1960s, then, Québec nationalism had a particular affinity for the state as a means of fostering economic growth and solving collective problems in a manner that strengthened the nation" (532). The ideal of subsidized tuition fees was discursively tied to Quebec's sense of nationhood, based on a social-democratic value system (Erk 2010). It coincided with the development of a welfare-state system and the nationalization of certain industries, notably hydroelectricity. The significance of Quebec's low tuition fees was also discussed as a key example of its distinctiveness within Canada, as a justification for a separate policy.

On the other side of the tuition fee debate were arguments calling for a need to hike tuition fees to finance the higher education system, which was considered in a state of crisis. Adjacent to the financial argument was the contention that heightening the cost of tuition would ultimately improve the quality of Quebec's higher education institutions, to the benefit of Quebec and its citizens. The tuition freeze was considered unfair to the Québécois nation by "condemning Quebec to mediocrity in terms of higher education" (Claude Ryan, MESS 1989). A similar conundrum is identified in the discussion over the AIEQ, and the cuts to the organization's funding over the years (chapter 7). The AIEQ is viewed as an indispensable public diplomacy actor for Quebec, raising awareness and understanding around the world of its linguistic, cultural, and historical attributes as a minority nation. It was seen as a key transmitter of Quebec's image abroad, and as serving an indispensable nation-building goal. Yet, against a backdrop of financial downturns and rising neoliberal policies since the 1990s, its funding by the government is also deemed difficult to justify.

These examples showcase how the pursuit of nationalist goals and the desire to preserve national distinctiveness for minority nations can come at a cost. As suggested by Hubert Rioux (2020), minority nationalism and economic policy are closely related. Indeed, as exemplified throughout this book, nationalism and economy are difficult to disentangle. The literature on economic nationalism tends to focus on how economic policies are either moulded by nationalist interests or how nationalism is promoted through economic policy. Understanding the variegated ways economy and nationalism interact provides a rich terrain for the theorization of economic nationalism in today's global system. Equally important is the need to consider how the balance between nationalism and economic interests is played out. Under what conditions are nationalism and economy mutually reinforcing, and when might they be at odds? In a study on the interplay between minority nationalism and regional economic policy in Quebec, Graefe (2005) contends that

> [c]ompetitiveness is an attractive strategy for nationalists, in that it mobilizes all social actors in a shared project of national development. Yet when the distribution of costs and benefits of that project is perceived as too one-sided, as in the Québec case- nationalist assertion may find itself undermined rather than advanced (544).

Graefe rightfully suggests that economic competitiveness goals can be both constructive and destructive to the nationalist cause. The longitudinal analysis of how higher education and nationalism interact in Quebec reveals that the cost–benefit view is not consistent over time or between different stakeholders or in relation to different policy issues. Further research geared towards explaining how and why nationalism overtakes economic interests or vice versa (in the event that they clash) could be incredibly valuable to the study of minority nations as well as the theorization of economic nationalism more broadly.

As substantiated here, regardless of where the pendulum falls on the economic competitiveness/nationalism equilibrium, both sides of the debate can be seen to be promoting economic nationalism. Indeed, if we consider economic nationalism in its broad sense as "a political claim that invokes national categories and attempts to mobilize national sentiments for a broad range of political projects" (Baltz 2021, 799), or as the "symbolic embeddedness of economy to nation" (Crane 1998, 67), whether economic interests come out on top or not, nationalism is a core argument promoted by political actors. This comes to support the notion that economic nationalism should be considered an ideology as opposed to solely an economic practice. Economic nationalism is promoted in symbolic ways as well as through more manifest policy decisions.

Studying Minority Nationalism beyond the "Usual Suspects"

By investigating empirically how nationalism influences policy decisions and discussions pertaining to higher education in Quebec, the book lends weight to the idea that nationalism is promoted in seemingly banal ways (Billig 1991). This finding comes to corroborate the literature linking social policy to nationalism (Béland and Lecours 2008; McEwen 2005; Lecours and Moreno 2003). For Béland and Lecours (2008), "states continuously engage in nation building through routine and seemingly innocuous practices" (218). Yet, "[t]here has been much less research conducted on nationalism and policy fields not directly related to language (or culture)" (Béland and Lecours 2006, 78). Higher education policy is especially valuable to explore the connection to nationalism given its relation to more explicit nationalist elements (culture, language), and to the "more innocuous practices" cited by Béland and Lecours (policy structures/models, tuition fees). As substantiated throughout the book, it is not solely the cultural and linguistic features of higher education policy linked to nationalism. While these are significant, the structural foundations of Quebec's higher education system were also found to be intertwined with nationalist discourse and ideals.

The Quiet Revolution and Parent Commission set the stage for the consolidation of Quebec's modern higher education system and the development of a *modèle québécois* in this sphere, predicated on widened access and democratization. The development of Quebec's higher education model and subsequent low tuition fees coincided with a broader welfare-state program, including the development of subsidized daycare schemes and drug insurance provisions. Taken together, these policy decisions were promoted as an indication of Quebec's distinctiveness vis-à-vis Canada, and importantly its "ideological distinctiveness" (Béland and Lecours 2006, 83) based on a social-democratic vision of society in contrast to the neoliberal model pedalled by the federal policy initiatives.

The policies themselves played an important part in showcasing Quebec's distinctiveness, whether in terms of the subsidized tuition fees, the Cégep system and the University of Quebec network, or the distinct image promoted to recruit international students. Yet, this distinctiveness was also exemplified by the very assuming of the higher education policy sphere as a Quebec authority. As noted by McEwen (2005) the desire and appeal for policy ownership over a specific field often does more for minority nationalism than the policies themselves. The discursive connection identified between higher education policy control and Québécois nationalism throughout this book substantiates this. Whether the policies enacted converge with or diverge from those in place at the federal level is less relevant to the question of nationalism. Quebec's distinctiveness is apparent from the onset as it demands control over higher education. The very arguments behind Quebec's appeal for control are based on the notion that it is a distinct society and, as such, necessitates its own strategies and policy institutions.

Higher education policy thus serves nationalist movements by promoting a particular culture or language as well as in more implicit ways, through discourse around the need for congruence between a polity's institutions and its national community. It provides another indication of the ways in which minority nations harness their policy-making authority to promote their nation-building efforts.

Promoting Political Perspectives on the University

By investigating how nationalism and higher education policy interact in Quebec, the research presented throughout this book also lends weight to the important discussion on how the university becomes entangled in broader political debates and scenarios. As argued by Pusser, universities should be understood as "politically constituted institutions of the state" (Pusser 2015, 62). They are embedded in broader power dynamics of the state and society in which they operate. While manifest, the significance of higher education policy for the politics of the state has been the focus of limited research so far. As McLendon argued in 2003, "the politics of higher education as a field of study has suffered a history of benign neglect" (186). The political dimension of higher education has since gained more profound attention (see, e.g., Cantwell et al. 2018; Weimer and Nokkala 2020), although a coherent and substantive field of research remains lagging.

The scholarship on the politics of higher education tends to take a state-theoretical approach, given the superseding role of the state in higher education policy and governance. By discussing the political discourse and policy discussions by state representatives and government officials around higher education in Quebec, this book also sought to promote a state perspective to the study on higher education. It does so however with a specific view of the state: that of a non-sovereign state home to a minority nation. By so doing, the book supports the need for a context-specific understanding of how state, power, and higher education interact. For Pusser (2015),

> the existence of a state, however, does not determine the nature of the state. There are many forms and permutations of states, with [the] state having more or less robust institutions and forms of governance emerging from [a] contest between the states and their respective civil societies, and various other social, institutional and political forces (14).

This is corroborated by Robertson and Dale (2009), who call for a departure from the *methodological statism* characterizing much of the literature on higher education. In their view, studies on higher education tend to assume that "all polities are ruled, organised and administered in essentially the same way with the same set of problems and responsibilities and through the same set of institutions"(1116).

An overarching argument put forward here is that as a minority nation, the relationship between nationalism and higher education takes on a distinct manifestation in Quebec. The advancement of research on the politics of higher education should be aware of the specificities of the states, or polities under scrutiny. Moreover, just as the specificities of states and political systems should be considered, so, too, should the specificities of nationalism under scrutiny. Quebec's higher education policy discussions and their connection to nationalism cannot be effectively understood without consideration of its minority nationalism and its power struggles with the dominant nation-building project occurring at the federal level. The situation of one minority nation will not necessarily be echoed in another, hence the importance of rooting any study on the politics of higher education in the historical and socio-political context of the case in question. Research on the connection between higher education and nationalism requires a strong reading of both the higher education system and the nationalism under investigation.

More broadly, the entanglement of higher education in Quebec's nationalist politics is demonstrative of the continued significance of territorial interests, and importantly state interests in the higher education domain. With marketization and globalization processes heightened, territorial borders between higher education systems and institutions have become increasingly blurred, and the role of public authorities are seemingly on the decline. It has been argued that globalization has "disembedded" universities from their national contexts in part by loosening the state's grip on higher education (Beerkens 2003, 146). The commodification of the university sphere has prompted a further decline of state mediation in this domain and a rise in private and market interests. Both trends are contributing to the view of an increasingly homogenized and standardized global system of higher education. According to some scholarly accounts, as pivotal to the development of a global knowledge society, universities today have found themselves positioned "beyond space and time" (Frank and Meyer 2020, 31) and bounded by a "homogenous culture" (42). The *Politics of Higher Education in Minority Nations* challenges this view of a de-territorialized higher education system by providing evidence of its sustained territorial significance, in this case for non-sovereign minority nations.

This is not to say that global and market forces are not having an impact. Evidently, and as evidenced throughout this book higher education policy and governance are significantly influenced by the intensification of global flows and penetration of market interests and neoliberal models. Yet these do not come at the expense of nationalist interests. They can come to challenge the pursuit of nationalism, but they can also work to propel it. This is certainly the case regarding globalization, which as the case of Quebec revealed, has both challenged and supported its nationalist ambitions. The case of minority nations provides a valuable illustration of the argument that nationalism and globalization are not in a zero-sum position – rather, they can be mutually reinforcing (Cox 2021).

Afterword

As this book was being finalized, new debates emerged around Quebec's international student fees. In October 2023, the CAQ-led Legault government announced its decision to increase tuition fees for "out of province" students coming to study in Quebec. Per the announcement, tuition fees for international students and for students from other

Canadian provinces would be raised 30 per cent. The decision was concomitant to the introduction of more stringent language policy measures put forth by the CAQ government prompted by concerns over the declining use of French in Quebec.

I was initially reluctant to incorporate this policy event in the book, as this is certainly not the only significant policy change occurring in the years following the study's empirical timeline. After all, in the world of policy and politics tides are constantly shifting and a researcher should be prepared to put her pen down so to speak. That said, this case is worth elaborating on as it crosses several themes raised throughout the book and offers a useful snapshot into the politics of Quebec in this moment, as the book is being finalized (April 2024).

The announcement continues the saga over tuition fees in Quebec and amplifies the existing language debates in Montreal. It is also reflective of the challenge Montreal faces in becoming a "world city." Quebec's anglophone universities, foreseeing the disastrous repercussions on their student numbers and overall financial well-being, were quick to challenge the government's decision. Montreal's status within Quebec was also of concern. with the city's mayor voicing concerns over the impacts on the city. Responding to the Mayor's comments, Jean-François Roberge noted: "Montreal is the francophone metropole of the Americas. This should be more than a slogan ... Montreal's mayor should be a government ally in this process."[1] For Roberge, the initiative towards maintaining Montreal's francophone character is one that should be shared by all, especially the city's mayor.

Of note, certain groups of students are exempt from the tuition fee hike – notably French and francophone Belgian students who are covered by the tuition exceptions in place. The long-standing friendship with France and Quebec's desire to forge additional bonds with other francophone communities safeguards students from these regions but also ensures Quebec retains a strong number of francophone students and potential immigrants to help balance the linguistic proportions.

The decision to hike tuition fees for out-of-province students was accompanied by a strategy to attract international students to French-language institutions in Quebec regions. Indeed, also exempt from the higher fees are "international students enrolled and accepted to a university of collegiate institute located outside the Montreal metropolitan area" (Quebec Ministry of Education 2024). These students must be pursuing their studies in French and, in key areas, be determined a priority for Quebec's labour market needs. The focus on regions harkens back to the development of Quebec's education system in the 1960s and the establishment of the University of Quebec Network and Cégeps. At the time of their development, these aimed to widen the accessibility of learning in peripheral regions of Quebec, to bring up the education status of its francophone population. Over sixty years later, government policy is turning to these regions as potential hubs for international students (and eventual immigrants). It is yet another indication of the long-standing interface between nationalist politics and higher education policy in Quebec, with policy ideas moulded and adapted to fit this moment in time.

Appendix: List of Primary Sources

Chapter 2: *maîtres chez nous*

Government of Quebec. Ministry of Education. 1978. "Les collèges du Québec : nouvelle étape : projet du gouvernement à l'endroit des CÉGEP".

Government of Quebec. Conseil supérieur de l'éducation. 2019. Avis au ministère de l'éducation et de l'enseignement supérieur. "Les collèges après 50 ans regard historique et perspectives".

Letter from Duplessis to Saint Laurent, 17 November 1951. Cited in Université de Sherbrooke, Bilan du siècle. "Interdiction aux universités québécoises d'avoir accès aux subsides fédéraux." (usherbrooke.ca)

Letter from Duplessis to federal Justice Minister Stuart Garson, September 15, 1954. Cited in Secrétariat aux relations intergouvernementales Canadiennes 2003. "Québec's Positions on Constitutional and Intergovernmental Issues from 1936 to March 2001. Second Government of Maurice Duplessis August 30, 1944 to September 7, 1959."

Minville Esdras. 1956. "Les universités en face des octroix fédéraux". *L'action nationale*, 4 December. Vol. XLVI No.4.

National Assembly of Quebec. Commission des institutions. Journal des débats. Wednesday 13 June 2018. Vol. 44, No.263.

Rocher, Guy. 2006. "L'engendrement du Cégep par la commission Parent." In Lucie Heon, Denis Savard, and Thérèse Hamel (eds). *Les Cégeps: une grande aventure collective Quebecoise*. Quebec City: Presses Université Laval.

Rocher Guy. 2017. "Naissance et implantation des CÉGEPS Québécois". Accessed through la féderation étudiante collégiale du Québec.

Royal Commission of Inquiry on Constitutional Problems. 1956. (Tremblay Commission) Report. Vol. 2. Accessed through la bibliothèque de l'assemblée nationale du Québec.

Royal Commission of Inquiry on Constitutional Problems. 1956. (Tremblay Commission) Report. Vol. 3 Part I. Accessed through la bibliothèque de l'assemblée nationale du Québec.

Royal Commission of Inquiry on Education in the Province of Quebec. 1963. (Parent Commission). Report. Vol. 1. Accessed through la bibliothèque de l'assemblée nationale du Québec.

Royal Commission of Inquiry on Education in the Province of Quebec. 1964. (Parent Commission). Vol. 2. Accessed through la bibliothèque de l'assemblée nationale du Québec.

Royal Commission of Inquiry on Education in the Province of Quebec. 1966. (Parent Commission). Report. Vol. 3.

Royal Commission on National Development in the Arts, Letters and Sciences. 1951. "Report of the Commission on National Development in the Arts, Letters and Sciences, 1949–1951".

The Legislative Assembly of Quebec. Journal des débats. Thursday 23 January 1964. Vo. 1 No. 8.

The Legislative Assembly of Quebec. Journal des débats. Wednesday 5 February 1964. Vo 1 No. 17.

The Legislative Assembly of Quebec. Journal des débats. Monday 9 December 1968. Vol. 7 No.100.

Chapter 3: Towards the Maple Spring Protests

Bouchard, Lucien. 1998, 30 November. Speech delivered at centre des congrès du Quebec.Accessed through la société du patrimoine politique du Québéc.

Bouchard, Lucien. 1999, 3 March. Discours du trône . Accessed through la société du patrimoine politique du Québec.

Comité consultatif sur l'accessibilité financière aux études. 2015. Avis au ministère de l'enseignement supérieur et de la recherche. "Droit de scolarité supplémentaires imposés aux étudiants français inscrits au premier cycle universitaire à partir de l'année scolaire 2015 2016".

Conseil des Universités. (Council of Universities) 1986. "Mémoire à la Commission Parlementaire de l'Éducation sur les orientation et le cadre de financement universitaire québécois pour l'année 1987–1988 et pour les années à venir".

Conseil des Universités. (Council of Universities) 1988. Avis au Ministre de l'Enseignement Supérieur et de la Science. "Le Financement du Réseau Universitaire en 1988–1989".

Conseil supérieur de l'éducation. 1990. "Le financement du réseau universitaire en 1988–1989." Avis du conseil des universités au ministre de l'enseignement supérieur et de la science.

Government of Quebec. 1989, 19 December. Ministry of Higher Education and Science. [Ministère de l'enseignement supérieur et de la science.] "Les droits de scolarité: une hausse nécéssaire". Déclaration de Claude Ryan ministère de l'enseignement supérieur et de la science.

Government of Quebec. 1988. Secrétariat du Québec aux relations canadiennes. "Le gouvernement fédéral ne respecte pas le consensus québécois en éducation." Press Release.

Government of Quebec. Ministry of Education [Ministère de l'éducation]. 2000. "Politique québécoise à l'égard des universités. pour mieux assurer notre avenir collectif."

Government of Quebec. Finances Québec. 2011. "Un plan de financement des universités équitable et équilibré pour donner au Québec les moyens de ses ambitions".

Government of Quebec. Finances Québec. 2014. Budget 2014–2015.

National Assembly of Quebec. Commission de l'éducation. Journal des débats. 16 September 1986. Vol. 29 No.4.

National Assembly of Quebec. Commission de l'éducation. Journal des débats. 11 October 1984. Vol. 27. No.3

National Assembly of Quebec. Journal des débats. Wednesday 9 March 2005. Vol. 38 No.124.

National Assembly of Quebec. Commission de la culture et de l'éducation. Journal des débats. Friday 11 November 2011. Vo. 42 No. 22.

National Assembly of Quebec. Commission de la culture et de l'éducation. Journal des débats. Tuesday 28 February 2012. Vol. 42 No.82.

National Assembly of Quebec. Commission de la culture et de l'éducation. Journal des débats. Thursday 19 April 2012. Vol. 42 No.35.

National Council of the Parti Québécois . October 1989. "Les orientations du programme electoral du Parti Québécois" Accessed through POLTEXT Université Laval.

Quebec Liberal Party (PLQ). 1985. "Sythèse du programme libéral". Accessed through POLTEXT Université Laval.

Quebec Liberal Party (PLQ). 2003. "Un gouvernement au service des québécois". Le Plan d'Action du Prochain Gouvernement Libéral. Accessed through POLTEXT Université Laval.

Chapter 4: McGill and Quebec's Nationalist Politics

Bélanger Mathieu. "Faculté de médecine : le quart de la formation en anglais". *Le Droit*. 17 March 2014.

Cabinet du ministre de la famille. "Francisation de l'année préparatoire en médecine à son campus de l'Outaouais : l'université McGill peut aller de l'avant grâce à une aide financière de 140,000 $.". Newswire. 10 February 2020.

Claude Ryan. "'McGill et son avenir'". 26 March 1969. *Le Devoir*. Accessed through Bibliothèque et Archives nationales du Québec.

Government of Quebec, Office Québécois de la Langue Française. 2021. "Scénarios de projection de certaines caractéristiques linguistiques de la population du Québec (2011–2036)".

Lapierre, Laurier. "McGill and Quebec Society". Text of a speech made by Laurier LaPierre, Director of the French Canada Studies Program. 24 March 1969. 9 pp. McMaster University Archives. Opération McGill Collection.

Marie-Claire Kirkland-Casgrain, Speech to McGill Graduates Society. 11 May 1969. McGill University archives. Series Title, Administrative Records, Records, Group 0049 Container 0068 File 01458 Date 1969–1969.

McGill Daily. 3 March 1969. "Bienvenu à McGill". McMaster University Library Archives. Opération McGill Collection.

McGill Daily. 2 April 1969. "Twilight of the Gods". Vol. 58 No. 88.

McDevitt, Neal. "New vic project reaches new milestone". *McGill Reporter*. 17 September 2020.

National Assembly of Quebec. Commission Permanente de la Culture et de l'Éducation. Journal des débats. Thursday 4 May 2017. Vo.44 No. 69.

National Assembly of Quebec. Journal des débats. Dépôt d'un projet de loi concernant l'accélération de certains projets d'infrastructure. Wednesday 23 September 2020. Vo. 45. No. 125.

National Assembly of Quebec. Journal des débats. Wednesday 21 October 2020. Vol. 45 No. 134.

National Assembly of Quebec. Journal des débats. Thursday 13 May 2021. Vol. 45 No. 191.

Perreault Jean Paul, Maxime Laporte, Éric Bouchard et Pierre Allard. "'Non à McGill en Outaouais!'". *Le Devoir*. 9 November 2016.

Press Conference of Prime Minister M. Pierre Marc Johnson, Thursday 3 October 1985.

Presse Conference. Sonia LeBel, ministre responsable de l'Administration gouvernementale. "Dépôt d'un projet de loi concernant l'accélération de certains projets d'infrastructure." Version finale Le mercredi 23 septembre 2020, 13 h.

Radio Canada. "Université McGill en Outaouais : Lisée estime "inconcevable" de ne pas offrir des cours en français". 3 February 2017.

Radio Canada. "Une 1ère année en anglais pour les cégépiens admis à la faculté de médecine en Outaouais". 2 November 2018.
Radio Canada. Archives. "La manifestation pour un McGill français". 27 March 2019.

Chapter 5: The French Connection

AFP, "Le Québec veut faire davantage payer les étudiants français". 31 March 2014
Charest Jean. 10 March 2009. Inaugural Speech 37th Legislature. Cited in Boudarbat Brahim and Maude Boulet 2010. Immigration au Québec : politique et intégration au marché du travail. Montréal : Cirano. (p. 15)
Gérin-Lajoie Paul. Allocution du ministre de l'éducation aux membres du corps consulaire de Montréal, lundi, le 12 avril à 12 h 30 de l'après-midi, à l'hôtel Windsor Accessed through la société du Québec aux affaires Canadiennes.
Gérin-Lajoie Paul. Allocution du ministre de l'éducation à un diner offert aux membres d'une délégation d'universitaires belges, français et suisses. Cited in Michaud Nelson and Jean-François Simard. 2018. Le défi de changer les choses : une anthologie commentée sure les disours de Paul-Gérin Lajoie. Montreal : Presses de l'université du quebec. (311–317).
Government of Canada. 1965. Cultural Agreement Between the Government of Canada and the Government of the French Republic.
Government of Quebec. Ministry of International Relations [Ministère des relations internationales] 1978. "Entente entre le gouvernement de la république francaise en matière de mobilité étudiante au niveau universitaire".
Government of Quebec. Ministry of International Relations [Ministère des relations internationales]. 1985. "Le Québec dans le monde, le défi de l'intérdépendence".
Government of Quebec. Ministry of Cultural Communities and Immigration [Ministère des communautés culturelles et de l'immigration du Québec]. 1990. "Au Québec pour batîr ensemble, enoncé politique en matière d'immigration et d'intégration".
Government of Quebec. Ministry of International Affairs [Ministère des affaires internationales]1991. "Le Québec et l'inderdependence : le monde pour l'horizon".
Government of Quebec. Ministry of Immigration Diversity and Inclusion .[Ministère de l'immigration, de la diversité et de

l'inclusion] (MIDI). 2010. "Programme d'experience Québécoise, evaluation de programme".

Government of Quebec. 2011. Ministry of Immigration and Cultural Communities [Ministère de l'immigration et des communautés culturelles]. "La Planification de l'immigration au Quebec pour la période 2012–2015".

Government of Quebec. 2015. Ministry of Immigration Diversity and Inclusion [Ministère de l'immigration, de la diversité et de l'inclusion.] (MIDI). "Politique Québéboise en matière d'immigration de participation et d'inclusion".

Government of Quebec. Finances et économie Québec. 2014. Discours sur le budget. [Budget Speech]. Prononcé à l'Assemblée nationale par M. Nicolas Marceau, ministre des finances et de l'économie. 20 February 2014.

Government of Quebec. Finances Quebec. 2014. "Le point sur la situation économique et financière du Quebec."

Government of Quebec. Ministry of Higher Education [Ministère de l'enseignement supérieur] 2017. "Pays et organisation internationale signataire d'une entente internationale en matière de mobilité étudiante à l'ordre universitaire".

Government of Quebec. Ministry of International Relations and La Francophonie [Ministère des relations internationales et de la Francophonie webpage. 2024. "Foreign Représentations".

La Presse. "Québec négociera lui-même les accords qui le concerneront". 23 April 1965 . Accessed through BANQ.

Legislative Assembly of Quebec. Journal des débats. 10 February 1965. Vo. 2 No.12.

Letter from Jacques-Yvan Morin to French Consul General Marcel Beaux. 1 June 1978. Office of the Minister of Education.

Lévesque René. Discours prononcé par le premier ministre, M. René Lévesque lors de la remise d'un diplôme honorifique à la Sorbonne, 15 décembre 1980. Accessed through Quebec Ministry of International Relations and La Francophonie.

National Assembly of Quebec. Commission permanente de l'éducation. Journal des débats. 22 April 2009. Vol. 41 No.4.

National Assembly of Quebec. Commission permanente des relations avec les citoyens. Journal des débats. 20 April 2016. Vol. 44 No. 56.

National Assembly of Quebec. Procès-verbal de l'assemblée. 4 November 2014 No. 37.

National Assembly of Quebec. Journal des débats. 5 November 2019. Vol. 45 No.77.

National Assembly of Quebec, Reading of Bill 33, 3rd reading. 13 April 1967.

Chapter 6: Marketing and Branding

Charest Jean. 10 March 2009. Inaugural Speech 37th Legislature. 2009 cited in Boudarbat et Boulet 2010.
Gervais Lisa-Marie. "Québec dénonce l'ingérence fédérale en éducation". 23 January 2014. Le Devoir.
Government of Canada. Global Affairs Canada. 2019. Canada's international education strategy.
Government of Canada. Department of Foreign Affairs Trade and Development. 2014. Canada's International Education Strategy. "Harnessing our knowledge advantage to drive innovation and prosperity".
Government of Canada. Department of Foreign Affairs and International Trade 2012. Advisory Panel on Canada's International Education Strategy. "International Education: a key driver of Canada's future prosperity".
Government of Quebec. Ministry of International Relations [Ministère des relations internationales]. 1993. "Rapport Annuel". 1992–1993. Accessed through Bibliothèque et archives nationales du Québec.
Government of Quebec. Ministry of International Affaires [Ministère des affaires internationales]. 1991. "Raport Annuel". 1990–1991. Accessed through Bibliothèque et archives nationales du Québec.
Government of Quebec. Secrétariat du Québec aux relations canadienne. 27 May 1998. "Le gouvernement fédéral ne respecte pas le consensus québécois en éducation".
Government of Quebec. Ministry of International Relations [Ministère des relations internationales]. 2001. Plan stratégique 2001–2004. "Le Québec dans un ensemble international en mutation". Accessed through Bibliothèque et archives nationales du Québec.
Government of Quebec. Ministry of International Relations [Ministère des relations internationales]. 2006. "La politique internationale du Québec: la force de l'action concentrée". Accessed through Bibliothèque et archives nationales du Québec.
Government of Quebec. Ministry of International Relations [Ministère des relations internationales] 2011. "Politique internationale du Québec. Plan d'action 2009–2014. Rapport d'étape mesures pour l'année 2009–2010."
Government of Quebec. Ministry of Higher Education [Ministère de l'enseignement supérieur]. 2015. Comité consultatif sur l'accessibilité financière aux études. "Droits de solarité

supplémentaires imposés aux étudiants français inscrits au premier cycle universitaire à partir de l'année scolaire 2015-2016".
Government of Quebec. Ministry of International Relations and La Francophonie [Ministère des relations internationales et de la francophonie] 2017. "Le Québec dans le monde : s'investir, agir, prospérer." La politique internationale du Quebec.
Government of Quebec. Ministry of Education and Higher Education. 2018a. "Étude de crédits du ministère d'éducation et d'enseignement supérieur 2019-2020 : réponses à la demande de renseignements particuliers du troisième groupe de l'opposition".
Government of Quebec. Ministry of Education and Higher Education. 2018b. "Trousse d'informations sur l'offre éducative du Québec, choisir le Québec". Accessed through Bibliothèque et Archives nationales du Québec.
Government of Quebec. Ministry of International Relations and La Francophonie. [Ministère des relations internationales et de la Francophonie]. 2022. "Rapport annuel de gestion 2021-2022",
Lisée Jean-François "Étudiants français : on peut faire mieux". Le Devoir. 6 November 2014.
Legislative Assembly of Quebec, Débats. 10 Feburary 1965. Vo. 2 No.12.
Parti Québécois. Press Release. "Le gouvernement du Québec s'oppose à la stratégie d'éducation internationale du gouvernement Harper et demande une pleine compensation financière". 22 January 2014.
Presse conference. Hélène David, Minister of Education and Higher Education. "Importante annonce pour l'ensemble des universités du Québec" Transcription of National Assembly of Quebec. Thusday17 May 2018.
Rainville Patricia. "Les étudiants africains francophones encore rejétés à la tonne". Le Quotidien. 18 August 2022.

Chapter 7 Promoting the Quebec Nation

Association internationale des études Québécoises (AIEQ). 2016. "Plan Stratégique 2017-2019".
Benoit Pelletier. 2006, 16 November. "Allocution du ministre Benoît Pelletier à l'occasion de l'annonce de la création du Centre de la francophonie des Amériques". Accessed through Secretariat du Québec aux relations canadiennes.
Centre de la francophonie des Amériques. 2023. "Rapport d'activités 2022-2023".

Centre de la francophonie des Amériques. 2009. "Rapport d'activités 2008–2009".
Centre de la francophonie des Amériques. 2019. Rapport d'activités 2018–2019.
Gaulin André. "Le rayonnement de l'AIEQ". Lettre. *Le Devoir*. 31 December 2014.
Gervais Lisa-Marie. "Coup dur pour l'image du Québec à l'étranger". *Le Devoir*. 24 December 2014.
Globe and Mail. "Understanding Canada no more." 19 June 2012.
Government of Quebec. Ministry of State for Cultural Development [Le ministére d'état au développement culturel]. 1978. "La politique québécoise du dévelopment culturel : perspectives d'ensemble : de quelle culture s'agit-il ?". Vol. I
Government of Quebec. Ministry of Intergovernmental Affairs [Ministère des affaires intergouvernementales]. 1985. "Rapport annuel 1983–1984".
Government of Quebec. Ministry of International Relations [Ministère des relations internationales]. 1986. "Rapport annuel 1984–1985".
Government of Quebec. Ministry of International Affaires [Ministère des affaires internationales.] 1992. "Rapport annuel 1990–1991".
Government of Quebec. Ministry of International Affairs. [Ministère des affaires internationales] 1991. "Le Québec et l'interdépendance. Le monde pour horizon, éléments d'une politique d'affaires internationales".
Government of Quebec. Ministry of International Relations [Ministère des relations internationales]. 2003. "Rapport annuel de gestion."
Government of Quebec. Secrétariat du Québéc aux relations canadiennes. 2006. Le centre de la francophonie des Amériques.
Government of Quebec. Ministry of International Relations [Ministère des relations internationales]. 2007. "La Politique Internationale du Québec. Plan d'Action 2006–2009. Rapport d'étape 2006–2007."
Government of Quebec. Ministry of International Relations [Ministère des relations internationales]. 2010. "Stratégie du gouvernement du Québec à l'égard des États Unis".
Government of Quebec. Ministry of Higher Education, Research, Science and Technology [Ministère de l'enseignement supérieur, de la recherche, de la science et de la technologie] 2013. "Priorité Emploi'. Politique nationale de la recherche et de l'innovation 2014–2019". Accessed through BANQ.
Government of Quebec, Ministry of Education [Ministère de l'éducation] 2024. "Exception des droits de scolarité supplémentaires selon le programme d'études et la région".
Graham John W. "Canadian Studies Abroad : Perils and Prospects". ACSUS Conference Montreal. November 13–16 2019.

Lévesque René. 25 January 1977. Speech delivered at the Economic Club of New York. "Québec : Good neighbour in transition". Retrieved from the Quebec Ministry of International Relations and la Francophonie webpage.

National Assembly of Quebec.Comission permanente des affaires intergouvernementales. Journal des débates. Friday 25 May 1979. Vo.21 No.97.

National Assembly of Quebec. Commission permanente des institutions. Journal des débates. "Crédits du ministère des relations internationales". Tuesday 18 April 1997. No. 72.

National Assembly of Quebec. Commission permanente des institutions.. Journal des débates. "Études des crédits du ministère des relations internationales". Thursday 7 May 1998. No. 125.

National Assembly of Quebec. Journal des débates. Wednesday 4 June 2003. Vol.38 No.1.

National Assembly of Quebec. Journal des débates. Thursday 23 November 2006. Vol. 39 No. 62.

National Assembly of Quebec. Journdal des débats de la commission des institutions. Monday 16 April 2012. Vol.42 No. 77.

National Assembly of Quebec. Commission permanent des institutions. Journal des débats "Études des crédits du ministère des relations internationales et de la Francophonie". Thursday 26 April 2018. Vo. 44 No. 251.

Parti Québécois. "Coupes à l'AIEQ- Le saccage du rayonnement du Québec à l'étranger continue". 14 January 2015. Newswire.

National Assembly of Quebec. Commission permanente des institutions. Journal des débats. Tuesday 28 November 2006. Vo. 39 No.31.

Symons. T.H.B. 1975. "To Know Ourselves. The Report of the Commission on Canadian Studies". Vol I and II.

Notes

Introduction

1 The distinction between internationalization and globalization in higher education is important to clarify here. Teichler (2004) offers a useful differentiation by which internationalization is defined as heightened cross-border activities between national systems of higher education, while globalization implies activities occurring alongside a blurring between national systems.
2 For a comprehensive list of primary sources used, see Annex I.
3 I am grateful to McGill University Archives and McMaster University Archives for access to their digital files.
4 For an application of the domestic/foreign policy framework on Wallonia's economic policy see Moscovitz (2021).
5 This is not to say that the link between Quebec's higher education policy and Quebecois nationalism is not discussed in the literature. Scholarship on both Quebec's higher education policy and Quebecois nationalism reference their intertwining (see, e.g., Beaulieu and Bertrand 1999; Bernatchez 2007; Balthazar 1986; Corbo 2002; Fournier 1987). What I hope to accomplish in this book is to offer a holistic view of this connection and one that extends beyond a particular moment in time to provide a historically ingrained understanding.

1. When (Minority) Nationalism Meets Higher Education: Concepts and Issues

1 A distinct sense of nationhood among French Canadians dates back centuries. A notable organized expression of French Canadian nationalism is the 1837–38 Rebellion of the Patriots. The idea that a minority group of francophones in North America form a distinct nation is a long-standing one (Balthazar 1986). This book is concerned with Quebec's modern political and territorial nationalism prompted in the 1960s.

2. *Maîtres Chez Nous*: The Quiet Revolution, Higher Education, and the Consolidation of Quebec Nationalism

1 The discussion on policy ownership and policy distinctiveness builds upon the analysis presented in Moscovitz, Hannah. 2020. "Between nationalism and regionalism: Higher education policy and national/regional identity in Quebec and Wallonia." *Nations and Nationalism* 26(3): 708–726.
2 University of Quebec Network, "General Presentation," accessed 18 July 2017, http://www.uquebec.ca/reseau/fr/reseau-de-luq/presentation-generale.

3. The University as Public Good: towards the 2012 Maple Spring Protests

1 The council was established in 1968 to advise on university issues and was abolished by the government in 1992.
2 It should be noted that opposition to the federal intrusion by the Ontario government has also been cited (Wellen et al. 2012).

4. McGill University and Quebec's Nationalist Politics

1 For a compelling account of the racial politics surrounding McGill University, see Hampton (2020).
2 A number of amendments were made to the university governance system including the possibility of turning in papers and conducting exams in either French or English.
3 The plan was a remnant of the PQ government – Marois had begun discussions in 2014.

5. Higher Education as a Catalyst to Quebec's 'Identity Paradiplomacy': The French Connection

1 In 1984, the Ministry for Intergovernmental Affairs was renamed the Ministry of International Relations and its focus turned to Quebec's external affairs exclusively.
2 A 2023 update to the PEQ provides a "fast track" route to citizenship for international students having graduated from a French-language degree program.

7. Promoting the Quebec Nation through Education Diplomacy

1 Part of this chapter was published in Moscovitz, Hannah, and Roopa Desai Trilokekar. 2024. "Does Soft Power Look Different in Multinational Federations? International Education and Soft Power Politics in Canada/Quebec." *Canadian Journal of Political Science/Revue canadienne de science politique*: 1–24.

Conclusion

1 François Carabin, "Valérie Plante n'est pas une alliée pour le français, dit la CAQ," *Le Devoir*, 8 February 2024.

References

Agnew, John. 1994. "The territorial trap: The geographical assumptions of international relations theory." *Review of International Political Economy* 1(1): 53–80.

Alexandre Couture Gagnon & Carol A. Chapelle 2019. " Opération Amérique: Québec's Soft Power Applied to French Language Teaching in the United States", *American Review of Canadian Studies*, 49 (3): 413-427.

Ancelovici, Marcos, and Francis Dupuis-Déri. 2014. *Un printemps rouge et noir. Regards croisés sur la grève étudiante de 2012*. Montreal: Écosociété Éditions.

Annick, Germain, and Damaris Rose. 2000. *Montreal. The Quest for a Metropolis*. Chichester: John Wiley and Sons, Ltd.

Arnott, Margaret, and Jenny Ozga. 2010. "Education and nationalism: The discourse of education policy in Scotland." *Discourse: Studies in the Cultural Politics of Education* 31(3): 335–350.

– 2016. "Education and nationalism in Scotland: Governing a 'learning nation'." *Oxford Review of Education* 42(3): 253–265.

Aronczyk, Melissa. 2013. *Branding the Nation: The Global Business of National Identity*. Oxford: Oxford University Press.

Badie, Bertrand. 1995. *La fin des territoires: essai sur le désordre international et sur l'utilité sociale du respect*. Paris: Fayard.

Balbachevsky, Elizabeth, and José Augusto Guilhon Albuquerque. 2021. "Bolsanaro's Brazilian neonationalism and universities." In John A. Douglass (ed). *Neonationalism and Universities: Populists, Autocrats and the Future of Higher Education*. Baltimore: John Hopkins University Press: 239–257.

Balthazar, Louis. 1986. *Bilan du nationalisme au Québec*. Montreal: L'hexagone.

– 2003. "Les relations internationales du Québec." *Québec: État et société* 2: 505–535.

Balthazar, Louis, and Alfred Olivier Hero. 1999. *Le Québec dans l'espace américain*. Vol. 4. Montreal: Québec Amérique.

References

Barbarič, Diane. 2020. "International education as public policy in Quebec." In Tamtik Merli, Jones Glen, and Roopa Trilokekar (eds). *International Education as Public Policy in Canada*. Montreal: McGill-Queens University Press: 288.

Barker, Fiona. 2010 "Learning to be a majority: Negotiating immigration, integration and national membership in Quebec." *Political Science* 62(1): 11–36.

Beaulieu, Paul, and Denis Bertrand. 1999. *L'État québécois et les universités: acteurs et enjeux*. Montréal: Presses de l'Université de Montréal.

Beerkens, Eric. 2003. "Globalisation and higher education research." *Journal of Studies in International Education* 7(2): 128–148.

Bégin-Caouette, Olivier, and Glen A. Jones. 2014. "Student organizations in Canada and Quebec's 'Maple Spring'." *Studies in Higher Education* 39(3): 412–425.

Béland, Daniel, and André Lecours. 2005. "Nationalism and social policy in Canada and Québec." In McEwen Nicola and Moreno Luis (eds). *The Territorial Politics of Welfare*. London: Routledge.

– 2006. "Sub-state nationalism and the welfare state: Québec and Canadian federalism." *Nations and Nationalism* 12(1): 77–96.

– 2008. *Nationalism and Social Policy: The Politics of Territorial Solidarity*. Oxford: Oxford University Press.

Bélanger, Louis. 2002. "The domestic politics of Quebec's quest for external distinctiveness." *American Review of Canadian Studies* 32(2): 195–214.

Bernatchez, Jean. 2007. « Priorités des politiques publiques de l'enseignement supérieur au Québec et problématique de l'accueil des étudiants internationaux ». In S. Mazzella (ed.), L'enseignement supérieur dans la mondialisation libérale (1–). Institut de recherche sur le Maghreb contemporain. https://doi.org/10.4000/books.irmc.731

Bérubé, Gérard. 2008. "Perspectives- le Québec en récession." *Le Devoir*, 11 December. Perspectives- Le Québec en récession | Le Devoir.

Billig, Michael. 1995. *Banal Nationalism*. London: Sage Publishing.

Biswas, Shampa. 2002. "W (h) ither the nation-state? National and state identity in the face of fragmentation and globalisation." *Global Society* 16(2): 175–198.

Blanchet, Alexandre, and Mike Medeiros. 2019. "The secessionist spectre: The influence of authoritarianism, nativism and populism on support for Quebec independence." *Nations and Nationalism* 25(3): 803–821.

Bloom, William. 1990. *Personal Identity, National Identity and International Relations*. Cambridge: Cambridge University Press.

Bouchard, Gérard. 2000. *Genèse des nations et cultures du Nouveau Monde*. Montreal: Les Éditions du Boréal.

Brenner, Neil. 1999. "Beyond state-centrism? Space, territoriality, and geographical scale in globalization studies." *Theory and Society* 28(1): 39–78.

Breton, Raymond. 1988. "From ethnic to civic nationalism: English Canada and Quebec." *Ethnic and Racial Studies* 11(1): 85–102.

Brøgger, Katja. 2022. "Post-Cold war governance arrangements in Europe: The University between European integration and rising nationalisms." *Globalisation, Societies and Education*: 1–15.

Brooks, Stephen (ed). 2019. *Promoting Canadian Studies Abroad: Soft Power and Cultural Diplomacy*. Cham, Switzerland: Springer.

Burgess, Michael. 2012. "Multinational federalism in multinational federation." In A. G. Gagnon and M. Seymour (eds). *Multinational Federalism Problems and Prospects*. New York: Palgrave Macmillan.

Calhoun, Craig. 2006. "The university and the public good." *Thesis Eleven* 84(1): 7–43.

Cameron, David M. 1997. "The federal perspective." In G. Jones (ed). *Higher Education in Canada. Different Systems. Different Perspectives*. New York: Routledge: 9–29.

Campbell, David. 1992. *Writing Security: United States Foreign Policy and the Politics of Identity*. Minneapolis: University of Minnesota Press.

Cantwell, Brendan, Hamish Coates, and Roger King (eds). 2018. *Handbook on the Politics of Higher Education*. London: Edward Elgar Publishing.

Caron, Jean Francois. 2014. "Québécois and Walloon identities: The shift from an ethnic to a civic identity." In M. Reauchamps (ed). *Minority Nations in Multinational Federations*. Oxon: Routledge: 44–60.

Carpentier, Vincent, and Aline Courtois. 2022. "Public good in French universities: Principles and practice of the 'republican' model." *Compare: A Journal of Comparative and International Education* 52(1): 1–18.

Cerny, Philip G. 1997. "Paradoxes of the competition state: The dynamics of political globalization." *Government and Opposition* 32(2): 251–274.

Charteris-Black, Jonathan. 2011. *Politicians and Rhetoric: The Persuasive Power of Metaphor*. New York: Springer.

Cheong, Pauline Hope, Rosalind Edwards, Harry Goulbourne, and John Solomos. 2007. "Immigration, social cohesion and social capital: A critical review." *Critical Social Policy* 27(1): 24–49.

Clift, Dominique, and Sheila McLeod Arnopoulos. 1984. *The English Fact in Quebec*. Montreal: McGill-Queen's University Press.

Corbo, Claude. 2002. *L'éducation pour tous: Une anthologie du Rapport Parent*. Montreal: Presses de l'Université de Montréal.

Coughlan, Sean. 2017. "Montreal ranked top city for students." *BBC News*, 15 February. https://www.bbc.co.uk/news/business-38959018

Couture Gagnon, Alexandre, and Carol A. Chapelle. 2019. "Opération Amérique: Québec's Soft Power Applied to French Language Teaching in the United States." *American Review of Canadian Studies* 49 (3): 413–427.

Cox, Lloyd. 2021. Nationalism: Themes, Theories, and Controversies. Springer Nature.

References

Crane, George T. 1998. "Economic nationalism: Bringing the nation back in." *Millennium* 27 (1): 55-75.

Criekemans, David. 2010. "Regional sub-state diplomacy from a comparative perspective: Quebec, Scotland, Bavaria, Catalonia, Wallonia and Flanders." *The Hague Journal of Diplomacy* 5(1–2): 37–64.

Cull, Nicholas John. 2008. "Public diplomacy: Taxonomies and histories." *The Annals of the American Academy of Political and Social Science* 616(1): 31–54.

Cull, Nicholas John. 2009. *Public diplomacy: Lessons from the past*. Vol. 22. Los Angeles, CA: Figueroa Press.

Dassylva Martial. 2006. "La naissance des cégeps: un exercise rationnel, coherent et urgent." In Lucie Heon, Denis Savard, and Thérèse Hamel (eds). *Les Cégeps: une grande aventure collective Quebecoise*. Quebec City: Presses Université Laval.

Davies, Scott, and Aurini Janice. 2021. "The evolving prism: The role of nationalism in Canadian higher education." *European Journal of Higher Education* 11(3): 239–254.

De Lima, Antônio F. 2007. "The role of international educational exchanges in public diplomacy." *Place Branding and Public Diplomacy* 3(3): 234–251.

Dinnie, Keith. 2015. *Nation Branding: Concepts, Issues, Practice*. Oxon: Routledge.

Donald, Janet. 1997. "Higher education in Quebec." In G. Jones (ed). *Higher Education in Canada: Different Systems, Different Perspectives*. New York: Routledge: 161–186.

Doray, Pierre. 2016. "Politiques universitaires et égalité des chances: les détours de l'histoire." *Education et sociétés* 2: 87–103.

Douglass, John A. 2021. *Neo-Nationalism and Universities: Populists, Autocrats, and the Future of Higher Education*. Baltimore: John Hopkins University Press.

Dupont, Louis. 1995. "L'americanité in Quebec in the 1980s: Political and cultural considerations of an emerging discourse." *American Review of Canadian Studies* 25(1): 27–52.

Dupuy, Claire, and Virginie Van Ingelgom. 2014. "Social policy, legitimation and diverging regional paths in Belgium." in S. Kumlin and I. Stadelmann-Stefan (eds). *How Welfare States Shape the Democratic Public: Policy Feedback, Participation, Voting, and Attitudes*. Cheltenham: Edward Elgar: 198–222.

Enders, Jürgen 2004. "Higher education, internationalisation, and the nation-state: Recent developments and challenges to governance theory". *Higher Education*, 47(3): 361–382.

Enders, Jürgen, and Ben Jongbloed. 2007. "The public, the private and the good in higher education and research: An introduction." In *Public-Private Dynamics in Higher Education: Expectations, Developments and Outcomes*: Bielefeld: Verlag, 9–36.

Erk, Jan. 2003. "'Wat we zelf doen, doen we beter'; Belgian substate nationalisms, congruence and public policy." *Journal of Public Policy* 23(2): 201–224.
- 2010. "Is nationalism left or right? Critical junctures in Québécois nationalism." *Nations and Nationalism* 16(3): 423–441.
Fairclough, Norman. 2001. *Language and Power*. New York: Longman Group.
- 2013. "Critical discourse analysis and critical policy studies." *Critical Policy Studies* 7(2): 177–197.
Fetzer, Thomas. 2022. "Beyond 'economic nationalism': towards a new research agenda for the study of nationalism in political economy". *Journal of International Relations and Development*, 25(1): 235-259.
Ferretti, Lucia. 1994. *L'Université en Réseau-Souple: Les 25 Ans de l'Université du Québec*. Montreal: Presses de l'université du Québec.
Fisher, Donald, Kjell Rubenson, J. Bernatchez, R. Clift, G. Jones, J. Lee, and C. Trottier. 2006. *Canadian Federal Policy and Postsecondary Education*. Vancouver: Centre for Policy Studies in Higher Education and Training, Faculty of Education, University of British Columbia.
Fitzgerald, Gerald F. 1966. "Educational and cultural agreements and ententes: France, Canada, and Quebec-birth of a new treaty-making technique for federal states?" *American Journal of International Law* 60(3): 529–537.
Foisy-Geoffroy, Dominique. 2007. "Le Rapport de la Commission Tremblay (1953–1956), testament politique de la pensée traditionaliste canadienne-française." *Revue d'histoire de l'Amérique française* 60(3): 257–294.
Fournier, M. 1987. "Culture et politique du Québec." *The Canadian Journal of Sociology / Cahiers Canadiens de Sociologie* 12(1/2): 64–82.
Freed, Josh. 2012. "Participation in strike shows linguistic divided." *Montreal Gazette*, 19 May.
Frank, David John, and John W. Meyer. 2020. *The University and the Global Knowledge Society*. Princeton University Press.
Frost, S. B. 1984. *McGill University: For the Advancement of Learning, Volume II, 1895–1971*. Montreal: McGill-Queen's Press-MQUP.
Gagné, Gilbert. 2004. "L'identité québécoise et l'intégration continentale." *Politique et sociétés* 23(2–3): 45–68.
Gagnon, Alain G. (ed). 2009. *Contemporary Canadian Federalism: Foundations, Traditions, Institutions*. Toronto: University of Toronto Press.
- 2001. "The moral foundations of asymmetrical federalism: a normative exploration of the case of Quebec and Canada". in Gagnon A-G. and Tully J. (Eds.) *Multinational democracies*. Cambridge: Cambridge University Press: 319–337.

- 2010. *The Case for Multinational Federalism: Beyond the All Encompassing Nation*. London: Routledge.
- 2013. "The five faces of Quebec." *L'Europe en Formation* 3: 39–52.
- 2014. *Minority Nations in the Age of Uncertainty: New Paths to National Emancipation and Empowerment*. Toronto: University of Toronto Press.
- 2018. "Political Dynamics in Quebec Charting concepts and Imagining Political Avenues" in Albert, R., & Cameron, D. R. (Eds.). *Canada in the world: comparative perspectives on the Canadian Constitution*. Cambridge University Press. Cambridge: 59-81.
- 2021. "Multinational federalism: Challenges, shortcomings and promises." *Regional & Federal Studies* 31(1): 99–114.

Gagnon, Alain G., and Raffaele Iacovino. 2006. *Federalism, Citizenship and Quebec*. Toronto: University of Toronto Press.

Gagnon, Alain G., and James Tully (eds). 2001. *Multinational Democracies*. Cambridge: Cambridge University Press.

Garland, Eric. 2012. "How Quebec's 'Maple Spring' Protests fit with the Arab Spring and Occupy Wall Street (Sort of)." *The Atlantic*, 12 June.

Gilboa, Eytan. 2008. "Searching for a theory of public diplomacy." *The Annals of the American Academy of Political and Social Science* 616(1): 55–77.

Gingras, Paul-Émile. 1992. "Les cégeps, d'hier à demain." *Vers la réforme scolaire* 6(1).

Giroux, Henry A. 2010. "Bare pedagogy and the scourge of neoliberalism: Rethinking higher education as a democratic public sphere." *The Educational Forum* 74(3): 184–196.

- 2013. "The Quebec student protest movement in the age of neoliberal terror." *Social Identities* 19(5): 515–535.

Gould, Karen L. 2003. "Nationalism, feminism, cultural pluralism: American interest in Quebec literature and culture." *Yale French Studies* 103: 24–32.

Graefe, Peter. 2005. "The contradictory political economy of minority nationalism." *Theory and Society* 34(5): 519–549.

Graefe, Peter, and X. H. Rioux. 2020. "What should be done with a 'house in order'? An economic perspective on post-liberal Quebec." *American Review of Canadian Studies* 50(3)" 293–308.

Guibernau, Montserrat. 1999. *Nations Without States: Political Communities in a Global Age*. Cambridge: Polity Press.

Gupta, Suman. 2019. "Indian student protests and the nationalist–neoliberal nexus." *Postcolonial Studies* 22(1): 1–15.

Habermas, Jürgen. 1975. *Legitimation Crisis*. Cambridge: Polity Press.

- 1984. *Communication and the evolution of society*. Oxford: Blackwell Publishers.

– 1991. *Communication and the Evolution of Society*. Cambridge: Polity Press.

Hampton, Rosalind. 2020. *Black Racialization and Resistance at an Elite University*. Toronto: University of Toronto Press.

Harvey, Andrew. 2010. "Nationalism and higher education: Emerging trends." *International Journal of Learning* 16(12): 355–364.

Harvey, Fernand 2001. "Le développement des études québécoises dans le monde." *Globe* 4 (2): 59-81.

Helleiner, Eric.2021. "The diversity of economic nationalism." *New political economy* 26, (2): 229-238.

Henderson, Alisa, and Nicola McEwen. 2005. "Do shared values underpin national identity? Examining the role of values in national identity in Canada and the United Kingdom." *National Identities* 7(2): 173–191.

Hillman, Nick. 2021. "International students are worth £ 28.8 billion to the UK." *Higher Education Policy Institute (HEPI)*, 9 September.

Hintz, Lisel. 2018. *Identity Politics Inside Out: National Identity Contestation and Foreign Policy in Turkey*. Oxford: Oxford University Press.

Hoerder, Dirk. 2010. *To Know Our Many Selves: From the Study of Canada to Canadian Studies*. Edmonton: Athabasca University Press.

Hsieh, Chuo-Chun. 2020. "Internationalization of higher education in the crucible: Linking national identity and policy in the age of globalization." *International Journal of Educational Development* 78: 102245.

Hurteau, Philippe, and Francis Fortier.2015. "État québécois, crise et néolibéralisme." *Revue Interventions économiques. Papers in Political Economy* 52: 1–18.

Jansen, Sue Curry. 2008. "Designer nations: Neo-liberal nation branding– Brand Estonia." *Social Identities* 14(1): 121–142.

John, Jojin V. 2015. "Globalization, national identity and foreign policy: Understanding 'Global Korea'." *The Copenhagen Journal of Asian Studies* 33(2): 38–57.

Jungblut, Jens. 2015. "Bringing political parties into the picture: A two-dimensional analytical framework for higher education policy." *Higher Education* 69(5): 867–882.

Keating, Michael.1997. "The invention of regions: political restructuring and territorial government in Western Europe." *Environment and Planning C: Government and Policy*. 15 (4): 383–398.

Keating, Michael. 1998. *The New Regionalism in Western Europe: Territorial Restructuring and Political Change*. Cambridge: Cambridge University Press.

– 2001. "So many nations, so few states: Accommodating minority nationalism in the global era." In Alain G. Gagnon and James Tully (eds). *Multinational Democracies*. Cambridge and New York: Cambridge University Press: 30–64.

– 2002. "Plurinational democracy in a post-sovereign order." *Northern Ireland Legal Quarterly* 53: 351.

- 2013. *Rescaling the European State: The Making of Territory and the Rise of the Meso*. Oxford: Oxford University Press.
Kerr, Clark. 1991. "International learning and national purposes in higher education." *American Behavioral Scientist* 35(1): 17–42.
Kirkey, Christopher, Stéphane Paquin, and Stéphane Roussel. 2016. "Charting Quebec's engagement with the international community." *American Review of Canadian Studies* 46(2): 135–148.
Koch, Natalie. 2014. "The shifting geopolitics of higher education: Inter/nationalizing elite universities in Kazakhstan, Saudi Arabia, and beyond." *Geoforum* 56: 46–54.
Kofman, Eleonore. 2005. "Citizenship, migration and the reassertion of national identity." *Citizenship Studies* 9(5): 453–467.
Kostov, Chris. 2008. "Canada-Quebec immigration agreements (1971–1991) and their impact on federalism." *American Review of Canadian Studies* 38 (1): 91–103.
Kwiek, Marek. 2005. "The University and the state in a global age: Renegotiating the traditional social contract?" *European Educational Research Journal* 4(4): 324–341.
Kwiek, Marek. 2013. "The university and the welfare state in transition: Changing public services in a wider context". in Epstein et al. (eds) Geographies of knowledge, geometries of power framing the future of higher education. pp. 32–49. World Yearbook of Education. London: Routelege.
Kymlicka, Will. 2000. "Federalism and secession: At home and abroad." *Canadian Journal of Law & Jurisprudence* 13(2): 207–224.
Lachapelle, Guy. 2011. *Le destin américain du Québec: américanité, américanisation et antiaméricanisme*. Quebec City: Les presses de l'université.
Lachapelle, Guy, and G. Gagné. 2000. "L'américanité du Québec ou le développement d'une identité nord-américaine." *Francophonies d'Amérique* 10: 87–99.
Laforest, Guy. 2005. *The Historical and Legal Origins of Asymmetrical Federalism in Canada's Founding Debates: A Brief Interpretive Note*. Kingston: Institute of Intergovernmental Relations, School of Policy Studies, Queen's University.
Laliberté, Robert, and Denis Moniére. 2004. *Le Québec au mirroir de l'Europe*. Quebec: AIEQ.
Lamonde, Yvan. 1999. "Pourquoi penser l'américanité du Québec?" *Politique et sociétés* 18(1): 93–98.
Laniel, Jean-François, and Joseph Thériault. 2018. "Comment se débarrasser de la Grande Noirceur sans se débarrasser du passé québécois?" *Mens: revue d'histoire intellectuelle et culturelle* 18(2): 67–107.
Lecours, André. 2001. "Political institutions, elites, and territorial identity formation in Belgium." *National Identities* 3(1): 51–68.
- 2002. "Paradiplomacy: reflections on the foreign policy and international relations of regions". *International Negotiation* 7 (1): 91–114.

– 2008. *Political Issues of Paradiplomacy: Lessons from the Developed World*. Netherlands Institute of International Relations' Clingendael' Discussion Papers on Diplomacy.

Lecours, André, and Luis Moreno.2003. "Paradiplomacy: A nation-building strategy? A reference to the Basque Country." In Alain-G. Gagnon, Montserrat Guibernau and François Rocher (Eds). *The conditions of diversity in multinational democracies*. Montreal: McGill-Queens University Press: 267-294.

Lee, Jenny J. 2017. "Neo-nationalism in higher education: Case of South Africa." *Studies in Higher Education* 42(5): 869–886.

Levine, Marc. 1991. *The Reconquest of Montreal: Language Policy and Social Change in a Bilingual City*. Vol. 43.Philadelphia: Temple University Press.

Lo, W. Y. W., and S.-J. Chan. 2020. "Globalism, regionalism and nationalism: The dynamics of student mobility in higher education across the Taiwan Strait." *Discourse: Studies in the Cultural Politics of Education* 41(4): 587–603.

Lomer, Sylvie, Vassiliki Papatsiba, and Rajani Naidoo. 2018. "Constructing a national higher education brand for the UK: Positional competition and promised capitals." *Studies in Higher Education* 43(1): 134–153.

Lukacs, Martin. 2012. "Quebec student protests mark 'Maple Spring' in Canada." *The Guardian*, 2 May. https://www.theguardian.com/commentisfree/cifamerica/2012/may/02/quebec-student-protest-canada.

MacLennan, Hugh. 2018 (first edition 1945). *Two Solitudes*. Montreal: McGill-Queen's Press-MQUP.

Malone, Gifford D. 1985. "Managing public diplomacy." *Washington Quarterly* 8(3): 199–213.

Marginson, Simon. 2006. "Dynamics of national and global competition in higher education." *Higher Education* 52(1): 1–39.

– 2014. "Higher education and public good." In *Higher Education in Societies*. Rotterdam: Sense Publishers: 51–71.

– 2018. "Public/private in higher education: A synthesis of economic and political approaches." *Studies in Higher Education* 43(2): 322–337.

– 2022. "What is global higher education?" *Oxford Review of Education*: 1–26.

Maroy, Christian, Pierre Doray, and Mamouna Kabore. 2014. *La politique de financement des universités au Québec à l'épreuve du «Printemps érable»*. Montréal: Centre interuniversitaire de recherche sur la science et la technologie. http://crcpe.umontreal.ca/documents/Note2014-02.pdf.

May, Stephen. 2012. *Language and Minority Rights: Ethnicity, Nationalism and the Politics of Language*. New York: Routledge.

McEwen, Nicola. 2005. "The territorial politics of social policy development in multi-level states." *Regional & Federal Studies* 15(4): 537–554.

– 2006. *Nationalism and the State: Welfare and Identity in Scotland and Quebec*. Brussels: Peter Lang.

McEwen, Nicola, and Luis Moreno. 2008. *The Territorial Politics of Welfare*. Oxon: Routledge.

McLeod Arnopoulos, Sheila M., and Dominique Clift. 1983. *The English Fact in Quebec*. Montreal: McGill-Queen's Press-MQUP.

Melissen, Jan. 2005. *The New Public Diplomacy: Soft Power in International Relations*. New York: Palgrave Macmillan.

Meren, David. 2012. *With Friends Like These: Entangled Nationalisms and the Canada-Québec-France Triangle, 1944–1970*. Vancouver: University of British Columbia Press.

Mesli, Samy. 2009. "Le développement de la 'diplomatie éducative' du Québec." *Globe: revue internationale d'études québécoises* 12(1): 115–131.

Metzgar, Emily T. 2016. "Institutions of higher education as public diplomacy tools: China-based university programs for the 21st century." *Journal of Studies in International Education* 20(3): 223–241.

Michaud, Nelson, and Jean-François Simard. 2018. *Le défi de changer les choses : une anthologie commentée sure les disours de Paul-Gérin Lajoie*. Montreal: Presses de l'université du quebec.

Michaud, Nelson, and Jean-François Simard. 2019. *Le défi de changer les choses: anthologie commentée des discours de Paul Gérin-Lajoie*. Publications Université du Québec.,

Miller, David. 1995. *On Nationality*. Oxford: Clarendon Press.

Mills, Sean. 2010. *The Empire Within: Postcolonial Thought and Political Activism in Sixties Montreal*. Montreal: McGill-Queen's Press-MQUP.

Moscovitz, Hannah. 2020. "Between nationalism and regionalism: Higher education policy and national/regional identity in Quebec and Wallonia." *Nations and Nationalism* 26(3): 708–726.

– 2021. "Regional identity and economic development in 'recovering' regions: Exploring the Walloon case". *Regional & Federal Studies*, 31(5):597-624.

– 2022. "Projecting the nation (s) in multinational federal systems: International education and nation branding in Canada/Quebec." *Publius: The Journal of Federalism* 52(1): 82–106.

Nakano, Takeshi. 2004. "Theorising economic nationalism." *Nations and Nationalism* 10(3): 211-229.

Norman, Wayne. 2006. *Negotiating Nationalism: Nation-Building, Federalism, and Secession in the Multinational State*. Oxford: Oxford University Press.

Nye, Joseph S. 2004. *Soft Power: The Means to Success in World Politics*. New York: Public Affairs.

– 2008. "Public diplomacy and soft power." *The Annals of the American Academy of Political and Social Science* 616(1): 94–109.

Oakes, Leigh, and Jane. Warren. 2007. *Language, Citizenship and Identity in Quebec*. London: Palgrave Macmillan.

Ohmae, Kenichi. 1995. *The End of the Nation State: The Rise of Regional Economies*. London: Harper Collins.

O'Malley, Brendan. 2021. "The mystery of Brexit: Tumult and fatigue in UK higher education." In John A. Douglass (ed). *Neonationalism and Universities: Populists, Autocrats and the Future of Higher Education*. Baltimore: John Hopkins University Press: 43–60.

Paquin, Stéphane. 2004. "La paradiplomatie identitaire: le Québec, la Catalogne et la Flandre en relations internationales." *Politique et sociétés* 23(2–3): 203–237.

– 2005. "Les actions extérieures des entités subétatiques: quelle signification pour la politique comparée et les relations internationales?" *Revue internationale de politique comparée* 12(2): 129–142.

– 2006. "La relation Québec-Paris-Ottawa et la création de l'organisation internationale de la Francophonie (1960–2005)." *Guerres mondiales et conflits contemporains* 3: 31–47.

– 2016. "Quebec–US Relations: The Big Picture." *American Review of Canadian Studies* 46 (2): 149–161.

– 2018. "Identity paradiplomacy in Québec." *Quebec Studies* 66(1): 3–27.

– 2024. "Quebec's Relations with the US under Jean Charest: Building a Special Relationship". In Abelson D.E. and Brookes S. (eds). *History has made us friends, reassessing the special relationship between Canada and the United States*. Montreal: McGill-Queens University Press: 212–230.

Paquin, Stéphane, and Annie Chaloux. 2010 "Le Québec sur la scène internationale. Les raisons de son dynamisme." *Globe: revue internationale d'études québécoises* 13(1): 25–45.

Paquin, Stéphane, and Guy Lachapelle. 2005. "Why do sub-states and regions practice international relations?" In Stephane Paquin and Guy Lachapelle (eds). *Mastering Globalization: New Sub-States' Governance and Strategies*. Oxon: Routledge: 77–89.

Pickel, Andreas 2003. "Explaining, and explaining with, economic nationalism." *Nations and nationalism*, 9(1) 105–127.

Potter, Evan. 2003. "Canada and the new public diplomacy." *International Journal* 58(1): 43–64.

Potter Evan. 2009. *Branding Canada: projecting Canada's soft power through public diplomacy*. Montreal: McGill-Queens University Press.

Pusser, Brian. 2006. "Reconsidering higher education and the public good." In William G. Tierney (ed). *Governance and the Public Good*. New York: State University of New York Press: 11–28.

– 2018. "The state and the civil society in the scholarship of higher education." In Brendan Cantwell et al. (eds). *Handbook on the Politics of Higher Education*. Cheltenham: Edward Elgar Publishing.

Pusser, Brian, and Simon Marginson. 2013. "University rankings in critical perspective." *The Journal of Higher Education* 84(4): 544–568.

References

Radio Canada. 2018. "Archives 1968: Une rentrée au cégep sous le signe de la contestation." 23 August. https://ici.radio-canada.ca/nouvelle/1119221/Cégep-greve-mouvement-etudiant-enseignement-college-universite-quebec.

Ratel, Jean Luc, and Philippe Verreault-Julien. 2006. *Le financement des universités québécoises: histoire, enjeux et défis*. Québec: CADEUL.

Reisigl, Martin, and Ruth Wodak. 2009. "The discourse-historical approach (DHA)." In R. Wodak and M. Meyer (eds). *Methods of Critical Discourse Analysis*. 2nd ed. London: Sage Publications: 87–121.

Rioux, X. Hubert. 2020. *Small Nations, High Ambitions: Economic Nationalism and Venture Capital in Quebec and Scotland*. Toronto: University of Toronto Press.

Rioux Ouimet, Hubert. 2015. "From sub-state nationalism to subnational competition states: The development and institutionalization of commercial paradiplomacy in Scotland and Quebec." *Regional & Federal Studies* 25(2): 109–128.

Rocher, Guy. 2006. "L'engendrement du Cégep par la commission Parent." In Lucie Heon, Denis Savard, and Thérèse Hamel (eds). *Les Cégeps: une grande aventure collective Quebecoise*. Quebec City: Presses Université Laval.

Ruggie, John G. 1993. Territoriality and beyond: Problematizing modernity in international relations. *International Organization* 47(1): 139–174.

Saarinen, Taina, and Tarja Nikula. 2013. "Implicit policy, invisible language: Policies and practices of international degree programmes in Finnish higher education." In Aintzane Doiz et al. (eds). *English-Medium Instruction at Universities: Global Challenges*. Bristol: Multilingual Matters.

Samuelson, Paul A. 1954. "The Pure Theory of Public Expenditure." The Review of Economics and Statistics, 36 (4): 387–89.

Sataøen, Hogne Lerøy. 2015. "Higher education as object for corporate and nation branding: Between equality and flagships." *Journal of Higher Education Policy and Management* 37(6): 702–717.

Scott-Smith, Giles. 2020. "Exchange programs and public diplomacy." In Snow Nancy and Nicholas J. Cull (eds). *Routledge Handbook of Public Diplomacy*. New York: Routledge: 38–49.

Shahjahan, Riyad A., and Adrianna J. Kezar. 2013. "Beyond the 'national container' addressing methodological nationalism in higher education research." *Educational Researcher* 42(1): 20–29.

Slaughter, Sheila, and Gary Rhoades. 2004. *Academic Capitalism and the New Economy: Markets, State, and Higher Education*. Baltimore: JHU Press.

Stein, Sharon. 2018. "National exceptionalism in the 'EduCanada' brand: Unpacking the ethics of internationalization marketing in Canada." *Discourse: Studies in the Cultural Politics of Education* 39(3): 461–477.

Szondi, Gyorgy. 2008. *Public Diplomacy and Nation Branding: Conceptual Similarities and Differences*. Waasenaar: Clingendael Institute.

Tamir, Yael. 1995. *Liberal Nationalism*. Princeton: Princeton University Press.

Tamtik, Merli, Roopa Desai Trilokekar, and Glen A. Jones (eds). 2020. *International Education as Public Policy in Canada*. Montreal: McGill-Queen's Press-MQUP.

Tange, Hanne, and Kirsten Jæger. 2021. "From Bologna to welfare nationalism: International higher education in Denmark, 2000–2020." *Language and Intercultural Communication* 21(2): 223–236.

Tannock, Stuart. 2007. "To keep America number 1: Confronting the deep nationalism of US higher education." *Globalisation, Societies and Education* 5(2): 257–272.

Taylor Charles. 1965. "Nationalism and the Political Intelligentsia: A Case Study". cited in Laforest Guy (Ed). Reconciling the solitudes: essays on Canadian federalism and nationalism. McGill-Queens University Press. 1993

Taylor, Charles. 1991. "Shared and divergent values." In A. Taylor et al. (eds). *Options for a New Canada*. Toronto: University of Toronto Press.

Teichler, Ulrich. 2004. "The changing debate on internationalisation of higher education." *Higher education* 48 : 5-26.

Thériault, Joseph Yvon. 2005. *Critique de l'américanité: mémoire et démocratie au Québec*. http://classiques.uqac.ca/contemporains/theriault_joseph_yvon/critique_de_americanite/critique_de_americanite.pdf

Trilokekar, Roopa & Glen A. Jones. 2020. "Federalism and Internationalization." In International Education as Public Policy in Canada, ed. R. Trilokekar, M. Tamtik and G. Jones. Montreal: McGill-Queen's University Press.

Tsygankov, Andrei P. 2019. *Russia's Foreign Policy: Change and Continuity in National Identity*. London: Rowman & Littlefield.

Tuathail, Gearóid Ó., and Simon Dalby (eds). 1998. *Rethinking Geopolitics*. London: Routledge.

Van der Wende, Marijk. 2021. "Neonationalism in the European union and universities." In John A. Douglass (ed). *Neonationalism and Universities: Populists, Autocrats and the Future of the University*. Baltimore: John Hopkins University Press: 117–140.

Van Dijk, Teun A. 1997. "What is political discourse analysis." *Belgian Journal of Linguistics* 11(1): 11–52.

Van Langenhove, Luk. 2011. *Building Regions: The Regionalization of the World Order*. Oxon: Routledge.

Varga, Somogy. 2013. "The politics of Nation Branding: Collective identity and public sphere in the neoliberal state." *Philosophy & Social Criticism* 39(8): 825–845.

Volcic, Zala, and Mark Andrejevic. 2011. "Nation branding in the era of commercial nationalism." *International Journal of Communication* 5: 21.

Wallace, William. 1991. "Foreign policy and national identity in the United Kingdom." *International Affairs* 67(1): 65–80.

Walter Rüegg. 2006. A History of the University in Europe. Vol. 3. Cambridge: Cambridge University Press.

Wang, J. 2013. *Shaping China's Global Imagination: Branding Nations at the World Expo*. New York: Palgrave Macmillan.

Warren, Jean-Philippe. 2008. "L'Opération McGill français. Une page méconnue de l'histoire de la gauche nationaliste." *Bulletin d'histoire politique* 16(2): 97–115.

Washburn, Jennifer. 2008. *University, Inc.: The Corporate Corruption of Higher Education*. Cambridge, MA: Basic Books.

Webber, Jeremy. 2015. *The Constitution of Canada: A Contextual Analysis*. Oxford: Hart Publishing.

Weimer, Leasa, and Aliandra Barlete. 2020. "The rise of nationalism: The influence of populist discourses on international student mobility and migration in the UK and US." In Weimer Leasa and Terri Nokkala (eds). *Universities as Political Institutions*. Leiden: Brill: 33–57.

Weimer, L., and T. Nokkala (eds). 2020. *Universities as Political Institutions*. Leiden, The Netherlands: Brill. https://doi.org/10.1163/9789004422582

Wellen, Richard, Paul Axelrod, Roopa Desai-Trilokekar, and Theresa Shanahan. 2012. "The making of a policy regime: Canada's post-secondary student finance system since 1994." *Canadian Journal of Higher Education* 43(3): 1–23.

Wodak, Ruth. 2009. *Discursive Construction of National Identity*. Edinburgh: Edinburgh University Press.

Wojczewski, Thorsten. 2020. "Populism, Hindu nationalism, and foreign policy in India: The politics of representing the people." *International Studies Review* 22(3): 396–422.

Yang, Rui. 2010. "Soft power and higher education: An examination of China's confucius institutes." *Globalisation, Societies and Education* 8(2): 235–245.

Zubrzycki, Geneviève. 2013. "Aesthetic revolt and the remaking of national identity in Québec,1960–1969." *Theory and Society* 42(5): 423–475.

Index

Agnew John, 11–12, 146, 148
AIEQ (association internationale des études québécoises), 135–138, 142, 147, 153
alliance française, 128
americanité, 16, 31, 118–119, 126, 140
americanization, 95
anglophone, 75, 76, 78, 79, 81–83, 85, 86, 88, 90, 115, 119–123, 143, 150, 158
anti-colonial, 79
Arab Spring, 3, 51, 66–67
autonomy, 19, 27, 30, 34, 36–37, 48, 57, 87

Balthazar Louis, 28–29, 91–92, 131, 146
banal nationalism, 5, 70, 154
BANQ (bibliothèque et archives nationales du Québec), 10
Béland Daniel, 13, 21, 22, 29, 54, 62, 69, 116, 154, 155
Belgium, 21, 22, 96, 130; Belgian students, 158
bilingual/bilingualism, 74, 76, 78, 82, 113, 116, 120, 130
bill 21 (loi des collèges d'enseignement général et professionnel), 44
bill 33 (for the establishment of a ministry of intergovernmental affairs), 93–94

bill 60 (for the creation of a ministry of education), 41
bill 66 (an act respecting the acceleration of certain infrastructure projects), 84–86
bill 101 (charter of the French language), 87
Bloc québécois, BQ, 122
BNAA (British North American Act), 26–27, 35
Bouchard, Lucien, 62
Bourassa, Robert, 58
British council, 128
Burgess Michael, 18, 19

Canada-France relations, 92–93
Canada's constitutional reforms, 26–27, 113, 116
Canadian studies, 78, 128–129, 135, 138
CAQ (Coalition Avenir Québec), 81–83, 85–87, 104, 105, 122, 157, 158
Catholic Church, the church, 4, 28–29, 34, 38–39, 41
CDA (critical discourse analysis), 10–11
Cégep, 43–50, 57, 64, 70, 76, 77, 81
centralization, 27, 28, 34, 36
CFA (centre de la francophonie des Amériques), 138–142, 147, 151

Charest, Jean, 51, 64–66, 100, 119, 136, 138–139
Charlottetown Accord, 27
Chrétien, Jean, 61
city of "two solitudes", 75, 88, 124
civil society, 88, 156
CMEC (Council of Ministers of Education, Canada), 113
collective mobilization, 14, 45, 48, 56, 57, 141, 142, 146, 151
Collen-Couture Agreement, 98
competition state, 106, 108
competitiveness, 7, 8, 9, 15, 34, 73, 105, 106, 108, 110, 111, 120, 121, 134, 153, 154
Concordia university, 70, 121
confederation, 26–27, 36
conservative values, 28, 29, 34, 39, 87
constitutional debates, 27, 36–38, 61, 90, 92, 114, 116–117
Couillard Philippe, 81, 103, 104, 137
council of universities 59–60
culture, 5, 13, 19, 20, 25, 26, 29, 31, 36, 37, 47, 48, 55, 59, 67, 70, 74, 80, 86, 97–99, 108, 112, 113, 117–119, 126, 128, 130, 132, 133, 136, 137, 139, 141, 142, 149, 150, 154, 155; political culture, 22, 65

Dawson college, 81, 84–85, 87
decentralization, 18, 20, 21, 27, 35
decision-making, decision-makers, 5, 9, 11, 53, 71, 77, 133, 137
de-colonial, 79
de Gaulle, Charles, 91, 95, 131
democratization, 14, 39, 41, 43, 52, 56, 57, 59, 66, 152, 154
demography, 20, 73, 99, 101, 104, 111, 147, 151
DFAIT (Department of Foreign Affairs and International Trade), 112, 113, 138

diplomacy, 92, 113; cultural diplomacy 130; education diplomacy, 16, 38, 126–130, 132, 134–135, 138, 140–141, 144, 147; paradiplomacy, 13, 15, 19, 24–26, 89–106; public diplomacy, 16, 25–26, 126–127, 132, 136–137, 142, 144
discourse, 7, 10, 11, 21, 23, 30–32, 43, 45, 50, 51, 53–57, 60, 61, 63, 65, 67–69, 71, 72, 76, 119, 130, 141, 142, 145, 154, 155
distinctiveness, 4, 7, 8, 14, 22, 24, 26, 37, 40, 42, 43, 47, 50, 52, 55, 60, 67–69, 71, 85, 86, 90, 99, 106, 115–119, 121, 125, 126, 135–137, 144, 147, 150–153, 155
distinct society, 29, 52, 59, 69, 146, 155
diversity, 6, 8, 18–19, 100, 141, 142
domestic/foreign binary, 6, 11–13, 23, 106, 144, 146–148
Duplessis, Maurice, 29, 33–34, 36, 38, 42

economic nationalism, 8, 153–154
edu Canada (brand), 112, 115–117
empire, 79
English language (lingua franca), 151
entente (France-Quebec), 89, 93–95
exchanges (educational, cultural), 25, 92–97, 105, 127, 141

federalism, 27, 37; multinational federalism, 6, 11, 14, 17, 19; territorial federalism, 18
federal spending power, 28
federation, 20, 31, 37, 91, 119, 130; multinational federation, 15, 19, 26, 76, 108, 147
financing (university), 9, 40, 53, 54, 56–64, 102, 120
Flanders, 21
founding nation, 19, 27, 116

France, 15, 76, 80, 89, 91–97, 103–104, 121, 131, 141, 146, 158
francophonie, 15, 16, 30, 89, 95, 96, 104, 106, 119–122, 126, 136, 139–143, 147, 151
Franco-Quebec education cooperation agreement, 91–95, 98
French Canada, French Canadian, 28, 29, 36–37, 133, 146
Front de libération du Québec, 78
Fulbright program, 127

Gagnon, Alain G., 6, 8, 18, 19, 26, 27, 29, 36, 106, 148, 149
Garson, Stuart, 36
geopolitics, 32, 147
Gérin-Lajoie, Paul, 42, 44, 90–91, 93–94; doctrine, 90–91, 97, 114, 115, 130, 148
Giroux, Henri, 51, 55, 66
global economy, 7, 8, 15, 31, 101, 106, 108, 112, 149, 150
globalization, 5, 7, 8, 9, 66, 148
grande noirceur, 33–34
grants, 35–38, 64

Habermans Jurgen, 21, 42
Hollande, François, 103
hydro-Québec, 49, 131, 152

identity paradiplomacy, 15, 25, 90, 96, 102, 105–106, 141, 147, 148
image, 15, 22, 23, 25, 34, 40, 67–69, 74, 79, 80, 94, 104, 107–108, 113, 115–124, 126–135, 142, 144, 146–147, 149, 153, 155
immigration, 5, 10, 27, 29, 73, 98–105, 121–123, 146, 147
impératif français, 83
international education, 15, 89, 96, 99, 105, 107, 109–121, 124, 150

international students, 15, 25, 71, 97–105, 144, 157; recruitment, 108–125, 147, 150
internationalization, 5, 9, 11, 109, 111, 115, 120

Janus-faced diplomacy, 144
Johnson Daniel, 94
Johnson Pierre Marc, 81

Keating Michael, 8, 17, 18, 24
Kirkland-Casgrain Marie-Claire, 79–80
knowledge economy, 4, 66, 98, 112
Kymlicka Will, 19

labour market, 104–106, 147, 158
l'action nationale, 37
Lachapelle Guy, 24, 30, 31
Landry Bernard, 64, 65
language; policy, 38, 70, 87, 158; rights, 151; minority languages, 150–152
Lecours André, 13, 21, 22, 24, 25, 54, 62, 69, 106, 111, 116, 154, 155
legitimacy, 20–22, 27, 31, 40, 42, 53, 54, 90, 147
Lesage Jean, 33–35, 38, 41, 42, 50, 91, 130, 131, 146
Lévesque, René, 81, 97, 131, 132
l'union nationale, 41, 44, 98

MacDonald John A, 27
maison du Québec, 91
maîtres chez nous, 30, 34–40, 54–56, 90, 91, 146
maple spring, 3, 12, 14, 51–57, 64–71, 102
Marginson Simon, 9, 52, 53, 75
maritime provinces, 27
marketing (education), 15, 107–124, 134, 144, 147, 152

marketization, 9, 53, 109, 157
Marois Pauline, 64, 68, 71, 102
massification of higher education, 35, 39, 76
McEwen Nicola, 13, 20–22, 38, 42, 54, 69, 116, 154, 155
McGill français, 14, 76–83, 150
McGill James, 74
McGill University, 14, 70, 72–88
methodological nationalism, 7
middle powers, 25–26
millennium scholarships, 61, 62, 65, 99, 114
Minville Edras, 37
modèle québécois, 14, 50–51, 70, 154
modernization, 29, 34, 38, 39, 44, 48, 56, 58, 84, 85, 92, 151
Monseigneur Alphonse-Marie Parent, 38
Montreal, 14, 47, 48, 70, 72–88, 90, 96, 117, 122, 138, 150, 158
Morin Claude, 93, 132
multiculturalism, 116, 131

nation branding, 15, 107–109, 112, 118, 124
nation-building (adj), 88, 89, 98, 109, 126, 146, 148, 153, 155, 156
nation building (n), 124, 149, 154
nation state, 7, 9, 10, 18, 23, 24, 53, 124, 149
NECQS (Northeast Council for Quebec Studies), 133
neoliberal/neoliberalization, 3, 51, 53, 58, 60, 61, 65–67, 87, 155, 157
neo-nationalism/new nationalism, 5, 6
New Brunswick, 26
North America, 28, 42–43, 47, 48, 62, 65, 68, 83, 90, 96, 99, 103, 118–119, 130, 133, 136, 141–143
Nova Scotia, 26
Nye Joseph, 25, 128

occupy wall street movement, 51, 67, 76
OECD (Organization for Economic Co-operation and Development), 47
opération amérique, 131–135
outaouais, 76, 81–83, 86

Paquin Stéphane, 13, 24, 25, 89, 91, 131, 132, 147, 149
party politics, 58, 62, 70, 71
PEQ (programme de l'expérience québécoise), 100, 101, 104–106
PLQ (Parti libéral du Québec), 3, 15, 29, 34, 48, 58, 60–62, 64–68, 71, 78, 79, 81–84, 87, 100, 103, 104, 110, 119, 123, 126, 136, 137, 143
policy ownership, 21, 22, 24, 38, 42, 53, 55, 62, 69, 114–116, 120, 122, 123, 130, 155
policymaking (n, adj), 7, 8, 13, 17, 18, 20, 22, 24, 29, 58, 61, 124, 145; policymaker (n), 6
populism, populist, 5, 29
post-war, 22, 33, 54
power-sharing, 20, 27
PQ (parti québécois), 29, 61–65, 68, 71, 82, 84, 85, 87, 102–104, 114–116, 121, 122, 129–132, 137, 139, 141
Protestantism, 28, 34, 75
public good, 40, 41, 52–71

QS (Québec Solidaire), 85, 87, 105, 123
Quebec Act (1774), 28, 73
Quebec-Ottawa relations, 28, 38, 93, 131
Quebec studies, 15, 126, 129–144
quiet revolution, 4, 12–15, 28–32, 34–35, 46, 48, 50, 56–58, 60, 62, 64, 66, 69, 73, 76, 89, 91, 95, 116, 129, 131, 145, 146, 152, 154

rankings (university), 72, 75, 86
regional development, 29, 45, 133

re-territorialization, 8, 17–18, 24, 157
Rioux Ouimet, Hubert, 8, 20, 24, 29, 87, 105, 106, 153
Rocher Guy, 43–46
Royal Commission on Education (Parent Commission), 39–50, 55–57, 92, 152, 154
Royal Commission of Inquiry into Constitutional Problems (1954) (Tremblay commission), 35–37
Royal Commission on National Development in the Arts, Letters and Sciences 1951 (Massey Commission), 35, 62
Royal Victoria Hospital, 84, 85
Ryan Claude, 58, 60, 79, 153

Saint-Laurent Louis, 35, 36
Scotland, 5, 54, 55, 106
secrétariat du Québec aux relations canadiennes, 62, 114, 139
secularism, 28, 29, 33
self-determination, 20
separatism/separatist, 20, 30
SNP (Scottish National Party), 54
social policy, 13, 21, 22, 148, 154
societal role, 39, 63, 76, 88; societal choice, 59, 63, 69–70
soft power, 25–26, 127–128, 134, 142, 144
solidarity, 64, 55
St. Lawrence River, 30
student strike, 52, 64–67, 70, 76, 77

sub-national, 10, 12, 13, 19, 21, 24, 30, 38
sub-state, 13, 17, 18, 22, 25, 111, 124, 149
supreme court of Canada, 27
symbolic, 21, 30, 43, 50, 76, 92, 97, 116, 154
Symons Commission, 129

Taylor Charles, 19, 30
territorial trap, 11, 12, 146
Toronto, 73, 79, 95
trade, 5, 7, 10, 11, 27, 74, 112, 114, 146
tuition fees, 14, 38, 45, 50, 51, 55, 58, 67, 69, 70, 77, 152, 152, 154, 155; exceptions, international student fees, 71, 95, 103, 122–124, 157, 158; freeze on tuition fees, 57, 63, 64; hike, 59, 60, 65, 66, 68, 158

understanding Canada program, 138
United Kingdom, 5, 22, 55, 106, 150
United States, 5, 18, 22, 43, 77, 131, 150; Quebec-US relations, 131–135
université de Montréal, 77
university of Quebec network, 43, 47–50, 155, 158

Wall Street, 51, 67, 131
welfare (ideals, politics, state), 5, 9, 21, 27, 33, 50, 53–55, 62, 65, 66, 148, 152, 155
world city, 74, 86, 87, 121, 150